EASY
KILLS

With special thanks to Richard Wyatt

EASY KILLS

SEBASTIAN MURPHY-BATES

MIRROR BOOKS

mB

MIRROR BOOKS

1

Published in Great Britain and Ireland in 2022 by
Mirror Books, a Reach PLC business,
5 St Paul's Square, Liverpool, L3 9SJ.

www.mirrorbooks.co.uk
@TheMirrorBooks

Print ISBN 978-1-913406-82-0
eBook ISBN 978-1-913406-83-7

Page design and typesetting by Danny Lyle

Printed and bound in Great Britain by
CPI Group (UK) Ltd, Croydon, CR0 4YY

Photos: Reach Plc, PA, Alamy, Rex/Shutterstock.

Every effort has been made to trace copyright and any
oversight will be rectified in future editions.

CONTENTS

ABOUT THE AUTHOR

Sebastian Murphy-Bates is Assistant News Editor
at the Daily Star. He was previously at the Barking and
Dagenham Post for two-and-a-half years, and was living
in Barking when Port was arrested. He previously worked
at MailOnline as a reporter.

PREFACE

INADEQUACY

Imagine the area, be it a town, city or village, in which you work. Picture its familiarity, its streets and landmarks. Think of everything that makes that place home. Now imagine that this scenery is rudely interrupted. The tableau that shatters it, in this case, is your discovery of a young man's corpse. His body is dumped in the street, in the middle of a modest housing development. The victim shows hallmarks of having been moved; his clothes are pulled up, exposing his midriff. His burst lip appears to have been bitten. He has died as the result of an overdose on a drug that has for years been associated with sexual predators, who use it to overpower their prey. So established is this reputation, that the substance – GHB – is, in common parlance, called a 'date-rape' drug. The reason you've arrived at this scene is that a concerned citizen has called the emergency services. You soon realise that this man had in fact hired the very same person, now reduced to a lifeless form, as an escort. He has lied about the circumstances in which he found the body and has dragged the corpse outside. Picture, if you're able, holding all of these details in your mind and taking the decision not to investigate the possibility that this was a murder, despite the protestations of devastated family members. Such is your assurance that there was no foul play involved, that you neglect to undergo rudimentary checks that could lead to such a conclusion. Now imagine yourself doing this three more times, with three more bodies, all of which turn up within 400 yards of the first body. All have overdosed on date-rape drugs. Every one of the victims is gay. Still, you do not investigate.

This is the story of how a serial killer whose crimes were so blatant and mind-numbingly inadequate that to place him in the category of criminal genius would be frankly insulting to hard-working psychopaths. It is a story of a police force who not only failed to perform their duties, but actually decided against doing so despite the pleas of devastated mothers and sisters begging them to display even just a cursory form of care. You may not be surprised to learn that phone calls from grieving mothers, fathers and sisters don't decide the scope of a police investigation. Fair enough, you may say. But think of ordinary people, in the throes of a sorrow so profound that most can hardly comprehend, not only urging the police on, but identifying gaping holes in their conduct. These were normal citizens, totally unqualified, telling the men and women assigned to protect them how to do their jobs. This was combined with questions from journalists who suspected that the police were wrong in their assertions that the deaths were not suspicious.

INADEQUACY

Such a case of neglect would surely shame the force in question into a proactivity in terms of protecting gay young men from sex attack killers. And yet, such hope may well be unwise. For as we shall see, this case was not the first one in which such people had been overlooked, forgotten, left to the non-existent mercy of a murderer. As a journalist who covered the case and lived in the borough that bore witness to these crimes, I feel it necessary to explore these failings. Never again must the police allow a rapist and murderer the freedom to target young gay men in a deprived, working-class area. The people who live in Barking and Dagenham don't just deserve a voice. They deserve authorities that will listen to that voice. It seems that, in order to realise this ambition, these failings must once again be laid bare. I hope, at the very least, that this book achieves that. This is the story of Stephen Port. And the gargantuan effort that it took to convince a flacid police force to finally arrest the man that one officer would later concede was "probably one of the most dangerous individuals" he'd ever met.[1]

1

PETER

Peter Hirons is preparing for company in his home, a modest council flat in the deprived borough of Newham. A towering man in his late forties, he exudes a confidence perfectly suited to his job performing as a drag queen in the capital's pubs. His sharp, yet kind face has a somewhat reptilian quality and his small eyes peer intensely underneath short, dark hair. He's looking forward to a quiet night off the stage. For tonight, Peter will have an audience of just one. Jack Taylor, 24, is coming from nearby Dagenham after a week or so of conversations on the gay dating app Grindr.

Jack, being significantly younger, is definitely Peter's type and the host's small, glittering eyes are pleased when he opens his front door to a short-haired, slim forklift truck driver for what he hopes is a hook-up. But it isn't. Sex isn't going to happen. "Maybe some drugs would help lower your inhibitions?" the host ventures in a voice that years of cigarette-smoking have

1

coarsened into a formidable rasp. "There are some, if you'd
–." But no. Jack just wants to talk. He's hoping to confide in
his host, to learn from his life experiences as an older gay
man and in so doing see himself more clearly. The guest sips
a whisky and coke and explains that his workplace isn't the
ideal environment in which to be open about his sexuality. Has
he come out to his family? No. Is he worried about doing so?
Not really, he just hasn't got around to it. Three hours pass
pleasantly before Peter calls a taxi for his guest, who leaves his
host with an impression of quiet confidence manifesting itself
in good humour and flirtatious charm.

October 15, 2015, Barking, east London

Stephen Port is in his flat at 62 Cooke Street, his gangly 6ft
3ins figure surrounded by *Transformers* action figures, amyl
nitrate and gay pornography.[2] Suddenly, he is startled as
he hears somebody break down his front door. Barking and
Dagenham police officers barge into his home, surrounding
him. They charge the bald 40-year-old with four murders,
the first of which they say occurred on June 19, 2014, when
an overdosed escort had been found outside this very flat. It
isn't the first time that officers have spoken to him about this.
It was Stephen who had fabricated an account of stumbling
across the body after calling 999.[3] Despite knowing this at the
time, the police had not considered him a suspect. Nor did
they suspect him when two more overdosed bodies turned up
within 400 yards of his home just three weeks apart.[4] They
didn't kick down his door when the drug-filled corpse of Jack

Taylor was found on the same spot as the second and third victims.[5] Yet here they now stood.

They soon learn that Stephen has been using fake identities, including the name Lance, to hide his true self when making contact with his victims. Once his targets were back at his flat, he had drugged them with GHB to render them unresponsive, in the lustful fulfilment of his rape fantasies.[6] Four days after his arrest, Stephen faces Barkingside Magistrates' Court, where he is remanded in custody to await trial at the Old Bailey in central London[7]. Though he is finally in custody, journalists wonder how he has been able to dump the bodies of four young men so brazenly while not being suspected of their deaths. Editors at the *Barking and Dagenham Post* wonder how local law enforcement didn't even treat the remarkably similar deaths as suspicious during the 15-month period in which the bodies dropped around Stephen.

October 2015, East Ham, east London

It's 3am and Peter is up a ladder, catching up on some DIY. Perched above a sea of bin bags, he eyes the 30 waistcoats which hang in his flat after he took it upon himself to repair them for friends. He isn't startled by the knock at the door – it's normal, even at this hour. The visitor, he suspects, is his next-door neighbour, who often comes over early in the morning if a strange sound has disturbed her. The area isn't exactly crime-free and is home to thousands of people who have yet to feel the benefits of local regeneration credited to the London 2012 Summer Olympics, the epicentre of which was at a brand new stadium down the road in the borough's flagship of gentrification, Stratford.

But Peter is confused when he doesn't find his quiet neighbour standing at the entrance to his home. Rather, it's a suited man who greets him, brandishing a warrant. He and his colleagues, now piling into the flat, are here about a murder. "Is there any contraband or sharp objects we might hurt ourselves on as we conduct our search?" the officer asks. 'Just that big bag of crystal meth at my feet', thinks Peter. Despite his confusion, he decides that it's best to be honest, given the seriousness of the investigation and points them to the amphetamines. "Can we have the password to your phone, sir?" the officer asks. "Of course," says Peter, aware that he's revealing a series of conversations largely centred on the bulk-buying of drugs for him and his friends.

The officers survey the room, eyeing the bin bags, waistcoats and sewing machine. A blackboard bears the instruction: 'Repair Lance's waistcoat.' They seize the garments as Peter wonders what they could possibly have to do with the death of anybody. The investigators grab his bag of meth and meet Peter's expectations by hauling him off for a night in the cells. Peter doesn't know that this murder investigation centres on the young man who graced his flat just a year ago. Jack is the final victim of a serial killer, who dumped his body in a graveyard of the neighbouring town, Barking, on September 25, 2015. Peter also hasn't learned that the murderer is one of the men to whom he's been dealing drugs. And he was in his flat just weeks ago. The killer must have been a truly remarkable individual to have gone unnoticed.

2

MUTE

Not exactly. Stephen, born in Southend-on-Sea, Essex, was not somebody known for excelling. He moved to Dagenham when he was still a toddler with parents Albert and Joan and cemented his reputation as a shy, silent pupil at Monteagle Primary School. The only thing that stood out about Stephen was the absences he brought to a room. The absence of noise. The absence of friends. The absence of interaction. He stood out for the things he didn't do, the words he didn't say. He was barely present.

A former classmate of his told me that Stephen was an extremely lonely boy. The former pupil in question spoke to me on condition of anonymity. He feared that an association with Port would distract from the work in which he is now engaged. Liam, as we'll call him, attended primary school with Stephen from 1979 to 1986 and may have been the closest thing to a friend the boy had. He first met him before they became classmates, as both boys had older siblings they would go to pick up with their parents.

Liam told me has 'hazy memories' of racing up and down the playground with Stephen, but said that even then there was no verbal communication. They just ran. This near-speechlessness continued once the pair began school, and the young Stephen adopted almost total silence no matter the person with whom he came into contact. Although a school photo shows the tall boy beaming as he towers over his peers in a West Ham United football shirt, the real Stephen was no more known for a jolly disposition than he was for his sportsmanship. "He was the quietest kid I have ever met," Liam said. "He was almost mute. He barely spoke to anybody in the seven years I was there."

Wearing a lumberjack jacket and large glasses till the age of 12, the gangly child Stephen would normally be found standing alone at breaktime while other pupils played in groups around him. "He just wouldn't speak to anybody," Liam said. "He was very much a loner. He would often be on his own in the playground. He wouldn't mix with people, engage with people."

But just because a child is quiet and retreating doesn't mean they go unnoticed. There must have been something, other than his being apart from others, that stood out about Stephen. Perhaps he excelled elsewhere. If he did, then Liam certainly didn't notice. Not once, in seven years. Summing up Stephen, he said simply: "It's kind of difficult to talk about his character because he didn't really have one." About the only thing that people did seem to notice was a quality that wasn't actually attributable to the boy. He was known as the deaf kid, despite being able to hear perfectly well, such was his quietness.

Liam doesn't recall other pupils being particularly cruel to Stephen, or any bullying on which it might be tempting to blame the warped future that awaited the boy. Far from the tormented youngster that media reports presented the boy as when his older self was arrested, Liam says at most there was a little teasing of a child who refused, for whatever reason, to engage from the start. Outside of school, all Liam ever saw of Stephen was him sheltering in the shadow of his mother as he walked alongside her through suburban streets lined with council housing. Though he was retreating, Stephen wasn't the obedient child you might associate with such a trait. Rather than realising that he wouldn't be bothered by as much social interaction if he simply complied with requests, he seemed intent on disobedience, but would try to dodge any confrontation by being covert in his deviation. If his father, Albert, asked him not to do something, he'd say 'yes dad, yes dad', only for Port senior to find his son carrying out said prohibited action in private later.[8]

* * *

The government built Dagenham up after the First World War in the hope that it'd become a destination for families not dissimilar to the Ports. Liberal Prime Minister David Lloyd George envisaged the area's future as one of a haven for men returning from the frontline. Keen that those who'd served wouldn't return to the slums of the East End, he ordered the country's first council estate to be built outside the capital, to the east, in what was then an agrarian Essex village. When development on the 26,000-home Becontree Estate began straight after the war, it signalled the birth of a suburban, working-class town as the estate would go on to rehouse 100,000 people.[9] Ford opened its Dagenham plant, becoming a focal point not just of employment but identity ever since the first car was produced there in 1931.[10] In 1965, Dagenham merged with Barking to its west to form the London Borough of Barking and Dagenham. Though officially east London, residents cling fiercely to its Essex identity. Eighty-eight years after the Becontree Estate began construction, it was still described as the largest public housing development in the world, its two-storey homes and front lawns a uniform of modesty, long after it had been the setting of Stephen's childhood.[11]

* * *

As a teenager, Stephen would work at a local ink shop for £9 a day, spending his money not on socialising with friends or on sneaking alcohol from a shop like some youths. Instead, he primarily spent them on sweet snacks such as Jaffa Cakes.[12] The teasing the lonely teenager received at school would later push him to work out and bulk up. After leaving school aged 16, Stephen enrolled in art college, but his family were unable to pay his fees. Stephen dropped out and began training as a chef, qualifying when he was 18 and beginning his career in kitchen work.[13]

3

STUNTED

In a job that necessitates the willingness to bark commands across the kitchen, Stephen struggled to work well with colleagues at bus depot kitchens in Romford and West Ham. Though he did not form personal relationships, he left an impression on co-worker Cynthia Adams during their bizarre, if limited, interactions. Recalling her time at Romford Bus Garage, she told me: "He was very quiet, he didn't talk. If he was spoken to, he would respond with a wink or a nod."

His limited capacity for conversation of any kind fostered tension with some colleagues, and his personal life was not without its difficulties. Stephen came out as gay aged 26 and, according to his sister, Sharon, their "old-school" mother had a problem with the revelation. The insecure chef worked out as he recalled name-calling at school due to his physique and wore what he'd boast was a £900 wig to disguise the baldness spreading across the top of his head. But no attempt at skin-deep self-improvement could hide his utter inability to form appropriate relationships with those around him. Stephen moved into a ground-floor flat at 62 Cooke Street in Barking after his parents secured the apartment in a shared ownership agreement with a housing association.[14]

* * *

Ryan Edwards met Stephen in April 2005, after seeing him move into the property, which was in the same housing development, diagonally opposite and a minute's walk from his front door. Ryan had moved from Canvey Island, Essex, and was keen to sound out whatever gay community there might be in his new hometown. Hoping for friendship with another gay man, Ryan was stunned by Port's sheer inability to communicate when they met for coffee.

The gay men became friends but, like many other people in Stephen's life, he found his neighbour strange and childlike. Initially, he reminded Ryan of Roald Dahl's Big Friendly Giant as he lumbered quietly through their interactions. "He came across as very gentle, very quiet – like a gentle giant," he told me. "He would always speak to you in hushed tones."

Happily extending his social circle to bring Stephen in, Ryan introduced him to his friends while hosting a party. But his guest was more interested in a toy truck lying among Ryan's boyhood belongings. Seeing his new friend's fascination, and familiar with his interest in collecting toys such as *Transformers*, he casually offered it to Stephen as a gift. Though he may have expected him to display the truck with great enthusiasm, what he didn't expect was the bizarre sight of a man with size 14 feet sitting on the floor and pushing the truck up and down 'in a world of his own' as though he were a child searching for amusement while the adults around him talked.

But the picture Ryan built of his new friend in other areas of his personal life wasn't one of childlike innocence. He destroyed his relationships with a violence that seemed to escalate over the years. One boyfriend came to Ryan with a cut to his head, explaining that Stephen had pushed him into a television. Another described him as violent. Although Ryan never worked with Stephen, he heard through him how he brought these antisocial, destructive tendencies into his inter-actions in the kitchen. "He had a terrible time at work," Ryan told me. "He got promoted so he was managing several women and it got really hairy – I wouldn't want him as a manager. Those women hated him."

He faced sackings, re-hirings, suspensions and workplace investigations as he fought allegations of theft. An unusual glimmer of glamour punctured this otherwise bleak existence when the BBC One reality TV show *Celebrity Masterchef* descend-ed on the West Ham Bus Garage to film an episode in 2014. Toupee in place, he served Stagecoach drivers meatballs along-side JB Gill, from the boy band JLS, and *EastEnders* soap actress Emma Barton. Clearly relishing what might have been his only chance to flicker rather than shine, Stephen smiled as he lurked in the background.[15] And once the camera crews and minor celebrities had left east London, Stephen had other means of escapism. Despite being utterly useless at mixing with others, he developed something of a reputation on Cooke Street for hosting parties with young men, who'd cram into his tiny garden and work out topless. From his flat, Ryan could see people coming and going. He knew that Stephen's sexual appetites were voracious and described it as like an insatiable thirst, remembering his partners as 'literally one after another after another after another.' More than that, Ryan started to notice the looming, muscular chef's type – vulnerable. Afflicted by his ever present deficit of social skills, Stephen had also developed ways in which to sidestep barriers to sexual encounters.

One was by working as an escort, selling his services for £150 on the website SleepyBoy, with an overnight 'full service' fee of £350.[16] Familiar with the impulses of a deviant mind, he would never accept anything to eat or drink from his clients and supplied his own lube, condoms and poppers (amyl nitrate). Social media and online dating also allowed him to construct facades of fiction for dating. A man incapable of holding eye contact with his neighbours can't seriously be expected to charm vulnerable victims in a gay bar on a regular basis. Instead, he created around 20 accounts and invented charm without having to look the people to whom he was lying in the eye.[17]

He reinvented himself in a variety of ways, including as an Oxford graduate and as a kind-hearted soul who taught children with special needs at Westminster Kingsway College in central London, betraying his lack of basic teaching skills by misspelling the word 'special'. He also claimed to be a 'former Naval flight officer' on Facebook. 'Romantic', 'caring', 'successful' and 'educated' was how he summarised his character on

Badoo. He was honest enough to include 'rape fantasy' under the 'what he's into' section of his Slaveboys account. Stephen specified that he was only interested in 'younger smooth slim guys 18-24' adding on one account: 'Please no fat or hairy guys as I won't reply.'[18]

And of course there were drugs. When he appeared on *Celebrity Masterchef*, he was already well into his use, having started experimenting around 2013.[19] Beginning with the amphetamine mephedrone, he moved onto GHB around six months later, which stimulated his sex drive and lengthened his desire for hours at a time.[20] The drug also acted as an attractive shortcut by which he could circumvent consent. Slipping some GHB into a drink guaranteed him gratification without struggling to make eye contact in a display of clumsy flirting that was doomed to fail.

He did, however, have boyfriends. Rafael Alves da Silva was 19 years old when he met Stephen through social media. Rafael had come from Brazil to study and believed Stephen to be aged 25. Port facilitated this lie by caking himself in make-up and, after a few dates, the teenager moved into his flat at Cooke Street. For the young student, his new boyfriend was a chance to sample the gay scene in London. Not used to going out, he immersed himself in the capital's nightlife. But he ended the relationship about a month after moving in, realising that Stephen wasn't for him. Rafael found him weird and couldn't escape the strange atmosphere that hung about the relationship. He learned that Stephen was heavily into using drugs and had graduated from a user to a dealer. He'd fund his procurement by prostituting some of the men with whom he was romantically involved. He clearly wasn't right.[21]

Days after they split, Stephen sent Rafael a message saying that he'd left his passport at the apartment. When the young man arrived, he was puzzled to see another male answer the door. The man let him in. As Rafael made his way through the flat, he noticed a 'young boy' lying on the bed in a 'strange position'. He looked as though he'd taken, or been given, drugs.[22]

* * *

Though Stephen was sounding out sinister ways to force inter-actions, he couldn't manufacture memories. A visit from his mother left a slightly disturbing impression on Ryan, who was at Stephen's having a coffee when Joan came over. Stephen had only fleetingly referred to his parents in conversations with his friend, leaving everything to the imagination about his child-hood and teenage years. Spotting an opportunity to find out more, Ryan asked Joan what Stephen was like as a boy. Until this question she'd been quiet, but when she began recalling her time with her young son, she lit up describing a smiling youngster who, with her at least, had been very talkative. But when she attempted to describe his teenage years, Joan went quiet. Recalling the exchange, Ryan told me: "She looked into the distance and her voice trailed off. Then she started talking about the weather. She seemed like a nice lady."

He believes that Stephen's claims to be '70 per cent more gay than straight' when he was before a jury were due to him not wanting to identify as fully homosexual in front of his parents, given the reception he'd had when he came out to his family. But Ryan said that this was a fiction and dismissed any attempt to portray his former neighbour as anything other than 100 per cent gay as 'complete fantasy'. As he put it: "Stephen was gayer than John Inman in *Are You Being Served?* There wasn't a heterosexual bone in his body."

Their friendship progressed. But the closer Ryan got to Stephen, the more concerned he became about this supposedly gentle giant as he saw a controlling, abusive side at odds with his initial impression. His neighbour's approach to relationships was that of an infatuated schoolboy. But a violent streak accompanied this and Barking and Dagenham Police attended his flat on 'multiple occasions'. His type was, by design or chance, easy to dominate as Stephen tended to go for vulnerable young men with little education. It was common for partners to move in at Cooke Street a week into the relationship. Within a month there could be a reasonable expectation of an engagement party, one of which Ryan attended and was confused that not a single member of Stephen's family was present.

His obsession with how others perceived him also fostered a strange competitive streak as he tried to keep ahead of Ryan by having a bigger television and inviting him for rides in his latest customised car – which Ryan said would change 'nearly as often as he changed his men'. During one such trip, to a McDonald's in Beckton, east London, he made clear that he also viewed the men in his life as objects to be used, flaunted and even sold. As Ryan drank a milkshake with Stephen, he asked why Port's boyfriend was sitting across the restaurant from them, by the door. Wearing a 'totally serious' expression, Stephen replied: "It's because I'm pimping him out." Ryan laughed nervously, hoping this was a failed attempt at humour and another damning indictment of his social skills. But his expression didn't shift. Ryan remembers: "He meant it. We finished our milkshakes and left him there. I remember talking to my friends about it at the time. You just don't do that."

* * *

Around 2013, Ryan started to notice Stephen's escalating drug use. His neighbour was looking increasingly tired at strange times of the day and had a near constant runny nose, which he presented as an apparently perpetual cold. "I'm knocking and he's usually really prompt to the door," he said. "I hear a shuffling. He eventually opens the door and looks wrecked. He looks like he's been up all night."

Disturbed by red rings round Stephen's bloodshot eyes, Ryan was horrified to be greeted by a Tupperware box the size of a coffee table. It was filled with sachets of white powder and bottles of GHB. Stephen, wearing his wig but without his usual layer of make-up, was saying even less than usual as he combatted the come-down his latest boyfriend was evidently struggling with too. Afraid to bring it up in person, Ryan confessed his concerns to Port in a text message. In his reply, Port insisted his drug abuse was nothing to worry about, while somewhat paradoxically claiming that the massive stash was all for his personal use. "I didn't really believe him," he said. "But I'm a liberal at heart so I was like if he's not harming anyone and doing it in the comfort of his own home then that's up to him."

Their friendship cooled afterwards and was largely restricted to the occasional text message. But even then, Ryan wasn't free from Stephen's strangely sinister behaviour. Stephen was engaged in 2014 when he sent Ryan a picture of an unknown man who, in Ryan's words, 'looked dead'. He asked Ryan if he wanted to come around and have some fun. Ryan stared, disturbed, at the man in the photo. He was naked and in the foetal position. It was around 10pm. But when he later asked Stephen about the incident, his friend told him that he and the man in the picture had just been 'messing around'.[23]

One of the people Stephen had started buying his drugs from was Peter Hirons. Peter's relationship with drugs wasn't what you'd expect from somebody who ended up selling them from his flat in East Ham. Despite being exposed to it from a young age and understanding it to be a 'big part of the gay scene', the then-club dancer wasn't interested in taking ecstasy in the nineties, when clubbers were popping pills with such fervour that the decade's cultural identity would forever be framed through dilated pupils. "When I was younger, it was just before E and that generation," he told me. "At the time I was dancing so I didn't want anything to do with drugs – I was keeping myself fit. And I didn't want to do a pill and dance my tits off all night after work – that was my job."

But at the age of 40, curiosity piqued his interest and he decided he'd give crystal meth and GHB, also known as G, a go. "I had a couple of weeks off work, some money in the bank and

I thought 'everybody goes on about it, let's give it a try," he said. The latecomer soon realised what he'd been missing. "Crystal meth makes you stay awake, keep going and quite horny – I can understand how people think they can never have sex again without it," he said. "It sobers you up like cocaine does, but makes you more energetic. With G it's more of a euphoric feeling – it lowers your inhibitions. To me, G is one of the best drugs, because if you're sensible you get a nice buzz, a nice warm feeling. After an hour it's out of your system."

From a purely financial point of view, it made sense for the now recreational drug user to get a large stash in at a reduced rate and have friends reimburse them for their share afterwards. The primary downside of this cost-cutting was that Peter was now technically a drug dealer. "If you buy five grams instead of half a gram of meth, you get it cheaper," he explained. "So I grouped together with friends, and that's how it started and how it continued, just getting it for friends so it's cheaper for everybody. It's like Costco. It's bulk-buying."

Peter came to know Stephen when one of his friends went to Barking to meet him for sex. "One of my friends was going to play with him," Peter told me. "The friend rang me up and asked if Stephen could come and get some stuff. I said I didn't know him and made my friend come with him. He came, got some meth, some G, and he came another couple of times after that. He just seemed a little weird, I thought it was just a confidence problem, a bit insecure. I didn't realise he wore a wig – and I'm one of the best people who can tell a wig. He wore it messy, he carried it off very well."

4

ANTHONY

June 19, 2014, Barking, east London

Cooke Street's quietest resident, Stephen Port, is panicking, which is understandable given the sight of a dead young man propped up against a wall outside the communal entrance to his block of flats. He dials 999 on his mobile phone, telling the call handler that the person looks to have 'collapsed or had a seizure or was drunk' in the street.[24] The lifeless 23-year-old in question is a fashion student from Hull, East Yorkshire. His name is Anthony Walgate. Before appearing in the street, he was in the flat owned by Stephen, who has now thrust himself into the middle of any investigation that may occur in his attempt to divert the eyes of the police away from him and his home just feet away from the corpse.[25] Stephen makes a hasty excuse as he tries to shuffle himself off the call in a manner that appears unsuspicious. He hopes the emergency worker on the other end of the line will buy that he's merely a concerned passer-by. But the words he uses betray the fact that he's not exactly adept at moving seamlessly through a situation like this. As the handler tries to elicit Stephen's mobile number from him, he botches his portrayal of a bystander worried about a dead body by placing something utterly trivial at the top of his priorities, saying: "I'm just to get in my car. I've got to get to my car, the parking." The frustrated operator says: "Right, don't worry about that – what's the telephone number you're calling from?"[26]

Stephen severs the line, ending their connection, and no doubt hoping that'll be the end of the matter. He must surely have passed as somebody who doesn't live in the area. Why else would he need to move his car? They'll never guess that call was made from Cooke Street. He should be fine. They'll be more concerned about the body than a weird phone call. But the operator traces his number and calls back to ask Stephen to confirm that the location is Cooke Street, only to be told: "Oh, I've just driven away now."

The handler then asks for the door number outside which the young man's body is lying. Stephen claims not to have looked – despite in the previous call saying it was somewhere between 47 and 58 Cooke Street. The operator reminds him of this and Stephen rediscovers his certainty. Rather than saying 'maybe' or 'it could have been', which would presumably fit better with the confusion from which he seconds ago was claiming to suffer, he says: "Yeah, 47, yep." Not only does he sound suspicious, but he leaves behind a scene that demands investigation. Anthony's underwear has clearly not been put on by the student. It is inside out and back to front, with his jeans zip open, in a scene that betrays the panic of a suspect hurrying to make it look as though the young man has fallen where he sits while missing details that show he has been dressed after the fact.[27]

Anthony's body also has 14 visible injuries, including classic signs that he's been dragged to the spot, namely bruising on the inside of his upper left arm.[28] As if this doesn't look bad enough for Stephen, he's left a digital paper trail showing that he hired the Middlesex University student as an escort, a fact sure to be of interest to police if they find out. Anthony had arranged to meet Stephen – who was using a pseudonym, Joe Dean, which looks suspicious even in the most generous interpretation of events – the previous night. Anthony was working as an escort while at university as a source of extra cash and Stephen offered to pay him £800 for a night's work after contacting him online.[29]

What else has Stephen left behind? Internet search history littered with some very specific pornography in the hours approaching Anthony's arrival. He looked for 'date-rape drug', 'unconscious porn videos', 'boys being drug raped', 'unconscious boys rape videos', 'sleeping boy' and 'taking date-rape drug'.[30]

Anthony, too, has left something of a trail, betraying not only his destination – 62 Cooke Street – but also a heartbreaking irony. Though he was working in a potentially dangerous industry, Anthony was anything but reckless. The 23-year-old wouldn't vanish off to a stranger's flat without telling anyone. He takes precautions, showing friends a picture of 'Joe' – who uses his real image – and tells them he's going to meet him on June 17. Anthony sends the location of the meeting to his friend, Ellie Dean, with the explanation: 'In case I get killed.' He also tells her he's taking scissors with him in case he needs to use them in self-defence[31]. But any weapon would have been insufficient to guard against the surreptitious way in which Stephen attacked Anthony. And the terrible irony of Anthony's careful attempt to leave a paper trail is that those for whom it was intended in the case of his death don't seem particularly interested.

* * *

Paramedic Antony Neil finds Anthony propped up in a sitting position following Stephen's 999 call. His phone is missing, and blood around his mouth causes Neil to believe that the death could be suspicious. The cause of death is GHB intoxication.[32] Police trace the number that made the 999 call, leading them to Stephen. They question him based on the messages Anthony had sent to his friend showing his picture, address and the fact that he was heading to Cooke Street to see a client. This is all a horrible misunderstanding, Stephen explains – a terrible accident. He tells the officers that Anthony took GHB of his own volition after he hired him for sex. He claims that after their time was up, he left the total stranger alone in his flat for eight hours believing him to be asleep. Stephen says he returned to find him dead, panicked and left the corpse in the street before calling the emergency services.[33]

On holiday in Turkey, Sarah Sak has her phone switched off and is unaware that the police have found her son dead. She returns to the UK to hundreds of missed calls and messages and learns that her child is dead. What is almost as devastating is the news that Barking and Dagenham Metropolitan Police Service are not treating the death as suspicious. Through her grief, she is astute enough to suggest they trace her son's phone and check the electronic devices belonging to the man with whom he'd been staying.[34] Barking and Dagenham officers tell her it would be 'too expensive' to trace the handset and give the same excuse as to why they wouldn't be forensically examining Anthony or Stephen's laptops. She presses them further, questioning Stephen's story and asking why he'd leave a stranger at home in bed while he went off to work. She cannot comprehend how the same police force that is capable of believing such an improbable claim isn't prepared to believe that this death could be suspicious. Even without a check of electronic devices, the police have seen the state of Anthony's body and clothing and are aware of Stephen's lies about being a passer-by.[35] The force goes on to splash £25,000 and 980 man-hours on enquiries, but never open a murder investigation.[36] Instead, police arrest Stephen for perverting the course of justice, a crime for which he will be sentenced to eight months in Brixton Prison after admitting his guilt on March 23, 2015.[37]

5

GABRIEL

July 2014, south London

While awaiting his court appearance for the charge of perverting the course of justice, Stephen is free. He continues to live in his flat at 62 Cooke Street, aware that he will only have to appear before a judge in nine months' time. It is in this period that he meets a young Slovakian by the name of Gabriel Kovari. The 22-year-old has left his conservative home country for the comparatively liberal London, hoping that he can embrace his gay identity in an environment in which it is safe to be open about such matters. Before he meets Stephen, he moves in with a man called John Pape in south London, just one month after the death of Anthony Walgate. He meets John on a gay dating site called Bender but, rather than pursuing a sexual relationship, the two decide to become flatmates in July 2014.[38]

John is a little older than Gabriel, being in his mid-30s. He finds his new housemate to be intelligent and sensitive, often stumbling upon poetry that the slight Slovakian had written and left scattered around the apartment. John is glad to have made such a charming new friend. But just six weeks after moving in, Gabriel abruptly informs him that he's moving out of the apartment. He's off to Barking, to live with a man called Stephen. For some reason, Stephen has offered the younger man of a boyish appearance the opportunity to stay for free in his flat. Not exactly flush with cash, the young shop-worker agrees and, on August 23, 2014, moves into 62 Cooke Street.[39]

August 2014, Barking, east London

Gabriel immediately realises why Stephen wants him there. The older host hopes that the agreement will revolve around regular sex. Seeing just one bedroom at the apartment, Gabriel makes his position clear by sleeping on the sofa. He texts a friend saying he does not want to share a bed with his new flatmate. But Stephen is undeterred.[40] The next day, Stephen sets about boasting about the new man in his life, inviting his neighbour, Ryan Edwards, to come and meet his 'twink flatmate' and adding that he is taking 'good care of him'.[41]

Ryan agrees to meet Gabriel, despite his friendship with Stephen having cooled somewhat. Though he is used to the 'ritual' of meeting the men on whom Stephen had designs, Ryan immediately recognises that Gabriel is different to the others. He is a 'breath of fresh air', articulate, intelligent and aspirational. Ryan can't spot any vulnerability in Gabriel. But he does note naivety, as the young immigrant clearly saw nothing untoward about being offered a place to stay for free in such an expensive city. Gabriel, however, is feeling somewhat vulnerable as he spots Stephen going to the toilet and decides to confide in Ryan, saying: "Stephen isn't the person you think he is – he's a bad man."

This disturbs the listener, who for some time has watched his neighbour descend into a vortex of drug abuse and strange behaviour. The assertion, combined with how uninterested Gabriel is in sex with Stephen, makes Ryan nervous. He quickly offers the opportunity to stay at his home instead. As Stephen makes his way back from the toilet, Gabriel finds a moment to hurriedly say he'll consider it. This is the last time Ryan will ever see Gabriel alive.

On August 25, Ryan asks Stephen how Gabriel is during a text message conversation, only to receive some strange news. He's gone to live with another local guy, Stephen says, adding it's 'some soldier guy he had been chatting to online'.[42] It's the second time that day that Stephen has made a claim about Gabriel's whereabouts. At around 5am, he'd used Gabriel's own phone to text one of his friends and claim that the Slovakian hadn't been at the flat for two days. The next day he uses a different phone number to tell another friend that Gabriel has left unexpectedly, heading to Spain to live with his boyfriend Thierry Amodio.[43]

On August 27 at around 5pm, Stephen speaks to his sister, Sharon, who phoned her younger brother to find him sounding stressed. He tells her in a panic that he can't wake a man who is lying unresponsive in his flat. He admits they've both had drugs. A confused Sharon asks how long the body has been there, to be told that Gabriel's been lifeless in his home for one day and one night, meaning that at the time of conflicting messages to friends, Gabriel was already dead.[44] Unlike his behaviour after the death of Anthony, Stephen is laying the groundwork. He's preparing stories before calling the police. Transparent tales, granted. But he's becoming more dangerous.

Sharon visits her brother's flat on August 28 to find her sibling subdued and tired. The body has gone. This tracks with her advice that he should call the police about the body.[45] But what she doesn't know is that Stephen has dumped the corpse just hours before her arrival. He has left it slumped in the grave-yard of St Margaret's Church in Barking, less than 400 yards from his home. She asks her brother who the young man was and what the police had said. Stephen lies, telling her that it was a Lithuanian national named Anthony and that he is now on bail.[46] This isn't the first time Sharon has received grim news from her brother. When the actual Anthony had died, he told her it had happened in his flat when the pair were taking drugs.[47]

* * *

Barbara Denham, a short-haired 64-year-old, is walking her dog across Abbey Green, next to St Margaret's graveyard, on August 28, when she spots a young man leaning against a wall. The well-meaning woman is immediately concerned and decides to check on him. The scene looks evermore bizarre the closer she gets, as she notices that a pair of dark sunglasses seem to have been jammed onto his face, given the awkward angle at which they sit. One eye is exposed and clearly glazed over. Barbara reaches out to gently touch him, on his ankle, hoping to jog him into a response. She feels the cold skin of an unresponsive body and calls the police.[48]

* * *

John Pape answers his door to the bemusing sight of police officers standing before him. Gabriel Kovari has died of an overdose, they tell him. His body has been found in a church-yard in Barking. The cause of death is clear. There was no foul play. No DNA tests have been run at the scene, not even on the sunglasses so clearly shoved onto his face by another man. John is stunned; something just isn't right. The quiet, poetry-writing Slovakian he'd moved in with had suddenly taken enough drugs to kill himself? He'd moved out just weeks before; where were the signs of a spiralling drug addiction, an appetite so insatiable it'd result in death? Aside from some medication he'd spotted in his flatmate's room, there seemed to be no real evidence of substance use at all, let alone something of this magnitude. And why would he experiment in a graveyard of all places? Unsure about the story that clearly has police who have now left his address convinced, he decides to investigate with the limited tools he has available. A cursory Google search of the phrase 'unexplained deaths Barking' reveals that another young man, Anthony Walgate, was found in incredibly similar circumstances just months before.[49]

John contacts Gabriel's boyfriend, Thierry, who is also exasperated about the lack of curiosity from the police. The most detailed account of what happened to Gabriel to reach

Thierry isn't from the police at all, but from a man called Jon Luck, who is actually Stephen Port. What he doesn't realise is that the story is a total fabrication. As far as he knows, Jon Luck is a Californian former porn star who for some reason now lives in London. He tells the bereaved boyfriend that Gabriel cheated on him as they had sex on August 24. Jon is concerned that the police might want to speak to him, because his DNA might be on Gabriel. For a man with a seemingly casual relationship with Gabriel, Jon seems pretty clued-up on his death, telling Thierry that he died as the result of a drug overdose while having sex in a graveyard.[50]

It's not just Gabriel's death that Jon seems to know about, but the wider context in which it occurred. He describes a veritable epidemic of deviants luring younger gay men to orgies. Once there, they drug and rape the invitees.[51] John Pape is disturbed that such things could be happening with no investigation from the police. 'They've clearly missed something,' he thinks, 'and what if I'm in danger, as Gabriel's friend?' John urges Thierry to get in touch with the police, fearing he can't do much as he's not next of kin. Despite these difficulties, John tried to raise the issue many times in the months that follow, keen to do whatever he can to alert the police. But Barking and Dagenham officers remain unmoved. Gabriel has not been murdered. There is no need to worry.[52]

So unmoved are the officers by the two deaths as many months apart, they do not perform any outreach into the community. They do not attract attention, for example, from Ryan Edwards, whose last meeting with Gabriel could well raise concerns. At the very least it might prompt an interview with Stephen, a check of his transparent attempt at a cover-up during his conversations with Thierry and a quick look at the other time this man was before them in an almost identical situation. A check of his phone records would reveal chats with his sister, Sharon, who has no reason to lie to the police and would explain that her younger brother was in a panic due to a corpse in his flat. Again. None of this happens. Ryan doesn't go to the police. He does not do so due to him making the reasonable assumption that the police would appeal for the public's help if there was a reason to do so. Stephen remains free.

All the while, John is keeping an eye on the death of his former flatmate. During the early stages of his search for the truth, he'd checked Gabriel's Facebook profile shortly after being told he was dead. John hoped to see warm tributes from loved ones, touching sentiments befitting of the bright young man he'd briefly known. There was nothing. Not a trace that he'd died. He concluded that the police hadn't bothered to contact Gabriel's family.

6

DANIEL

September 2014, Barking, east London

In the weeks following Gabriel's death, Stephen contacts a young chef named Daniel Whitworth. He speaks to the 21-year-old chef from Gravesend, Kent, on the website Fit Lads. Apparently emboldened, Stephen suggests something at odds with his shy, indoors persona as he proposes they meet in the open for a drink before going to his flat. He reassures the young man that he thinks it best they meet outside his home first 'so you know I'm not some psycho'.[53] On September 18, Daniel tells his boyfriend, Rick Waumsley, that he'll be home late from his job in Canary Wharf, east London.

* * *

Cynthia Adams is walking through the grounds of St Margaret's two days later, performing her church warden duties. She sees what looks like a drunk, sleeping man with a bottle in his hand.

He's sitting against a wall. 'He must have drunk himself silly and is pausing for a rest,' she thinks. Though there's nothing particularly unusual about that scenario, something about this scene in particular strikes her as odd as she continues about her day. She has no idea that he is dead. Nor has she any notion that her former colleague, Stephen, murdered the young man she now walks past.

* * *

Barbara Denham is once again taking her daily walk through the grounds when she spots the second man she'd seen slumped over in St Margaret's graveyard in just over three weeks. Beneath him is a blue bedsheet and he is holding a piece of paper, protected by a plastic wallet, in his left hand. 'Not another one,' she thinks in utter disbelief as she once again makes her tentative approach. Barbara touches Daniel's stomach, which is exposed due to his t-shirt being pulled above it. Again, her hand meets cold flesh. Again, she calls Barking and Dagenham Police to tell them that a young man has died.[54]

Officers arrive on the scene to find the piece of paper bearing a hand-written note along with Daniel's corpse. Purporting to be from the deceased, it says that Daniel killed himself with an overdose of GHB. The reason? He killed Gabriel Kovari. They were having sex at a friend's house, the note says, when he'd given his lover some GHB only for him to overdose. The note's author is Stephen, who has concocted a cover story that not only contradicts the one ostensibly from Jon Luck, but contains blatant and obvious clues as to foul play that should, in the mind of any competent officer, raise questions as to the authenticity of this alleged suicide. Its contents cannot be believed by a thinking person.[55]

In the scrawled 'confession', the apparently suicidal Daniel expresses guilt at hurting his family by taking an overdose, but doesn't mention a single relative by name. Its tone is impersonal and its length doesn't cover a side of A4 paper. But it gives the police an explanation as to the death that was bugging the likes of John Pape. Here's their answer. Daniel killed him. The truth abounds, with zero detective work. One might be tempted to forgive a face-value reading of the note from trained officers, were it not for the inclusion of this line from the author: 'BTW [by the way] please do not blame the guy I was with last night, we only had sex and then I left, he knows nothing of what I have done.'[56]

Who is the guy from last night? The police do not ask. Why would he be blamed when there's a suicide note? The police do not ask. Why would a desperate young man, suffering suicidal guilt, take up almost half of his last testament exonerating this supposedly inconsequential mystery man? The police do not ask. The note that should have aroused so much suspicion and confusion instead clarified the brutal scene onto which they'd stumbled. Daniel had noticed that Gabriel had stopped breathing during sex, dumped his body in a panic and now returned to that same spot to kill himself in a ritualistic repentance. Of course, despite being distraught at what he'd done, he'd carefully placed the note in a clear plastic wallet to ensure that it wasn't damaged when officers discovered his corpse and, along with it, the exoneration of an anonymous 'guy'.

So incurious are the police about this bizarre note, they do not carry out a fingerprint test on the note, or wallet, which would match those of a certain man presumably on their books as he awaits his day in court for perverting the course of justice.[57] The note, taken as credible, also provides a situation in which the blue bedsheet need not be tested. Stephen's DNA – specifically his semen – goes undetected. His ploy succeeds. Daniel's family will now have to learn that not only is he dead, but that he took his own life after killing a man with whom he'd cheated on his boyfriend.[58]

* * *

Mandy Pearson is at home in Gravesend, Kent. She is at the front door, which is open, wondering why two police officers are standing before her removing their helmets. They tell her that her stepson is dead. Her husband Adam Whitworth's only child overdosed in a graveyard in Barking. The devastated couple, like John Pape and Sarah Walgate before her, cannot comprehend what they are hearing. Suicide? There was a note? They need to see it. None of this makes sense. Despite their grief, or perhaps because of it, they proceed to exercise more scepticism than the entire Barking and Dagenham Metropolitan Police Service. Their questions only increase when they get hold of the note. Or at least, part of it.[59]

For reasons that would surely confound any rational being should they ever be known, officers scan and email just a scrap of the note to Mandy and Adam. The portion they send is the note's conclusion, in which Daniel was thought to have said an emotional goodbye to his family. The parents are not convinced by the sign-off. Surely the police cannot be taking the word of this note as proof of suicide. For one thing, they can't even be sure that it's Daniel's handwriting. Like most families who live apart from their child, their communication is usually through phone calls, text messages and social media. In order to help the police, the couple send them a birthday card containing a message written by Daniel's hand.[60] Perhaps an expert can look into it? They also press police to see the full suicide note. When Adam finally sees it, he cannot believe that it is being taken at face value. The full note, riddled with spelling and grammatical errors which appear here uncorrected, reads:

'I am sorry to everyone, mainly my family but I cant go on anymore. I took the life of my friend Gabriel Idine, we was just having some fun at a mates place and I got carried away and gave him another shot of G. I didnt notice while we was having sex that he had stopped breathing. I tried everything to get him to breath again but it was too late, it was an accident but I blame myself for what happened and I didnt tell my family I went out. I know I would go to prison if I go to police and I cant do that to my family and at least this way I can at least be with Gabriel again, I hope he will forgive me.

'BTW. Please do not blame the guy I was with last night, we only had sex then I left, he knows nothing of what I have done. I have taken what g I had left with sleeping pills so if does kill me its what I deserve.

Feeling dizzy now as took 10 min ago so hoping you understand my writing.

'I dropped my phone on way here so should be in the grass somewhere.

'Sorry to everyone

'Love always

'Daniel P W.'

Adam is overcome with incredulous suspicion. He's being expected to believe that his son was so desperate not to hurt him by going to prison that he'd killed himself, all the while knowing that nothing could hurt him more than the death of his child. This central claim of the note seems totally implausible. Perhaps a claim that he was too scared to face jail, or that he was too scared to face his family when this terrible secret came out would have been more understandable. But this just doesn't make any sense. Mandy is similarly confused as to how a death linked to this note can be regarded as non-suspicious. At the very least, the man with whom Daniel had been spending the night before he'd supposedly written this suicide note should surely be worthy of tracking down. Perhaps questioning him could provide some clarity. But the police are resolute – there is nothing suspicious about Daniel's death. Perhaps they'll never know the full story. These things happen.

* * *

It's not just the families of the dead asking questions. The appearance of three bodies of similar age in almost identical circumstances, with two of them dumped in the same grave-yard, is raising suspicion at the local paper by September 2014. *Barking and Dagenham Post* news editor Ramzy Alwakeel tells his reporter, Freddy Mayhew, to put in a call to the police and ask whether or not the deaths are linked. Detective Chief Inspector Tony Kirk tells him that the deaths are 'unusual but not suspicious'.[61] Ramzy, an incredibly rational young man whose reasonability results in a usually calm disposition, is shocked. 'There are so many unanswered questions here,' he thinks. 'The police are unconcerned but they seem to be on shaky ground telling us that the public has nothing to worry about. How can they know that when they know so little?'

There's clearly a story here, despite the police not seeing it. But Ramzy and Freddy know almost nothing about the victims. They don't even know that all three were gay. Nonetheless, they decide the deaths warrant attention, even if the latest development in the story is the police's assurance that there's nothing to worry about. Ramzy commissions a story that both highlights the apparent danger and the strangeness of the police response thus far. The baffling headline on the September 29 story reads: 'Unusual but not suspicious' says Met detective about three Barking bodies.[62]

* * *

An already frustrated John Pape hears about Daniel's death while keeping an eye on the police response to Gabriel's. He's still in touch with Thierry, who in turn is still speaking with Stephen Port posing as Jon Luck. The supposed ex-porn star has been in touch regarding the death of Daniel, once again linking it to Gabriel's. Jon claims to have seen Gabriel and Daniel at one of the orgies of rape he's mentioned. Thierry, who is living in Spain, urges him to contact the police. As far as he knows, Jon never does so. An increasingly desperate Thierry takes action. He contacts Barking and Dagenham Police himself, repeating the rape orgies narrative. He includes a link to Jon Luck's Facebook profile.[63]

John, meanwhile, contacts *Pink News* to report his concerns in the hope that media exposure can force an investigation. His email to the gay news website reads: 'My biggest fear is that vulnerable young gay men are being taken advantage of in Barking with fatal consequences. I do not trust the police to give this their full attention without someone pushing for answers.'[64]

Nicky Duffy, the site's UK Editor, calls the police in October 2014 and explains John's fears about a threat facing gay men. Having weighed up whether they should investigate reports of exclusively gay drug-fuelled orgies in Barking in light of two GHB overdoses in the area, the police decline and reaffirm that the deaths are not suspicious. This leaves Nicky with what appears to be rumour and an article from a local newspaper confirming a lack of investigation. *Pink News* decides not to run a story.[65]

John is also in contact with human rights campaigner Peter Tatchell, who is somewhat legendary in gay activist circles for his bravery and outreach. Peter fears that a serial killer is at large, given the identity of the victims. He tells John to contact

Galop, an LGBT+ anti-violence charity.[66] Galop's brief is to assist members of its community who feel let-down by the police. If ever Barking and Dagenham Police needed an outside force to kick them into action, it was now. Their indifference to vital clues strewn about the crime scenes had caused them to abort any lines of enquiry before they'd even had a chance to manifest in the minds of the officers who'd attended the scenes.

This third tragic death isn't just something that seems suspicious to the grieving family of Daniel Whitworth. It isn't just something that seems to be more than a suicide to local journalists who'd seen two remarkably similar deaths. It is a case that is arousing suspicion in anybody who came into contact with it, including in the mind of Barbara Denham as soon as she discovered Daniel's body.[67] This ordinary member of the public, without the training of Barking and Dagenham's finest, without the opportunity to forensically analyse the crime scene, is at this moment in time exercising more critical thinking than the force that is paid to do so. As Barbara watches the case – or lack thereof – unfold, she's left with the impression that the police involved don't really know what they're doing. This incompetence, the finer details of which are only known by those close to the non-investigation, are soon to be laid bare at the inquest into the deaths of Gabriel and Daniel.

7

UNANSWERED

The inquest into the deaths of Gabriel and Daniel was only the second I'd attended as a journalist. I came to Walthamstow Coroner's Court six months into my first reporting job at the *Barking and Dagenham Post*. Having joined in December the previous year, I'd had no involvement in stories covering the discovery of the bodies. Ramzy, who had commissioned the 'unusual but not suspicious' article had since left for the *London Evening Standard* and my new editor, Janine Rasiah, and I, were new to the case. But even without an intricate knowledge of the background, or of the back and forth between the police and our paper, this inquest, and its outcome, struck us as bizarre, incomplete and unsatisfactory. From the back of the court, I watched the disbelief spread over coroner Nadia Persaud's face as a police officer admitted that he hadn't carried out basic tests. Daniel's loved ones sat at the front of the court, having been granted the displeasure of a front-row view of this stupidity.

Daniel's boyfriend, Ricky Waulmsley, a short-haired and slight man of a meek appearance, looked exhausted as he sat beside the towering figure of Adam Whitworth and his partner, Mandy. John Pape was the only person who was able to turn out for Gabriel, his family being far away in their home country.

But his brother, Adam, had sent an email that the coroner read aloud. It described a caring, inquisitive and artistic young man robbed of his chance to make a mark on the world. 'He wanted to make a difference,' it read. 'He was full of love and care for others, loved the company of his friends. He had excellent relationships with all his relatives and the desire to prove himself to the world was so strong he probably made a fatal mistake and left for London on his own.'[68]

John confirmed his former flatmate's creative, gentle side, telling the inquest that he'd noticed poems on the theme of loneliness. He also made it clear that Gabriel wasn't known to be a drug user. John said that while Gabriel was staying with him, he'd signed up to the gay dating app Grindr to meet new people. "His plan was to make a go of it in London," he told the inquest. "He wanted his life to begin in London. I think the intention was, as a young gay man, lots of people come to London because it's an open, tolerant place."

Indeed, he'd been so determined to live in the capital that he'd previously stayed in a hostel on the Isle of Dogs and was prepared to sleep on the streets. Originally, John had offered him a room for two weeks. But, when it became clear that Gabriel had nowhere to stay and was willing to sleep rough, he felt it only right to let him stay for longer. His lodger had also been facing cash flow problems, claiming that his boss at an eastern European store where he'd been doing shifts had failed to pay him. Once Gabriel had moved to Barking, John said, he'd been unable to contact his friend. He confirmed that after his death, he'd become aware of rumours that Gabriel had been having sex at orgies. Though it was clear that Gabriel had died of an overdose, the coroner had no CCTV footage with which to determine if he'd taken himself to the graveyard.

The most damning details of the inquest surfaced during the examination of the police's actions when they found Daniel's body. Despite there being clear signs that Daniel had either been dragged, or found himself in some sort of struggle with another person before his death, Acting Detective Inspector Rolf Schamberger told the coroner that there was nothing to suggest that the fatal dose of GHB had been administered by anyone other than Daniel himself. He was also the officer on hand to explain, to the bewilderment of everybody in the room, that no DNA testing had taken place. Not even on the bottle of GHB resting by Daniel's crossed legs.[69]

Despite the 'suicide note', those present at the inquest heard that Daniel had never shown any desire to end his life. Though his medical history included mild self-harm, these acts contained no suicidal intent, the coroner said. At the time of his death, he'd been working as a chef de partie at the ISS restaurant in Canary Wharf. His colleagues described him as happy. His father said he'd had a 'happy childhood' and described an 'active, intelligent outdoor boy' who 'loved days on his bike exploring leafy byways'.[70] 'Daniel also made sure he kept in contact with his grandmother, helping around the garden,' his statement, read aloud to the inquest, said. 'He kept his love of nature and other life and travel. Those who knew him well were shocked by the terrible news.'

A pathologist told the inquest that marks on Daniel's body indicated he may have been man-handled, another sign suggesting foul play.[71] The pathologist said: "There was bruising below both arms in the armpit regions which is unlikely to have been caused accidentally and may have resulted from manual handling of the deceased, most likely prior to death".[72] The police admitted at the inquest that they had been unable to rule out the possibility that Daniel had been moved by someone else.

The coroner, with far fewer tools with which to determine what had happened to Daniel, was unable to do what the police had done so easily and did not record his cause of death as suicide. Ms Persaud recorded an open verdict, which essentially meant that the inquest was unsure as to the reason for Daniel's death. She did the same for Gabriel.[73]

After specifically raising 'the question of someone moving'[74] Daniel, Ms Persaud made her closing remarks. She said: "I don't have sufficient evidence to have any conclusion other than an open conclusion. I find that Gabriel Kovari died on the 28th of August in the grounds of St Margaret's Church of a mixed drug overdose – my conclusion is an open conclusion. I do have some concerns surrounding Daniel's death that have not been answered by the police investigation. My concerns of a third party being involved in Daniel's death can't be allayed by the evidence brought to the court.

"I can't say I'm satisfied he took his own life or was unlawfully killed. The only conclusion I can make is an open conclusion. Daniel Whitworth, born 22nd December 1993 in Gravesend, Kent, died on the 20th September 2014, found deceased in St Margaret's Church yard. My conclusion is an open conclusion. I'm sorry to the family."

Hardly closure for the families. Mandy took the chance to press police further, understandably unsatisfied with the open conclusion. She hoped that the police would investigate further now that a conclusion of suicide had not been reached. John was also left with questions. The note's veracity had been totally undermined. And if Daniel didn't murder Gabriel, then who did? And was he still at large?

But neither John nor Daniel's family would get their investigation. Despite the police admitting at the inquest that all they'd done with the fake suicide note was take it down to the station for a look, the case, as far as they were concerned, was closed. It was difficult for John not to conclude that the police had reasons that were nothing to do with actual evidence for reaching their conclusion. In his words: "How can they not have linked those first three deaths? You've got three young gay men propped up, dead, within 300 metres of each other, within four months of each other. In my opinion, it seems as if the police just went 'oh well, that's what young gay men do – they take drugs and they die in grave yards.'"[75]

Even if the police thought they had these deaths figured out, even if they were utterly convinced themselves that these three young men had overdosed by their own hand and they did not suspect murder even in the slightest, they should have been more proactive. Peter Tatchell pointed out to me that even if the police didn't regard them as suspicious, protocol requires them to circulate information among the gay press in order to appeal for witnesses to find the answers to unanswered questions. Like John, Peter was left with the impression that a misplaced belief that it is common for gay people to do drugs and find themselves in this situation. He also believes police ineptitude, negligence or outright homophobia could have played their parts. But Peter also laid some of the blame at the coroner's door. He said Ms Persaud was wrong to press ahead with the inquest in the face of the obvious gaps in evidence that surfaced in the police's testimony and should have demanded an adjournment until the officers found answers to the many questions surrounding the deaths. With the Met clearly unwilling to do this without a strong arm pushing them to do so, this could have kickstarted a fresh investigation.[76]

The open conclusion inevitably affected the write-up after I returned from the inquest to the *Post*'s office in Ilford, east London. With hindsight, it's difficult to understate how much more use the local press might have been had the case been adjourned due to gaps in evidence. An article explaining this decision, plus the circumstances surrounding the deaths of Daniel and Gabriel, would surely have aroused suspicion across the community in Barking, rather than restricting it to those directly involved in the case. Most importantly, it would have left nowhere to hide for the police. What happened in reality was that Stephen Port got free promotion of the false narrative that he'd put out to Gabriel's boyfriend, Thierry; drug-fuelled orgies were feared to be responsible for the deaths of two innocent gay men.

This was because my news editor and I wanted to do our best to highlight the apparent dangers the inquest threw open. The main concern was that there was an underworld that neither we nor most of our readers knew about; an underworld of unregulated, orgy-based drug-taking that had cost two lives. I figured it was better to risk an over-the-top warning about that than ignore it. With no prior knowledge of the case, no police outreach raising the alarm and the need to produce an accurate report of the proceedings as opposed to a list of things that didn't happen, such as proper police investigation, we took the only line we felt was strongest and put out the open conclusion. We had little else to go on as the inquest was not a forum for Mandy, Adam, Ricky or John to vent their various suspicions. And Adam politely refused to speak further about his son's death after the inquest when I approached. Seeing his grief, and awed at how measured he was in dealing with a stranger asking if he'd like any pictures of his dead son in the final piece, I felt it best not to press the matter. I did speak to John briefly at the coroner's court, but I don't recall him saying anything that I could latch on to during that conversation either. A more experienced reporter would, and should, have pointed out the lack of DNA testing and that the police could not rule out the fact that the bodies had been moved. But, just like Ryan Edwards, I deferred to the police, concluding that if they had needed to carry out such tests, they wouldn't be admitting, in an inquest open to the press, to not doing so. And John himself, as suspicious and concerned as he was, had bought at least part of Stephen's story – that young gay men were being drugged and raped at parties run by something of a rapist ring, as opposed to being targeted by a serial killer, which he'd relayed to the inquest.[77]

In the end, we ran the story with the headline: 'Double drug overdose killed Barking lovers found in church grounds'. Though correct in the cause of death, it lent credence to Stephen's account that Daniel and Gabriel had been romantically involved. It may as well have carried the byline Barking and Dagenham Police (additional copy by Stephen Port). At the very least, the story made clear that the coroner had not reached a conclusion of suicide, which caused a lot of confusion in our newsroom. The publisher's London-wide website, *London 24*, picked up the *Post*'s story, and the editor, Kate Nelson, had some questions.

In any mention of drugs, sex or suicide during the rest of the article, we were careful to point out that it was the note that made the claims, not necessarily Daniel. We also substantiated claims made in the note with phrases such as 'Walthamstow Coroner's Court heard'. This is common practice in journalism when reporting on things that are said as part of a legal proceeding, that might not necessarily be proven as true. Reporters and editors take this very literally as meaning that the thing was said in court and heard by those present, but stop short of reporting it as fact. You may have spotted this during murder trials. Before a killer is convicted, the copy will read 'x murdered y in cold blood, jurors heard today'. If x is later convicted, you can remove the subordinate clause, because it is now established fact. The average reader may not pick up on these nuances, but Kate certainly had. She made her way over to me from the other end of the office wearing a look of frustrated exasperation she was struggling to mitigate with a kind smile. She asked why an open verdict had been recorded if a suicide note had been found. The inclusion of such a note in proceedings would usually mean that we could call a spade a spade and run a headline that mentioned suicide. But the fact was that we couldn't say it was a suicide, we could simply say that claims of suicide were heard in court. It resulted in a story almost as confusing as the previous article carrying the police's unusual but not suspicious line. It didn't smell right. However, with a lack of any real investigation, we did not know why.

* * *

In the same month we were unwittingly publishing a rapist's lies, Stephen was released from prison with an electronic tag. In March of 2015, he had been sentenced to eight months in Brixton Prison for perverting the course of justice after fabricating the story of stumbling across the body of Anthony Walgate. Eleven days after the story appeared on the *Barking and Dagenham Post*'s website, Stephen sexually assaulted a man, who fled from his flat in terror.[78] With three lives taken, there was still no murder investigation in sight. That summer, he forced syringes of GHB up the anuses of two men against their will.[79] The first of the two slipped into a drug-induced daze after being penetrated with the syringe despite making clear through Grindr conversations that he did not take such substances. He was unable to fight back, or even fully understand where he was, as he lay face-down while Stephen raped him.

* * *

Let's at this point pause to consider the kindest interpretation of the perspective of the police force not bothering to investigate these deaths. In order to show just how egregious their disinterest was, I'm going to grant them the benefit of the doubt for the sake of argument, purely to show that even if we do so, it's still utterly unacceptable that they didn't focus their attention on the possibility of a sinister explanation. To this end, I'll imagine that well-meaning officers were innocently unfamiliar with the gay community to the point that they couldn't tell the difference between a cultural norm and an obvious red flag. Such officers, in their ignorance, may well assume that taking dangerous amounts of GHB is just something they don't understand and that it fits that a community that engages in such behaviour is beyond their understanding. I'll consider, as part of this thought experiment, that this baffles them. In finding the bodies of Anthony, Gabriel and Jack, they have confronted scenarios so bizarre, unchartered and confusing that we can, in the context of this exercise, forgive them for attributing the tragedy to a world which they simply do not understand: the world of the drug-taking homosexual. Let's say that on top of that, Barking and Dagenham's less-than-cosmopolitan image makes it conceivable that any drug-using homosexuals would find themselves outside the mainstream. As such, they may be forced to move in darkness, taking drugs at one another's homes and in churchyard corners. Officers not familiar with seeing a vibrant gay scene in the borough may find it completely fitting that such a scene operates as a parallel society they are not capable of understanding. Entertain this possibility – and consider how it just might make you think it perfectly unsuspicious that this unseen, unreachable and unregulated underground had, as a result of its inherent danger, burst forth as a rude interruption of normal society.

Put all of this in your mind, then imagine yourself looking at each of the bodies of Stephen's first three murder victims. These mental acrobatics might, just might, change your perspective entirely. That is, until you spot a single similarity at each of the crime scenes. The common feature of which I write is the fact that Anthony, Gabriel and Daniel all had their clothing pulled upwards, exposing their midriffs. The question to be asked at this point is: 'How did the bodies get there?' Answer: They were dragged.

Stephen left this clue – so obvious it doesn't require DNA testing – and still the police didn't catch him. Factor into this that Gabriel's body was found less than a month after police had charged Stephen over lying to them about the circumstances of Anthony's death. Might it not occur to you, even if you were a well-meaning, sheltered cretin that it could be worth speaking to that dodgy bloke who's been convicted of lying? Apparently not. In the words of my former editor, Ramzy: 'How smoking does a gun have to be?' Far more, it would seem, to stop Jack Taylor dying.

8

JACK

July 23, 2015, Barking, east London

Stephen is back at 62 Cooke Street, having served under three months in Brixton Prison, south London, for perverting the course of justice. He could have faced another five months inside, had his full sentence been served. That would have put his release date at November 23. But none of that matters now. He's free to invite whomever he pleases to the flat in which he's already killed three men.[80]

September 13, 2015, Barking, east London

Jack Taylor is out drinking early into Sunday morning when he decides to call time on his night on the town. He opens the Grindr dating app on his phone and speaks to Stephen. Is he around? They arrange to meet outside Barking train station at 3.15am.[81] From there, the new acquaintances walk across the town centre to Stephen's flat. Stephen's Grindr account vanishes from the platform after he blocks Jack's profile at around 7.20am.[82] For the fourth time, Stephen has a corpse in his apartment. He stays with Jack's body for the day while he tries to figure out what to do, though he will eventually settle on a disposal that so far seems to have worked in his favour.

Dagenham, east London

Donna and Jen Taylor aren't worried when their younger brother doesn't return to the family home on Sunday. He's a grown man, perfectly capable of getting himself back when he's good and ready. Any 25-year-old male living in London would surely find it slightly overbearing if their sisters were pestering them to come back when the most likely reply they'd receive would reveal him to be nursing a hangover on a friend's sofa after a good night out. For all they know, their younger brother had come back and then rose early despite his night out and slipped away before their mother, Jeanette, could notice. It isn't unusual. But the day stretches on. And by the afternoon, Jack still isn't home.[83]

* * *

Donna is speaking to her mother on the phone when she learns of her brother's death. The knowledge comes courtesy of her mother's screams when the police come in to tell Jeanette that Jack has been found. Binmen discovered his body, they explain, in a seated position, propped up in the grounds of St Margaret's Church on September 14. He had taken an overdose in Barking. Jen races to Jeanette's when she hears the news. She walks through the front door to find her mother enveloping her face in a shirt that Jack had worn on Friday. Jeanette is wrapping the garment around herself, clinging to an expiring sense of closeness to her dead son. Jack had been their world. He had elicited all of the compassion expected toward a youngest sibling, while displaying all of the protective gallantry of an older brother. His death shatters the Taylors.[84]

* * *

Donna and Jen simply cannot accept that their brother died of an overdose by his own hand. This unacceptance is not borne of grief. Rather, disbelief, doubt and scepticism pierce the fog of their torment. Why would a family-oriented young man, so beloved by those closest to him, take his own life? Why, if he were so inclined, would he do so in a public churchyard? It could have been an accident, you might say. But if he had died of an overdose, the result of getting carried away with drugs, why was he taking them next to London Road, the busy driving and walking route that leads to the rest of the capital? Why was he even at St Margaret's? It was hardly a regular haunt. Even if they could believe that he was into drugs – which they don't, by the way – to conclude that he would have taken them in this setting is inconceivable. The police must have got it wrong.

Eleven days after Jack's death, Dagenham, east London

Donna and Jen contact the Met for an update, demonstrating more proactivity than the entirety of their local police force.

Their reward is hearing that the investigation about which they are enquiring doesn't exist. Not only do police inform them that they aren't investigating, they categorically state that Jack had not been drugged or raped. Donna and Jen start their own investigation.[85]

They stay up till 5am some nights, completing the grim jigsaw of events that led to their brother's body being found. The sisters place pieces of paper on the floor in an attempt to piece everything together. A quick Google search reveals the deaths of Anthony Walgate, Gabriel Kovari and Daniel Whitworth in sickeningly similar circumstances. About the only thing notably different in the first three deaths from Jack's, save for Daniel's 'suicide note', is extremely trivial geography. Anthony had been found in Cooke Street. Gabriel and Daniel's bodies were found, yes, in St Margaret's, but on the opposite side of the wall that surrounds the graveyard. All of this tragedy within 400 yards. They are stunned by the similarities. And they are aghast that the police aren't connecting the deaths.[86]

The sisters contact police to point out these glaring similarities, for officers to repeat the well-worn line that the deaths are not connected. Even for officers incapable of spotting a pattern, this conclusion demonstrates a shocking lack of competence. For even if it is accepted that none of the fatalities were suspicious, two of them were most certainly linked, even when interpreting their deaths through the eyes of the police. The fake suicide note explicitly linked Gabriel and Daniel, albeit through a false allegation designed to destroy the reputation of one of the two. There really is no excuse for the conclusion that none of these deaths are linked at this point, a fact obvious to the sisters. Donna and Jen are familiar with the *Barking and Dagenham Post*'s report on the inquests into the deaths of Gabriel and Daniel, which also links the two via the fake suicide note.

The note – visible to anyone who is familiar with the four deaths – sparks more questions. Has this been checked for DNA? It must surely have been, with the handwriting properly scrutinised. It looks too suspicious to be taken at face value and further investigation is obviously required. But the police's insistence that the deaths are not suspicious, a conclusion that could only be reached by some sort of rudimentary investigation, given the unusual nature of the deaths, leaves three options to consider. Option one: They checked the note, but Stephen had somehow erased every trace of his DNA, or left none behind. Option two: They checked the note, found Stephen's DNA, but didn't have a match in their system. Option three: Any claims that the note had been DNA tested only for officers to reach the conclusion that the deaths were not suspicious were false.

Option one is difficult to believe, given that Stephen was so stupid as to implicate himself directly in the scrawled suicide note and even called 999 himself after dumping his first body. Option two should be unlikely, given that Stephen had been arrested on June 26, 2014, for perverting the course of justice. At this point, the police were entitled to take a DNA swab, which would later be a match for the note. It's possible that they did not do this. But option three seems the most likely. After all, why would they bother DNA testing the fake suicide note, when they hadn't thought to test the blanket on which Daniel's body lay? Option three also fits with the inquest testimony of Acting Detective Inspector Rolf Schamberger.

Undeterred, the Taylor sisters press on and soon unearth contradictions so basic that it's a wonder the officers involved don't blush, bolt and hand the case over to the pair. Donna asks the police about a syringe that had been found with her brother's body, perhaps not even aware of drug paraphernalia found on the other bodies. Officers tell her that the syringe had not been used. This is the same police force that had previously told her Jack had injected himself and overdosed. Jen, meanwhile, is struck by the strangeness of the scene that was being presented. The sisters went to St Margaret's to the precise spot at which Jack's body had been found. They were being asked to believe that his final living moments were spent in the dirt, with sodden leaves for a seat – when there was a bench nearby. That he also chose a spot which would have had less light than the nearby seat also struck her as incorrect – he was terrified of the dark.[87]

After some time, the officers manage about the only useful thing they have so far achieved regarding the death of Jack Taylor; they tell the sisters that there is CCTV of their younger brother walking from the station. The force allows the sisters to view the footage. Donna and Jen are disturbed to see a tall, blonde man looming over Jack as the pair make their way through Barking town centre. Their suspicion of foul play becomes terrifyingly credible. Or at least they think so.

Barking and Dagenham Police are still sticking to their theory that Jack took an overdose, despite being the people who shared the footage with the sisters. Such is the fervour with which they push this narrative, that Jen feels as though she and her family are being brainwashed. But at least they now have the footage. The police knew they'd seen a strange man towering over their brother. They'll understand their suspicions and, even if they don't believe them, exhaust the line of enquiry. Right? Wrong. The force are not investigating the mystery man and the sisters are faced with the prospect that they might never know the identity of the stranger. His meeting with Jack, his intentions, his very identity could remain a mystery to the very officers tasked with crime detection. There are many mysteries in life. Identifying a male who is fresh from a custodial sentence and has already been linked to the starkly similar death of Anthony Walgate is not one of them. It becomes even less of a brain-stumper when the suspect is captured taking a direct route to his own flat through a well-lit town centre in the English capital.

It isn't just the inclusion of an unknown subject in the footage that disturbs Donna and Jen. The police's interpretation of another moment in the video was key to their theory and the sisters can't help but feel that a certain outcome is being taken for granted with no evidence. Cameras captured Jack walking toward Barking Town Hall – which is on the most direct on-foot route to Cooke Street. Officers tell Donna and Jen that around the town hall, the cameras lose the mystery man. It is through this CCTV blackspot that Jack supposedly walked, heading for Abbey Green, separated from St Margaret's graveyard by a stone wall. But there is no actual footage of Jack going to the green. And it boggles the mind that if he was seen heading there on September 13, it would be September 15 until somebody stumbled across his corpse. This gap in chronology doesn't stop the police's theory, though. Their interpretation of events holds that, after Barking Town Hall, Jack carried on toward the green, and died at some point. They don't once consider that he may have spent the intervening period somewhere else. Despite it being highly unlikely, for the reasons laid out here, that he headed straight to the green, the police never entertain the question Donna and Jen now ask: 'What if Jack turned left?'

Turning left would take Jack to Cooke Street. It would have taken him in the direction of the home of a man whose recent prison sentence was directly linked to the death of Anthony Walgate. Not that Donna and Jen know who Stephen is, but it's surely worth considering that Jack turned left, with the mystery man, rather than parting company with him and ending up on the green. This man needs identifying. The siblings suggest releasing the footage to the media. They tell the family that releasing the CCTV footage would not be something they usually do in circumstances that do not appear to be suspicious. Despite this initial obstruction, the sisters finally secure an appeal in the local paper. This is, of course, after enduring the police going through a strange throat-clearing exercise in which they tell the Taylors such an appeal probably isn't possible because Jack's death definitely wasn't – wait for it – suspicious. Nevertheless, the *Barking and Dagenham Post* and *London Evening Standard* run stills of the CCTV footage in the hope of identifying the man seen walking with Jack hours before his death.[88]

Within hours of the images being published, the identity of the supposedly elusive man is revealed through a tip-off. Two days after the pictures first circulate, Barking and Dagenham police officers finally arrest Stephen Port. It is one month to the day that Jack's body was found. The Metropolitan Police's elite murder squad immediately takes over the case from its Barking and Dagenham division, assigning a specialist homicide unit. Local police refer themselves to the Independent Police Complaints Commission. Questions needed to be answered, for the sake of the victims' families.

It isn't just the bereaved who are left feeling frustrated. The fact that a serial killer has been at large for more than a year leaves gay men asking why the police didn't protect them from a murderer. They couldn't rely on the police performing basic outreach unless harangued into doing so by grieving sisters displaying exemplary grit. Journalists are similarly infuriated. For, in such an environment, the media cannot do its job in raising an effective alarm. When the police are onside, reporters get a green light to warn people of any danger they may or may not be facing without being accused of whipping up fear unnecessarily. But all the police had allowed the *Barking and Dagenham Post* to do was put out the line that everything was fine. True, an astute reader may have taken from a story in which a police officer refers to three similar deaths as not suspicious that said officer is incompetent, which is why Ramzy Alwakeel was correct to commission the *Post* article after Daniel's death. But the more likely reading was that you have nothing to fear if you do not take drugs in graveyards.

But for all the anger coursing through those closest to the case, at least Stephen is now in custody. In a strange show of proactivity, Barking and Dagenham Police telephone Amanda Pearson. Somebody has been arrested for the murder of her stepson, Daniel. As though still somehow in doubt as to what had happened, the officer tells her not to get her hopes up.[89]

9

CAPTURE

The police finally did what Barking and Dagenham officers had neglected to do for 15 months – they charged Stephen Port with murder.[90] Finally, they checked his phone in its entirety. It revealed an incredibly discerning taste in pornography in the form of 83 videos that provided a blueprint for who he would target and how. The clips centred on drugging young men to the point of unconsciousness before raping them.[91]

Once the police had Stephen, he didn't seem to be going anywhere. Aside from the fact that there was a world of untapped evidence to explore, he was an utterly unconvincing car crash of an interviewee. He displayed constant tell-tale signs of anxiety, scratching an apparent itch on his nose. Confidence, as ever, evaded him as he lowered his voice, which was taken as showing he just didn't have conviction in his version of events. Wearing a grey prison jumper, he placed an emphasis on the word 'no', which he used as a response 40 times out of 47 questions. His keenness to place importance on this denial was, for detectives, something of a giveaway, and must have seemed especially odd when set against his mumbling, otherwise unsure performance. There was no incredulity, no 'just what the hell are you accusing me of?'. Just a repetitive 'no', which reduced in volume with each utterance. He also had a habit of crossing his arms and closing his lips, as though there was something within him that he couldn't risk coming out. His hands clenched, squeezing up with tension as he squirmed in his chair. Adrenaline was clearly coursing through his leg as it vibrated in a movement indicative of pressure. And interrogation experts also picked up on a particular statement he uttered when challenged on the deaths. After granting them that he knew of the circumstances surrounding Anthony Walgate, which they already knew, of course, he said that he didn't know how the other three died, adding that everything he had told them up until this point was true. Again, he was betraying a lack of confidence by qualifying his false statement. Those in the know believe a more convincing statement of innocence would simply have been: 'Everything I have told you is true.'[92]

Now that Stephen was in custody, the investigation was picking up, which wasn't difficult compared to what had come before – ie nothing. It speaks to the shoddiness of Barking and Dagenham Police that the thing that first impressed Sarah Sak about the specialist officers now handling the investigation was their ability to take notes. She hadn't seen so much as a scrap of paper on officers until the specialist unit got involved.[93] The downside of this was that the Taylors were rewarded for their hard work by suffering the traumatic indignity of their loved one's body being dug up so it could actually be tested for DNA evidence.

10

AVOIDANCE

Stephen now finds himself facing questions about crimes for which he's not previously had to scrape together a proper explanation. Unlike the people he's dealt with during the non-investigation, these officers are very interested as to why he was the last person to see Jack Taylor alive.

The shy killer, without the option of incapacitating his interrogators with GHB, scrambles for a get-out. Foolishly, he denies ever having spoken to the young man on Grindr. He certainly has not invited him to his flat. Then, in an incredibly crass move, he tells them that Jack isn't even the sort of man he'd usually be sexually attracted to.[94] How can he possibly be suspected of the murder of this man when he isn't even keen on his photo?

But he does give them some information. Stephen points the police to a man from whom he has bought crystal meth, GHB and a 'cock ring' sex toy, with which he hoped to maintain a drooping erection. He was round there the other day, in fact, in East Ham. The dealer's name is Peter. Peter Hirons. Stephen insists that the sole purpose of his last visit was to return the apparently unsatisfactory, and so presumably used, sex aid. What he definitely does not tell them is that during that visit he dumped a black bin liner among the many already strewn about the flat. It contains evidence Stephen hopes will frame Peter for Jack's death, police later tell Peter. The bag retains its anonymity, he hopes, going unnoticed as it sits among the other bags while Peter decorates his apartment.

Stephen begins to drop clumsy clues in the hope of making Peter the focus. He admits to knowing Jack, telling the officers that the young man had also gone to Peter's flat to buy drugs. He tells his interrogators that Peter has young men brought to his flat for sex and drugs. Before the police head to Peter's flat, with Stephen hoping they'll arrest him instead, he tells them that Peter knows him as Lance. But police never find the bag. Peter threw it out by mistake. They instead discover conversations on Peter's phone between him and Jack in which the younger man refused to take drugs. They also take a random man's waistcoat, wrongly believing it to be Stephen's.

His unsophisticated plan fails. Stephen appears at Barkingside Magistrates' Court on October 19, 2015, charged with four counts of murder and four counts of administering a poison with intent to endanger life or inflict grievous bodily harm. Following his hearing, he is remanded in custody and told that the next time he'll be out of prison will be to face trial at the Old Bailey.[95]

Stephen's arrest shocked his Cooke Street neighbours, for whom it was beyond strange that a quiet man who wouldn't even make eye contact with them was accused of such brutal crimes. One of the street's residents told me: "He was really quiet, didn't say 'boo' to a goose and was never in any trouble. He was a bit odd looking and didn't even say hello. He used to walk along with his head down."

Cynthia Adams, the church warden who'd found Daniel's body, was disturbed when she realised that she knew the man who'd been arrested. He was the same, strange colleague she remembered staring at the floor when she worked in the kitchen at West Ham Bus Garage. "I realised I knew the guy," she later told me. "I couldn't believe he'd do these things because of how quiet he was."[96]

But the closest person he'd had to a childhood friend, Liam, the boy with whom he'd spent hours running races in the playground, was less perplexed. "You're always going to be surprised if one of your schoolmates is revealed as a serial killer," he said. "But if someone said you have to pick someone you went to school with, he would be in the frame."

11

ALIBI

Inside the walls of Belmarsh prison[97], south-east London, Stephen had even more time to peddle falsehoods and revel in escapism. From his cell, he cultivated the portrait of a wrongly accused man. Letters from jail paint a picture of a misunderstood celebrity missing the comforts of home and hoping that one day the world will understand how absurd it is that he's facing murder charges.[98] And, as ever, he can't resist boasting in his letters to the outside world.

Clearly viewing himself as something of a conversationalist, he regales one pen pal with claims that he's had sex with politicians and a BBC television presenter. The politicians hired him as an escort. He and the presenter met on holiday, but he won't be giving out any names – just in case the letter is intercepted by his guards. The accounts are unverified, but a report of the correspondence did mention that Stephen named the show which the presenter was fronting. He claims that they even dated for a time.[99] It could well be true and it seems befitting of Stephen's bumbling stupidity that he would go to great pains not to name the man in question before pointing directly to him by mentioning the name of his show. Whether or not he mentioned the name, it's unlikely that national news media would take the word of a serial killer and risk linking an innocent man to a murderer by prying into his private life. Or rather, it's unlikely they'd come out of such an exercise looking good.

Despite facing such egregious charges, Stephen still manages to have some fun with his notoriety, calling himself a 'celebrity' and speculating as to whether there are any others in the prison. He can't see anybody else on his wing that he recognises from television.[100] The tone of his letters reveal a man apparently oblivious to the graveness of his situation. Instead of facing it, he seems determined to engage in escapism, just like he did by setting up fake social media profiles. Stephen uses his time inside as an opportunity to add to this ever-growing, ever-unlikely CV, by claiming to have modelled Jasper Conran underwear for the department store Debenhams. He claims it was his 'slim, toned' physique and 'really good six-pack' that landed him the job. Writing that his role models were action stars Jean-Claude Van Damme, Arnold Schwarzenegger, Chuck Norris and Sylvester Stallone, he says that he's a 'senior belt' in taekwondo with five silver medals at 'British nationals' behind him as well as 'a bronze in English championships'. Predictably, Debenhams said it had no record of Port working for the chain.[101]

The severity of the situation clearly hasn't hit Stephen. He clearly doesn't understand that the only reason he's been getting away with murder is because of an inept police force. He seems to think that he might have actually been adequate at covering up his crimes. That suicide note. The lack of a murder charge despite his 999 call. Perhaps he was on to something. He could get himself out of this. He just had to get his side out there.

* * *

Cody Lachey, an ex-gang member, drug dealer and prisoner, took it upon himself to write to Stephen because, in his own words, he's a 'nosey bastard'.[102] The former inmate of Manchester's Strangeways prison had also exchanged letters with Moors Murderer Ian Brady. Now he wanted to know what Stephen was all about. He wrote under the pretence of someone keen to extract legal advice from Stephen's case and also claimed to want advice on escorting. Stephen saw his chance to tell his incredibly unlikely side of the story: he was innocent.

What follows in their correspondence is something utterly bizarre that is testament to Stephen's failure to grasp reality. While pointing out that it's 'ridiculous' that he's facing four murder charges, he casually slips in that other inmates ask him to sign pictures of himself in their newspapers. There's a paradox for you: wrongly accused yet revelling in the attention.

Early into his remand, in November 2015, Stephen writes to Cody that it is 'so ridiculous' he is being described as an alleged serial killer. He says that to be a serial killer you have to have an intent to kill, and questions how you could possibly intentionally murder someone with GHB. Making a less-than cast-iron case for his acquittal, the former chef writes: 'If I wanted to kill someone, I would use an easier method – like hitting over the head with a rolling pin or something.'[103]

It's possible because of his ignorance that a verdict of murder does require an intent to kill, but can also apply in cases in which the killer intends to seriously injure somebody that ends in death, that Stephen is utterly convinced that he'll get off. But his confidence, when looking at the letters in retrospect, only incriminates him further as he openly discusses his familiarity with GHB and varying levels of tolerance with the drug. Nevertheless, he seems so sure of his release that he talks about selling his flat before he gets out. After all, he says, he couldn't possibly come back to Barking following the media's vilification of his character.

In imagining his new life, he lays what he evidently believes is groundwork that will build toward a verdict of innocence. In a revoltingly insensitive and arrogant passage, he claims to care deeply for the families of Anthony Walgate, Gabriel Kovari, Daniel Whitworth and Jack Taylor. He even implicates Anthony in his own death, telling his pen pal that the student took his own GHB and seemed to know what he was doing because he was measuring out quantities of the drug. Stephen theorises that his escort was 'on other pills', perhaps prescription tablets that didn't mix well with GHB. He even criticises journalists for not engaging in speculation as to this unproven theory, writing: 'They didn't mention that in the papers.'[104]

He insists that he called an ambulance when he realised Anthony wasn't well and helped him outside to get some fresh air. Stephen describes seeing the young man sitting down against a wall. His excuse for not being present when the paramedics arrived? He panicked when he saw police officers and an ambulance and fled to the confines of his home. The level to which this is at odds with not just the evidence, but Stephen's own account, is astounding. Bear in mind that at this point emergency services have a recording of a 999 call in which he claims to have stumbled across an already collapsed young man outside his flat. In the letter he makes no mention of Anthony being unconscious, yet in his call he reports that the young man looked as though he'd had a seizure.[105]

Still peddling the myth that orgies are to blame for his destruction, Stephen tells Cody that he met another of the victims at a sex party. He admits that he cannot remember much of the imaginary event in question, but says that's due to the amount of drugs that were on offer. 'I did overdo it a bit,' he writes. In yet another example of completely turning the tables on the part he played in a young man's death, he plays the victim as opposed to the predator. Stephen says that he began feeling sick at the party and the 'boy', along with another man, asked where he lived before helping him home, where he passed out. To his horror, he awoke the next day to a loud bang and a smashing glass. He heard shouting but found himself unable to intervene in whatever was happening in the next room. Nevermind standing up, he couldn't even turn his head. Stephen fell back asleep. The following morning, he found his apartment empty with signs of a struggle – a broken glass and spilled coffee. 'I cleaned up and thought no more of it,' is how he concludes this clumsy attempt to point the finger to a mystery assailant, who presumably dumped Daniel's body in the St Margaret's graveyard.[106] It's as though he hasn't even considered the wonder of DNA evidence. In fact, he says his link to the cases has been fabricated by the media. You know, the same media for which he was a virtual ventriloquist in the write-up of Gabriel and Daniel's inquest. Those same journalists who either reported that the police saw nothing suspicious, or abandoned the story altogether when the Met told them there was nothing to see here.

'I've told my parents not to speak to the press after all the lies,' he writes. 'They twisted everything to make it look certain that I did it when there's no evidence linking me to two of them [victims]. I would never harm anyone – I would sooner kill myself than take another's life.'[107]

It's worth lingering on the stupidity of Stephen's claim that there is 'no evidence' linking him to two of his four murder victims. He's already conceded that there is a link between him and Anthony, and his link to the student is established by his conviction for perverting the course of justice. He's fresh from an arrest secured through a police appeal that rested on CCTV of him and Jack. And in his letter to Cody, he appears to have linked himself to a third – the man who helped him home from a party, only to vanish after the sound of smashing glass. Such a weak grasp of the basic components of his own defence is truly astounding. His complacency is second only to that of the police force under whose noses he committed these crimes. It's a wonder that he retains any confidence in his acquittal.

Aside from his cast-iron cover stories, Stephen's self-assurance lies in the quality of his legal team. 'My QC is one of the best in the country,' he writes. 'He's amazing and he's confident he can prove my innocence.'[108] Without wishing to impugn the intelligence of English lawyers, I'm not confident that the level of skill required for that outcome currently exists.

But he continues to pave the way for a reality in which he may be seen as a caring innocent, caught up in a bleak tragedy. Stephen's primary concern, he tells his pen pal, is the impact that drugs are having on gay people. In a suggestion that would be funny were it not so perverse, he writes that once he's out of prison he'll tour universities and colleges as an expert lecturer, warning gay men about the risks of the substances in which he and those around him have dabbled. Presenting himself as a saviour made wise with experience, he is getting an alibi down in writing should the letters get out, which they did, on Cody's YouTube channel as well as in the tabloid press.

As for his life before all of this chaos descended, Stephen presents a happy home life overseen by supportive parents. He says both – including the father who would tell journalists he was 'against' his son's homosexuality – welcomed his boyfriends despite an initial shock. The inmate says that he came out as gay when he was around 20 after his mother asked him about a man who was in fact his first boyfriend. When he admitted that he was gay, he said his mother was a little upset because she'd wanted grandchildren. His father said nothing. His sister had already guessed, based on the Boyzone posters that adorned his wall growing up. But he and his partners would nevertheless be welcomed warmly to Sunday dinner. 'My parents are standing by me,' he writes. 'My mother has taken it hard but my dad writes to me. They know I'm not guilty of murder as I've always treated my boyfriends well.'[109]

Stephen asks for a similar solidarity from Cody, asking that he prays for him while he is awaiting trial. Unable to resist yet another insulting statement, he says: 'I do [pray], not just for myself but for my family and for the boys and their families and the truth to be known and my innocence to be proven.'[110] His advice on escorting is similarly insensitive, as he shares a tip with Cody on how not to be drugged, writing: 'Never accept a drink from a client.' Stephen also tells him to let someone he trusts know where he will be working in an instruction eerily redolent of Anthony's actions before he died. He claims that he and another escort would always swap job details, including addresses and hotel room numbers to look out for one another. He would also send hourly updates to his colleague in the form of a text message. Most of the time, he says, he'd have little to worry about as the men he'd go out with would simply ask him to dress up in uniforms and take pictures. Others would simply want to have dinner with him, raconteur that he is. Some wanted to 'touch him' and he claims to have been nervous when he started having sex with older men for money. He says he met clients through SleepyBoy and even recalls accompanying a boyfriend to an appointment. Ever the caring partner, he says the motivation for this was that he didn't want his boyfriend going it alone, which seems at odds with the casual way in which he told Ryan he was pimping a boyfriend out while they sat in a McDonald's in Beckton.[111]

He talks about one client in particular, referring to him only as Mike. Stephen has known Mike for about 10 years. Mike was married with three children when he began paying him for sex, but later moved in with his escort when he got divorced.[112] Stephen also tells Cody that he used to have a boyfriend that liked taking GHB and mephedrone and then receiving anal sex from him.[113]

'He would take mephedrone and we would go for hours,' he writes. 'But I didn't try GHB as I touched it once and it burnt my skin so I was always worried what it must do to your insides. I just stuck to mephedrone by snorting.'[114]

At some point, Stephen also started using Grindr to buy drugs. Though he claims to have not trusted GHB because it burnt his skin, he says that he enjoyed snorting mephedrone. He claims a man offered him three 'bags' of mephedrone in exchange for bringing guys to a party.[115]

His revelations into life in Belmarsh prison and its everyday stresses are surprisingly trivial for somebody facing charges so egregious. Rather than agonising about a life behind bars, he complains that the prison governor won't let him have the *Star Wars* annual Cody sent him. He's even written to his solicitor in the hope of securing the book on the grounds that he has not shown any aggression to anybody in prison and has no history of violence whatsoever. Until then, he's managed to find a large-print *Star Wars* book in the library that he can read without the reading glasses he doesn't have inside. The down side? No pictures.[116] Stephen asks Cody if it'd be possible for him to send a magazine about a car show, *Top Gear*, and expresses regret that he won't get to see the new *Star Wars* film while he's on remand.[117] He laments not being able to see ex-boyfriends and says he misses going out drinking, shopping and being with his action figures and DVDs.[118] With the festive season approaching, Port asks Cody to send him a Christmas card to brighten up his cell.[119]

12

TRIAL

October 5, 2016, central London

Stephen's eyes were down as his first day at the Old Bailey began. He looked down, past his blue tie and white shirt with purple stripes, at the floor as proceedings got under way. His wig no longer in place, the bald top of his head was the main view that I and the other journalists gathered had of him. It had been 10 months since his first Christmas in prison and, since he'd been arrested, a slew of charges had piled up. Rather than just facing the surely watertight four murder charges that he'd spent his time in jail denying, he now faced a total of 29 charges. Stephen stood accused of seven rapes; four counts of administering a substance with intent to endanger life or cause grievous bodily harm; six counts of administering a substance with intent to overpower to allow sexual activity and four counts of sexual assault by penetration. He also faced four counts of manslaughter relating to Anthony, Gabriel, Daniel and Jack, just in case the jury wasn't convinced that he was a serial murderer. It might have been prudent for him to admit these four lesser charges if he hoped to convince a jury that he had not murdered the four young men. But he astounded everyone by entering 'not guilty' pleas on every single charge.[120]

It was up to Jonathan Rees QC to explain to the jury, in graphic detail, why they shouldn't believe Stephen. Mr Rees set out the Crown's case in stark terms. Here was a defendant, he said, who had a sexual obsession with younger men. The men he favoured invariably had a boyish look and were known by the slang term 'twinks'.[121] But there was a dark component to Stephen's fascination, he claimed, a fantasy so central to his psyche that he'd murdered four men in pursuit of its realisation. Stephen liked to rape incapacitated men. He used drugs, such as GHB, in order to live out this fantasy. "The prosecution say it's a case about a man who, in the pursuit of nothing more than his own sexual gratification, targeted, sexually assaulted and in four cases killed young, gay men he had invited back to his flat," Mr Rees said. "The prosecution suggest that it is not a hard case to understand because we say all of the offending behaviour was driven by one main factor, namely the defendant's appetite for having sexual intercourse with younger, gay males while they were unconscious through drugs."[122]

Stephen's gaze being apparently rooted to the carpet reassured me that he was feeling a sense of shame. Perhaps being here, in this most serious of legal institutions, had humbled him. Maybe his twisted fantasies being laid before the court had embarrassed a man incapable of even asking a stranger for a drink without the crutch of a narcotic to knock them out later. Could it be that guilt was weighing his neck down as he wished for nothing more than to disappear?

He shattered this illusion by lifting his head and wearing the expression of a stroppy teenager. Stephen wasn't ashamed – at least, he didn't look ashamed. He looked *bored*. All of a sudden, his stripy shirt seemed inappropriate in its flamboyance. But most jarring was the moment at which he sprang out of his seat and delicately pranced, smiling across the dock to speak to his barrister. It baffled me as to how a man facing such a deluge of charges could appear anything other than desperately frightened.

Sat in the press pit, I noticed that a *Channel 4 News* reporter next to me was scribbling in his notepad, prepping his broadcast. I searched the printout of the prosecution's opening statement to identify a top line for the story I'd shortly be filing on a laptop in the hallway. Speed would be key, especially with an agonisingly inadequate internet connection using a mobile phone hotspot. But the statement, which Mr Rees was using as a script, provided so many lurid details that it was difficult to separate out the most newsworthy aspects.

Not only did it explore Stephen's drug rape fetish, it revealed just how terrible he'd been at hiding his preferences. The way in which he'd dealt with this in his police interviews was utterly incriminating. Officers quizzed him as to why he, a man suspected of raping and murdering four younger men, had searched the internet using phrases such as 'gay teen knocked out and raped' and 'drugged and raped'.[123] His brilliant curveball to the police when questioned? He was just looking for 'general porn'. Anybody who considers that general porn in the context of a rape-murder case would be suspect to a juror totally ignorant of other facts. He'd also listed 'rape fantasy' under the 'what he's into' section on a dating site called Slaveboys. Meanwhile, on his Flirt profile, he said he preferred younger-looking men.[124] Court papers revealed that Stephen had also been accused of raping a 19-year-old in 2012.[125]

The opening statement also sketched out the circumstances surrounding the deaths of Anthony, Gabriel, Daniel and Jack. It made clear to jurors that Stephen had hired the first young man as an escort, then lied to police about stumbling across the body. It mentioned the supposed suicide note found in Daniel's hand, saying that it did not match the handwriting of the victim. An expert had compared it with samples of Stephen's handwriting provided by the defendant in police interviews. They had also compared the note with letters he'd written. Police had further taken two pads from 62 Cooke Street, which were composed of the same paper on which the 'suicide' note was written. Removing any doubt, officers found indentation marks on one pad which were a direct match to the note, concluding it had obviously been written on the preceding page before the paper was planted on Daniel's body. They also found plastic sleeves bought from Woolworth's that matched the sleeve in which the note was preserved. There was, Mr Rees said, 'conclusive support' to the proposition that Stephen had faked the suicide note. Daniel had not killed himself. And he certainly had not admitted guilt relating to Gabriel's death.

The document also revealed how condemnatory the DNA evidence was once the police had finally secured samples from the victims' bodies. A perianal swab from Anthony contained Stephen's DNA. Swabs taken from Gabriel led investigators to conclude it was 16,000,000 times more likely that Stephen had contributed DNA to that particular crime scene than that he hadn't. Swabs taken from the palm of Daniel's right hand showed that it was more than 10,000,000 times more likely that Stephen had contributed traces than that he hadn't. A sample from the inside of Daniel's right trouser pocket was even more damning, showing it was 100,000,000 times more likely that Port had contributed DNA to the pocket than hadn't. Investigators reached the same figure of likelihood that Stephen had left semen all over the blanket on which Daniel was found. The chance that he'd contributed to DNA found on the left side of Daniel's neck was even greater.

* * *

Already facing the prospect that they'd let a serial killer go unchecked, the police were now confronted with the fact that the defendant may have been a rapist-at-large long before his first victim was found dead. The prosecution now honed in on the allegation that, more than two years before he'd been arrested for lying about his connection to Anthony, Stephen, the prosecution said, had raped a 19-year-old man. This was on February 25, 2012, when Stephen was aged 37. He met the teenager through Grindr, when the younger male – referred to as Victim A in court – was supposed to be meeting a date in central London. Having travelled from Epsom, he found that he'd been stood up and instead arranged to meet Stephen at Barking train station around 10pm. They went to his flat, where his host gave him a glass of red wine. It was the teenager's first drink of the evening and he drained the glass only to be horrified by a mound of congealed powder at its base. Panicked, he tried to make himself sick as Stephen encouraged him to go to bed. Victim A blacked out. He awoke naked to find that he was being raped in the middle of the night.[126]

* * *

Less than two weeks before Stephen had contacted Anthony Walgate, he'd also been spotted struggling to guide a disoriented young man to Barking train station. Police officers saw him dragging Victim B on June 4, 2014. Stephen, the prosecution said, had drugged the man. He'd offered him water at his flat, only for the younger man to black out. He woke up naked, physically aroused and terrified. He needed to get out. Stephen walked him to the station, but had also taken drugs and the pair were a conspicuous sight. Police stopped Stephen and questioned him. He admitted to taking crystal meth and told them he'd found the struggling man at his flat. The police took no action against him. He returned to his flat alone.[127]

The prosecution accused Stephen of drugging and assaulting by penetration a man he met at KFC just two days before he met Jack Taylor. The indictment against Stephen also said he'd drugged and raped a 24-year-old just weeks after he killed Jack. It seemed not even four deaths were enough for the police to stop him being a further danger to the public. He was said to have raped Victim H on a weekend in October 2015. Three further charges alleged that he had assaulted the man by penetration on a second weekend in the same month, when he was also said to have drugged and raped him.

October 6, 2016

In the unlikely event that anybody was in any doubt as to who had written the note found in Daniel's hand, their illusions would have been eradicated by the second day of the trial. The combination of the prosecution's opening statement coupled with Mr Rees articulating for the jury what was at this point obvious: The scrawled ramblings were a 'wicked attempt' to frame the deceased.[128] The fact that it was still in Daniel's grasp after his body had gone cold spoke to another party jamming it in there. This fact was also at odds with the clumsy attempt on behalf of the writer to convince the reader that the person who penned this confession was slipping out of consciousness. Were we really supposed to believe that an intoxicated chef was so drowsy that he worried about his family being able to decipher his statement, but then mustered the wherewithal to jam it into a plastic wallet and grip it tightly until his life expired? Absolute nonsense. If Stephen was still holding out on such hopes, surely examination had comprehensively dashed them.

Similarly, if there was anybody in the courtroom under the impression that Stephen's early morning walk with Jack as captured on CCTV was innocent and coincidental, they were enlightened as to the defendant's motives. Mr Rees revealed that in the lead-up to meeting Jack at Barking train station, Stephen had searched the phrase 'drugged sleeping gay twinks' online.[129]

But what those present could not have grasped was the insidious way in which Stephen's depravity had infected every aspect of his life. Sex and drugs weren't enough for him – he *had* to rape. This necessity seemed to have transformed what should be a profoundly evil act into something that was, for him, routine. To Stephen, rape seemed to have been viewed as a kink more important than the lives of those it could destroy. It wasn't sufficient to satisfy this through roleplay or pornography with consenting actors. He wanted to make his own films – of real rape, Mr Rees told the court. The defendant, he said, had filmed himself having sex with two men in the grips of drug-induced unconsciousness.[130] Obviously proud of his inclinations, Stephen was also said to have shown pictures of young men he targeted to another man, who he would also later drug and rape.[131]

October 12, 2016

Stephen finally got to tell his side of the story seven days into his trial. This was a chance for him to hit the jury with a red pill; it was his opportunity to rewire their perceptions and show that he was *obviously* innocent. But he faced yet another obstacle as the jury heard his bizarre 999 call the very same day.

The conversation was heard in all its incompetence: The defendant calls emergency services to report finding a body in Cooke Street that would later be identified as Anthony Walgate.

He theorises that the young man has collapsed, had a seizure or is just drunk. The caller reckons the body is outside either 47 or 48 Cooke Street (better not mention *his* door number). Anyway, what's more important is that he must get his car. Why? 'The parking.'[132]

One can only imagine what was going through the jurors' minds when they heard the second call, after the phone handler rang Stephen back. They heard the operator double-check the location of the body only for Stephen, who for some reason has answered his phone in this genius cover-up, to tell them: "Oh, I've driven away now." Some concerned bystander. Luckily, he can remember that it was on Cooke Street. But suddenly he can't answer the question of which door numbers the young man was lying by. He says: "I don't know, I didn't look." Then, when the call handler suggests that he heard 47 during their previous conversation, Stephen's memory returns: "Yeah it was 47, yep."[133]

Imagine hearing all of this for the first time and then being told that the person who'd made the call lived yards from the spot on which Anthony was found. And that, far from being a confused and worried member of the public, the caller had calmly gone back to bed, leaving police to find the student.

Stephen would have to smother his pill with sugar if he hoped to guide it deep down the throats of jurors. Instead, he showed each and every one of them how plausible it was that he should be blamed for Anthony's death. Stephen's whole strategy after leaving Anthony in the street, and after being found to have hired him for sex, was to lie about his original lie.[134] He had admitted to police that he'd moved the body from his flat. But he said that he had done so for fear of being wrongly accused of murder. He tried it again on jurors and journalists on October 12, telling the court: "He's in my bed, they are going to think I did this to him."[135] The prosecution couldn't have put it better. Yes, Stephen. There's a chance the jury might think you did this.

The court also heard the chillingly prescient text message Gabriel had received before he took the life-changing, and ultimately life-ending, decision to move in with Stephen. When the Slovakian told his friend about his plans to move to Barking, the recipient had concerns. Their reply read: 'Are you sure he's safe? There are some crazy people out there lol. Sorry, I don't want to sound like your mum.'[136]

If there could be anything to humanise the man sitting in the dock, it would surely be hearing from a friend of the accused. Ryan Edwards gave evidence that day, but his contributions offered an eerie insight into the life of his neighbour. He recalled the moment that he received a message from Stephen telling him that Gabriel had moved out. But he was worried not just by the randomness of the departure, days after he'd come to live at the apartment, but also by an instruction to keep quiet about the matter. He told the court that he was 'disturbed' by a request not to mention anything about it on Facebook. Ryan also mentioned his former friend's love of children's toys. Stephen's passion for *Transformers* figurines bought from Toys R Us was a "love bordering on obsession"[137], he said, painting a strange portrait for the families who'd gathered to see justice dealt to a man whose evil had left them hollow. Stephen appeared ever stranger to his former friend, too. Ryan looked over to see him sitting in the dock of the Old Bailey, only to see him offer up a 'half-smile'. He would later describe it to me as redolent of "a child who has been naughty and found out".

October 13, 2016

Stephen's sister, Sharon Port, did little to contradict the image that was very quickly taking hold in the minds of anyone following the trial. Giving evidence, she described the unnerving moment that her younger brother had told her that Gabriel was dead. She told the court that she sensed something was wrong with Stephen when they were speaking on the phone. He sounded tense. "I just asked him to tell me why he was stressed and what was wrong," the 44-year-old said. After meeting initial reluctance, she got her answer: "He just said there was a body in his flat."[138]

If this conversation was anything like Stephen's bungling 999 call, he would have given his sister the impression that he wasn't equipped to handle the situation. So Sharon took control. "I just told him to go to the police straight away," she said. "I was in a bit of a shock."[139]

The story that Stephen spun his sister was that Gabriel had stayed the night, as opposed to the reality that he'd moved in and immediately found himself in his new flatmate's carnal crosshairs. He claimed to have awoken to the worrying fact that his guest, supposedly a Lithuanian called Anthony, was not moving. He admitted that they'd been taking drugs, then told her that he'd gone straight to work, surely an unfathomable thing for a caring, innocent person to do. Sharon said the news made her feel ill.

"I was sick about it," she said. "It's not the sort of thing you hear every day. I was very worried. I wanted him to drop everything and go to the station, then ring me when he got out and tell me what happened."[140]

Later that afternoon, she received a text message in which Stephen said he was on the way to the police station. But she couldn't get through to him on the phone and was so worried that the next day she drove 66 miles with her boyfriend from Clacton-on-Sea, Essex, to Barking. "He just said he was on bail and that was that, really," she told the court. "He had to go back in a month or two. I just assumed it was all sorted. I came home, and that was that really."[141]

But rather than leave it at that, Stephen changed tack with his sister and decided to tell her that he'd been lying about the dead man. The reason for this lie? He was feeling guilty about *another* man who'd *actually* died in his flat. *He* was the one named Anthony.[142] This story, however unbelievable, would at least square with his upcoming conviction for perverting the course of justice in relation to Anthony Walgate's death.

October 14, 2016

The fabricated notion of a one-off mishap was fast coming apart in the trial. And helpfully, for anybody deluded enough to believe his lies, he'd kept a record of certain sex attacks, the living victims of which are anonymised here as is their right under the law. Police recovered 83 home videos of the serial killer having sex with young men. One clip in particular was definitely not showing consensual intercourse.[143]

Jurors endured 18 minutes of disturbing footage found on Stephen's mobile phone. One six-minute clip showed him having sex with a 24-year-old man who appears to be either asleep or unconscious during a celebration to usher in the New Year of 2015. A third man watches as Stephen rapes the still man before telling his friend to do the same, which he does. A fourth man leaves the party, saying: "I'll leave you guys to carry on, I have got work in the morning." Stephen asks his remaining friend if they should "do more stuff", a reference to drugs. His remaining friend replies: "Yeah babe."[144]

The same 24-year-old featured in six of the videos played to the jury. Though he admitted that on some occasions he would allow Stephen to have sex with him while knocked out, he was adamant that the New Year's Eve incident was rape. Three days after the clips horrified jurors, the man gave his evidence to the court. He said that, as far as he knew, his relationship with Stephen had been friendly and any sex was consensual. They would take drugs together and as far as he was concerned, Stephen had never been violent. So out of it was he at the party in question, that he had no idea the attack had occurred until police showed him stills of the video after Stephen's arrest and asked him to identify himself in the clip. When questioned by the prosecution, the man told Mr Rees that he had not given permission for Stephen to have sex with him while unconscious at the party.[145]

The defence pointed out that the man had told Stephen he felt "weirdly good" about one clip that he received. They also revealed that he'd given permission at some point for him to "carry on" should he fall asleep. But he insisted that no consent was given at the New Year's Eve party. And he was hurt by the suggestion from the defence that he'd enjoyed the videos, despite his reply to Stephen.[146]

It also emerged that day that Stephen was accused of raping a man identified only as Victim D, aged 22. He told the court that he went to the Cooke Street flat to get revenge on his boyfriend, who had been sleeping with Stephen. He ended up staying at the apartment for a week in January 2015. One evening, they were drinking vodka and coke when the guest began to feel ill after just three drinks. Thinking that it must be the combination of alcohol with some medication he was taking, Victim D decided to go straight to bed.[147]

Another night, they finished a bottle of vodka between them. They started having sex, but D passed out and, as far as he knew, sleep interrupted the session. But, when he woke up the next morning, Stephen told him that he'd carried on. The witness told the court that Stephen had left him feeling angry and recalled telling him: "You're disgusting."[148] He also said that Stephen had offered a graphic rationale for the rape when asked why he'd done it: "He said because it feels better when I am passed out. I am looser."[149] Stephen showed his victim the video he'd made of the assault. Victim D was not moving.[150]

A brief point of clarification is worth making regarding Victim D. During the trial, the news sites *Metro* and *London Evening Standard* reported that it was a transgender man who had given evidence at the Old Bailey, meaning a person born with a female body who was identifying, and living, as a man.

This is not correct. Victim D was born male, but was identifying as a *woman* while staying with Stephen and was therefore a trans woman. I do not point out this error to glory in the erroneous reporting of a news organisation, but rather because I think the biological sex of the victim is incredibly important in this case.[151]

If *Metro*'s article was correct, Stephen would have raped somebody with a female body who later presented in court as a man. This would be a stark aberration from his usual behaviour. It would mean that he had not solely targeted gay men. If this was correct, it would be of vital importance because it would mean that his predations constituted not just assaults on younger men, but that he was also guilty of sexual violence against a female. It's necessary to point out that this was not the case because any obfuscation of his crimes against gay men lessens the understanding of the impact that his rapes had on a specific set of people. When dealing with a case in which one of the chief concerns is that the police may have treated the appearance of dead bodies differently due to their sexual orientation, it would be unacceptable to contribute to a narrative that lessens the impact on the gay community by falsely reporting that Stephen also targeted a biological woman, or women. His crimes, it appears, were solely directed at gay, or bisexual, men. His motivation, too, was driven by his sexual desire, which, as far as we can tell, was not toward females. To deny or water down this fact is to diminish and obscure the nature of his crimes. It would be comparable to a report about a white supremacist attacking black people mistakenly reporting that one of the victims was white. Even if we can imagine a scenario in which the 'white' victim was in fact a black person who identified as white, the skin colour that the attacker and the reading public saw is still centrally important to understand what has happened and why. Victim D had a male body. Stephen targeted him for that reason, no matter how D identified, and that is of utmost importance. It's also worth noting that Mr Justice Openshaw referred to the person in question as a 'he' in his sentencing remarks. At the time of giving evidence, Victim D had interrupted his gender reassignment programme due to a head injury sustained in a separate assault. Due to the right to anonymity of victims of rape, I have no idea as to how D now identifies, but during the trial it was as a 'he'.

October 18, 2016

A slight, yet confident, effeminate man took the stand on October 18. The short-haired 35-year-old, referred to as Victim E, told a terrifying story of how he'd come to meet the defendant. Protected from Stephen's glare by a screen, his pithy account cut through the formality of the Old Bailey as he recounted the events of July 4, 2015. He'd made contact with Stephen on Grindr that day and was impressed with the profile picture, which showed a man with dark features and stubble corresponding exactly to his type. He arrived at Cooke Street to be welcomed into a darkened apartment, so dimly-lit, in fact, that he could only make out the shape and size of the man who welcomed him. As Stephen slipped into the shadows, another, overweight man emerged and told the pair to 'have fun' before exiting the flat. Stephen's shape re-emerged, still concealing his appearance, and the two men entered his bedroom. Victim E then heard his host explain that he was going to get some lubrication before they started, but told him: "I don't like lube – just use spit." He explained to the court: "I prefer it natural."

He told Mr Rees that he laid on the bed in the darkness with his legs open, adding: "I assumed he was going to fuck me." Sensing a fumbling beneath him, he thought that Stephen was trying to apply a condom. But then he felt a click in his anus as he realised a plastic object was being forced inside. Victim E asked him what it was and was told that it was lubrication. He protested, pointing out that he'd specifically told him that he didn't want that. But Stephen told him he'd feel 'really good' in a couple of minutes. A burning sensation spread through his anus and he panicked as he realised he'd never had this sensation when he'd used lube before. It occurred to him that the feeling was redolent of an injection and that there was no need for a syringe if what was invading his body was actually lube. Stephen was apologising now. He told his guest that he was putting the lube away. But 'very quickly' he came back and shoved the object inside him again, leaving the same pinching feeling. Again, he heard the click.

By this point, Victim E was furious. He'd been insulted, disrespected and violated. He leapt from the bed and turned on the light only to see a totally different face to the one he'd favoured on Grindr. "Who *are* you?" he asked, as his exposed host apologised. E grabbed his clothes and made a break for it as quickly as possible, chastising Stephen as he did so. His terror overrode his host's attempts to get him to stay and he was out of the door just 15 minutes after arriving. As soon as he got home, he jumped into the shower. Thankfully, he began to feel better a short time later. What Victim E didn't know at the time was that Stephen was still on an electronic tag after getting out of prison early for perverting the course of justice. Despite being rattled, Victim E didn't know for sure that he'd been injected with GHB, or any drug, at the time and didn't call the police. He only got in touch when he saw a Facebook post linking to an article about Stephen's arrest for murder.

* * *

A nervous, quiet and smartly dressed young man was next to accuse Stephen of rape. The bespectacled witness spoke softly as he explained to the court that he'd also met the defendant through Grindr. During their conversations, he made clear that he wouldn't use drugs – even if they were legal highs – during sex. He didn't mind if Stephen took legal highs, that was his business. Stephen reassured him that he'd lay off substances if they met. With the ground rules in place, the young man, identified only as Victim F, got on his motorbike and drove down the A13 to Cooke Street, arriving at about 2pm on August 2, 2015.

Victim F was keen to have sex when he got to the flat. But, after he'd made this plain, Stephen insisted that he wasn't that kind of guy. The host rebuffed his offer of consensual sex, suggesting that they sit down and have a chat first. After discussing their favourite sexual positions, Stephen's reason for waiting would become clear. His guest told him again that he wanted to have sex: "I don't want to wait."

Stephen then admitted that he was waiting for a drug dealer to come and sell him something. This shocked Victim F, given their previous interactions. It really wasn't a big deal, Stephen tried to explain. It was just that he didn't want to cancel an appointment he'd already made. And besides, the drugs in question were *definitely* legal. The dealer would be here shortly, with his boyfriend. Stephen thought the best way to pass the time, and forget this awkward encounter, was to play some eastern European porn for his guest. Once this was done, he got his phone out and started sharing homemade videos of him having sex with men.[152] Ever the charmer.

Two long hours after Victim F had entered the flat, the dealer and his boyfriend turned up at the door. He didn't know their names, noting only that they were both black and appeared to be in their twenties. The dealer, who claimed to be a nurse, hurried into the bedroom with his boyfriend and Stephen, leaving the guest alone. Ten minutes later, Stephen emerged holding a box. Syringes, pills and what appeared to be a plastic transfusion tube around 2.5ft in length lay within. He returned to the bedroom to complete the transaction. Once again, he came back into the living room. He took a white pill that he insisted was Viagra, famed for its blue colour, and bluntly told his guest: "We can start having sex now."[153]

Victim F was a private person and it would have been understandable were he anxious that the two strange men who'd sold his date drugs still hadn't left. But they were in the bedroom and the curtains looking out on the street were closed. He and Stephen began removing their clothes in the darkened living room. Just as he believed Stephen was going to penetrate him, his host left once again for the bedroom and told the student he was getting a lubricant. The guest waited on the sofa, with his legs in the air and his glasses removed. Two minutes later, his blurred vision made out a shadowy Stephen coming toward him. "He was holding something but I couldn't see what it was exactly," Victim F said. "He moved closer to my anus and said it was lube but then I noticed there was a bite around my anus – it was like a needle or pin."

Horrified, he realised it must have been one of the syringes he had seen moments earlier and said: "No drugs!"[154]

It was too late. Stephen had injected him. He struggled to comprehend the situation as he heard the predator drop all pretence as to having already applied lubrication by telling him he was going to get some baby oil. The drug started to take hold as Stephen penetrated his dizzy victim. Despite F's state, his attacker was undeterred, applying more baby oil. The drug dealer and his boyfriend left the bedroom and entered the living room, leading Victim F to weakly protest their presence. He begged for their removal as they watched the sordid attack. The dealer's boyfriend then asked Stephen if he could join in. Receiving permission from the least appropriate person to consent, he then shoved his penis into F's mouth. The student said that by this point his mind had gone blank and he was in no position to make a decision as to whether he wanted to give oral sex, even if he had been asked. His head began to hurt and he tried to explain to the trio that he was feeling disoriented. Then he fell unconscious, slipping from the sofa onto the floor. It was not yet 6pm.[155]

A pain in his anus woke Victim F at 5am. "Do you like that?" a voice asked. Stephen was raping him. He mustered the strength to tell him "no". Stephen stopped. His victim had no memory of the previous day's attack. He fell asleep again. His rapist woke the student two hours later. He couldn't sit up. It couldn't be a hangover as he was certain he hadn't drunk alcohol. And there was a crusty substance around his nose. As he struggled to gather himself, his host told him: "You come a lot."

They had taken drugs, he explained, which had knocked them both out cold. It seemed strange to Victim F, who'd never taken any such substances in his life. They lay in bed drinking tea and eating biscuits. They had protected, consensual and unenjoyable sex for about five minutes. When Victim F left at 10.50am, his head was still hurting and he was suffering from dizziness. He rang in sick to work to be met with an unsympathetic ear convinced he was just looking for a day off. He reported to a sexual health clinic.

* * *

Another encounter with Stephen heard in court that day also painted a deviant picture. A woman named Paige was rattled after her friend, Connor, had moved into the Cooke Street flat. Her written statement described how she met Stephen at the apartment in January 2015. Living in Dagenham, she'd decided to visit for a catch-up over drinks with Connor. But she was less-than-enthused when her friend welcomed her into a smelly flat. And when Stephen returned from work, she realised that the stench wasn't the worst thing about the living situation – it was the creep who owned the place. She found him 'strange' and 'shifty' as she sipped vodka Red Bulls with her friend. Though she felt uncomfortable, she stayed the night and spent the next morning walking around Barking town centre with Connor. The pair returned to the flat once more and again endured Stephen's antisocial stylings upon his return from work. His silence was unnerving, even as he helped Connor to walk her to the bus stop outside Barking train station.

* * *

Connor called Paige a few days later. He'd had drinks with Stephen the other night, but could not remember anything beyond his first. Connor was convinced that his drinks had been spiked. Paige told him to get out of the flat. He escaped. The next time Paige saw Stephen's face, it was in a message from her friend showing him on television during a report into the allegations he was facing.

October 19, 2016

Throughout all of this horror, through each and every sordid detail of Stephen's life being made plain to the court, the families of the men he killed were the embodiment of dignity. They sat calmly as they learned the full monstrosity of the man who'd been with their loved ones in their final moments, knowing full well that he may have done the same to their sons or brothers.

And on October 19, the Taylors had to steel themselves for more pain as they witnessed Jack's meeting with his killer.

Despite Stephen's earlier claim that the forklift truck driver wasn't his type, the jury now saw this statement exposed for the lie that it was as the defendant walked alongside the 25-year-old through Barking town centre. The Taylors watched in tears as the now familiar scene played out. They also learned that in the hours after Stephen had tried to erase evidence of their meeting through Grindr, he had been seen drawing £100 out of a cash point. He then headed to Peter Hirons' flat in East Ham with the mysterious black bag that was never recovered.[156]

October 27, 2016

It was Stephen's personal drug use that now became the focus of the trial. His appetite for 'chem sex' – sexual activity with the aid of drugs – was voracious. Sitting in the dock, he explained how he began by taking mephedrone. He said that he'd begun using the synthetic amphetamine before he started to include GHB in his sessions. And he shared with the court what he saw as the benefits of mixing chemicals with intercourse. "You could have sex for hours," he said, adding: "We would have a hyper-high for about an hour."[157]

But he denied using the drug to render Anthony, Gabriel, Daniel and Jack unconscious in order to rape them. Or anyone else, for that matter. Not only did he say he wouldn't have sex with somebody while they were unconscious, he told a court that had witnessed him do precisely that on homemade video that he just wasn't that into it. This weird obfuscation makes you wonder whether he was paying attention when his internet search history came to light. "I did like doing it but it was not a preferred experience," was his risible summary as he said he'd only have sex with an unconscious boyfriend who'd previously consented to it taking place.[158] I'd be fascinated to meet the man who records scenes on his phone to watch over and over again despite them not being his preferred experience.

More galling than this dismissive defence was his version of the events that led to Anthony's lifeless body being dumped outside the communal entrance to his block of flats. Again, oblivious to the sensitivities of his victim's family, he prioritised portraying himself as something of a desirable date. After telling the court he got on 'really well' with his escort, he bragged that Anthony had asked to see him again – and this time he wouldn't require payment.[159]

Moreover, the sex worker had taken the drugs that killed him of his own accord, he said. Ever the concerned host, Stephen only offered him a place to stay, he said, when his guest had vomited. He was free to leave whenever he felt better. According to his account, they both went to bed and Stephen went to work as normal the next day. When he returned home, he checked his Facebook and had a shower. He saw that his guest was still sleeping in his bed. So he leaned over him, he said, and he still seemed warm and was making gurgling noises, leading him to assume that he was in a deep sleep. Stephen supposedly decided to join him in slumber, only to wake up and find that Anthony was rigid. He claimed to have been shocked that the escort wasn't moving.[160]

"I didn't want to think he was dead, obviously," he said. "I thought there's no way, he's going to wake up any second. I tried to lift him, tried to get him to walk but I couldn't bend his legs. [He was] very rigid."[161]

He claimed to have then called an ambulance and moved the body outside. Up until this point, his version of events is roughly consistent with what he told the police in 2014. But then he gave a very strange excuse as to *why* he moved the body. He told the court that he was scared his partner would leave him, as opposed to the previously expressed fear that he'd go to prison for murder. And he then made the bizarre claim that he didn't want to get into trouble at work. When asked if he gave Anthony "anything that could have accounted for his death", Stephen said: "No I did not."[162]

October 28, 2016

Stephen's involvement with each victim was indisputable. And his proximity to the victims when they died left him very little space in which to manoeuvre. But his determination to be acquitted meant that he had to, leading to excuses characterised by cartoonishly complex absurdities. In making concessions to the prosecution, he invariably had to admit to things that he'd previously denied. His old lines just wouldn't work in the face of the prosecution's evidence. So he contorted himself by sketching out unlikely scenarios in an idiotic attempt to convince observers of his innocence.

These stories plunged to their nadir on October 28, when the suicide note found in Daniel's hand became the focus of the case. Stephen *had* to address the fact that it matched *his* handwriting and not Daniel's. He *had* to acknowledge that if he'd written it, he'd probably also encased it in the plastic wallet. Even Stephen realised he was backed into a corner. He was wise enough not to dispute these facts, because it was even more futile than his previous attempts at obfuscation. Instead, he crafted an excuse for *why* he'd written the suicide note. And in doing so, he once again tried to shift the blame for Gabriel's death away from himself.

Stephen told jurors that he'd written the note while Daniel was still alive. Daniel had asked him to write it and offered him sex if he complied. The reasoning behind this bargain, Stephen said, was to help the young man get Gabriel's death "off his chest". Explaining away both victims' deaths in this way was hardly a masterstroke, as it was never explained why Daniel couldn't write it himself. It may be considered unlikely that, upon meeting a stranger at his apartment, one would confess their role in the death of another man. Indeed, it is unlikely that this would turn out to be a man who just weeks ago was sleeping in the very flat where Stephen was taking dictation. It's even more unlikely, however, that Daniel would dictate such an inarticulate and odd note, though understandable that, if he had, Stephen wouldn't make corrections. And why would he mention that he's dropped his phone nearby if he wasn't writing it after stumbling over the grounds of St Margaret's? Like most of Stephen's attempts at an alibi, this story raised more questions than it answered. But he had a go nonetheless.[163]

After admitting writing a note that clearly expressed suicidal intent, Stephen maintained that he had nothing to do with Daniel's actual death. He also tried to explain away the supposed coincidence that both Gabriel and Daniel had been in his flat. It all started, he claimed, at a 'sex and drugs party' in Ilford, east London, which he said he'd attended with Gabriel. His then-flatmate left the party early, with somebody called Dan. By sheer chance, he later met the young chef on Fitlads. Daniel confided in him at Cooke Street, telling Stephen that he and Gabriel had gone to St Margaret's to take drugs and have sex in the churchyard. According to the defendant, Daniel said he'd woken up to find Gabriel dead in the churchyard. This fictional Daniel became fearful, terrified at the prospect his DNA would be at the scene, and began to despair. He poured out the story to Stephen in an act of catharsis, while his scribe joked that police might link the note's writer to Daniel's death if he *actually* committed suicide.[164] This detail was presumably an attempt to explain away the incriminating 'don't blame the guy I was with last night' line, but contradicts the note's assertion that 'he knows nothing of what I have done'.

Despite his clumsy attempt to convince jurors that he'd been the victim of the exact misfortune about which he'd joked with Daniel, Stephen was also adamant that he didn't think 'he was actually going to do it'. He said that he put Daniel's dictation down to the GHB he'd taken and that he was just getting emotions out of his system. He wanted the court to believe that he had no idea that Daniel would actually kill himself. So desperate was he to distance himself from the death that he said: "I would have stopped him. I would have done anything to prevent him from doing it."[165]

None of this made sense and Stephen's incapacity for basic coherence would continue to dog his defence. This incompetence was again displayed three days later, when he admitted lying to police about not knowing three of his victims – Gabriel, Daniel and Jack. Now he said that it was only two of the men he did not know – Gabriel and Jack. It was already known that he'd hired Anthony for sex and he'd conceded that he was with Daniel. This concession was necessary to reconcile his supposed innocence with the fact that he'd definitely written the suicide note. But why had he lied at all, if he was innocent? Jurors may well ask such a question. Luckily, Stephen had a catch-all answer for this that was sure to put any doubts to bed. He did it because "the truth sounded like a lie, so I lied to make it sound like the truth".[166] He no doubt hoped that if this sounded like total bollocks then that would prove his point. And with it, his innocence.

This tactic was a curious one. Stephen was clearly saying to the court that it was understandable that he was a suspect. His need to lie arose from the reasonability of the assumption that he could be seen as guilty. Of course, the problem with this line of defence is that if jurors actually took it at face value then they would be compelled to acquit the most guilty of people. The very grounds of suspicion are subverted into a defence. And so, the more guilty somebody looks, especially somebody who has lied consistently about the cases in question, the more innocent they could appear. Innocence demonstrable by suspect circumstances, thankfully, didn't seem to be an argument particularly rousing to these jurors. Even after constructing this topsy-turvy get-out, Stephen admitted that it might also be reasonable to conclude that he'd been lying to keep out of prison.[167]

* * *

Stephen was finally ready to admit that he had indeed met Jack Taylor. With his credibility in tatters as a result of the slew of concessions that the evidence had forced him into, he at least hoped to convince everyone present that his interactions with Jack during his final hours were harmless. But in order to do that, he'd have to convince them that the tragic fate Jack suffered was by his own hand.

Imagine being the Taylors at this point. Imagine sitting in the court, hearing a rehashing of the nonsense story that the police fed to you. Imagine remembering all of the nights you spent debunking this fiction, despite those in power patronising you while you struggled with such profound grief. Imagine being told, once again, to accept this narrative. To accept that a man so uninterested in drugs that Peter Hirons, who met him a grand total of once, knew of this aversion, was actually injecting crystal meth in the hours before he died. Stephen set about conjuring yet another unlikely story.

After Stephen and Jack had entered his flat, he said, the host casually asked if he'd like some crystal meth. Given that we know what his response to a similar inquiry from Peter was, we can probably assume that the guest wasn't interested. Nonetheless, Stephen insisted that not only had the young man been up for it, but that he'd proceeded to inject it into his ankle.

His date, meanwhile, injected two syringes of meth. "We were extremely high, extremely horny," he told the court. "We just wanted to have sex straight away."[168]

After they'd had sex at about 4am, he said, Jack had transformed from somebody who wasn't keen on illegal highs to the sort of person keen to slam in a second round of meth at 9am. Stephen claimed that he picked up a second batch at Jack's request. He headed to Peter's, where he also bought some mephedrone and GHB. So keen was Jack to pursue this new interest that he handed Stephen his phone to take to East Ham as collateral for more drugs, the defendant claimed.[169]

In the interests of briefly checking back into reality it's worth pointing out that Jack was most likely already dead when Stephen went to East Ham. Because this was the trip on which he planted a bag at the flat in an attempt to frame Peter for Jack's murder.

But Stephen's story had him returning to his flat in Barking to find his date calmly preparing a drink. Laying it on thick, Stephen told jurors that Jack asked him if he "wanted to get mega-high". They each necked a shot of GHB, then injected a mixture of crystal meth and mephedrone before having "rampant" sex, he claimed.[170]

This might be the point at which somebody so obviously guilty of murder might try and get off on a lesser charge, arguing his victim died in the flat and he dumped him outside in a frantic panic. But he'd already worn that excuse thin over the death of Anthony Walgate. So instead, he told the jury that Jack suggested a casual jaunt for some churchyard sex. This didn't exactly gel with his previous claims that Jack had told him he had a girlfriend. Nor did it square with Stephen's assertion that Jack wasn't comfortable with his gay identity. Stephen also told the court that he wasn't keen on having sex in the grounds of St Margaret's, because he was well aware that this was where Daniel had died. "I didn't want to go in the churchyard for obvious reasons – obviously I remember Daniel was in there – so I walked around that part to a dark area in the corner," he claimed. After taking yet more drugs and having sex, Stephen said he left Jack alive in the church's grounds on North Street.[171]

* * *

Peter Hirons had never been in trouble with the police in his life before he met Stephen Port. He'd certainly never seen a dead body. But that was what greeted him as Jack Taylor's lifeless face stared up at him from the pages of an evidence pack at the Old Bailey. Peter had been called as a witness and was desperate to help find out what had happened to Jack, though he feared he would be of little use to the case. When police first told him that Jack had died from an overdose, he was shocked as he remembered the young man who so decisively turned down drugs when they met at his flat. The only conclusion that made sense to him was somebody had put GHB in his whisky and coke without him knowing. Unlike the police, he had suspected foul play from the start.

Totally unprepared as he sat in court, Peter had been told to turn to a certain page, and there it was. The body of the man he'd entertained in his home. The corpse of somebody who stood out in his mind as strong, care-free and full of life. Murdered. Struggling to compose himself, Peter noticed that there was a bottle beside the body. The same vessel appeared in an enlarged version of the image and was the focus of the prosecution's questioning. Peter was asked if the receptacle, which looked like the kind that holds GHB, could have been supplied by him. He said that it could have been, but that then again it could be from anyone who sells the drug. Peter was relieved to see his former client keeping his head bowed in the dock as he too avoided looking at Stephen, all the while haunted by the reality that it may well have been his drugs that had been used to murder a man he so fondly remembered.

November 2, 2016

Stephen's lack of sense of accountability continued to insult and baffle observers of his trial. It seemed partly as if he was gloating, but mostly that he just didn't see what all the fuss was about. Not content with the false accounts he had used to smear the dead, he also tried to downplay the seriousness of the sexual assaults of which he stood accused.

Perhaps the most vulgar instance of this behaviour was when he was asked how he'd feel if Daniel Whitworth had drugged and raped him. His response? He wouldn't have minded. Rather than call into question the seriousness of rape as he'd no doubt hoped, this reaction further exposed his detachment. It reinforced the impression that he was capable of dehumanising young men to the point at which he didn't care if they died. His sole concern was that they facilitated his fetish.

But he went even further by suggesting that Daniel could well have raped *him*. This defamation of the dead was strikingly ugly. Yet Stephen mentioned it nonchalantly. He couldn't be sure, he said, that he'd not been raped.

The fact that Stephen seemed to have no particular conviction about the possibility he'd been raped seemed to imply it wasn't something worth troubling over. This was clearly a man who either didn't understand the seriousness of rape, or did and feigned indifference. The conclusion in both cases was clear; here was a dangerous individual. Stephen also claimed to have passed out after Daniel gave him a glass of wine containing GHB. Mr Rees challenged this, asking: "Why did you raise the suggestion this young man may have raped or sexually assaulted you? Against this dead boy?" Stephen replied: "I wouldn't have minded if he did." This, as Mr Rees pointed out, contradicted his fetish, which relied on him playing the dominant role.[172]

November 7, 2016

In his closing statements, Mr Rees said it would be 'inhuman' not to feel for the families who'd sat through the trial in court and emphasised that the aggravating factor in these crimes was Stephen's appetite for dominance. This drive lurked beneath a shy, cringing exterior and the easiest way to satisfy his relentless appetite for younger men was by slipping them drugs against their will. This ensured that they would be knocked out as the predator sought to treat them as mere vessels in his fetish for having sex with unconscious men. Had he not administered the drugs, he would be raping a struggling victim. Perhaps he wouldn't even accomplish the rape. Drugs guaranteed a success that mirrored the disturbing videos he watched online.[173]

In a question that had already been answered in the mind of any reasoned observer, Mr Rees asked the jury to consider two possibilities. Was it more likely, he asked, that they had in front of them a 'dreadful series of coincidences' in which four men who died in the same manner were linked to an innocent suspect whose panic had driven him to lie? Or was it more likely that Stephen, the man at the heart of each and every one of these horrific cases, *was* guilty? Rubbishing the notion that the defendant could be so unbelievably unlucky, he rejected the risible notion that circumstances had rounded upon him in several instances of gross misfortune. Stephen Port, he said, was a "habitual and compulsive liar".[174]

13

VERDICT

November 23, 2016

Stephen had been sitting in his cell knowing that his fate was solely in the hands of the jury, who had been sent out of the courtroom to reach a verdict. Having denied all 29 charges against him, he should have known that he would receive no leniency on any offences of which he was found guilty.

I, meanwhile, was back in Barking at the *Post*'s new offices, an eight-minute walk from the location at which Anthony's body had been dumped and a five-minute walk from the place in which Gabriel, Daniel and Jack had been found. Not knowing when the jury would return a verdict, I was ringing the Old Bailey every couple of hours to see if its members had made a decision. Each time, a tired man named John would pick up the phone and tell me in the same exasperated yet bored tone that no verdict had yet been reached. I'd have gladly spared him this tedium and would much rather have spent my time hovering around the court and reporting from the scene as the verdict came in. But local journalism's funds were strained and we couldn't afford to have a reporter out of the office missing stories in such a crime-ridden patch. Instead, I spent my time prepping articles that we'd been building about Stephen that explained his back story, what his neighbours thought about him and how Cynthia Adams had felt when she discovered that the man she'd discovered dead may have been killed by her former co-worker. Now we just had to wait and hope that I called at the perfect time for John to tell me, no doubt to his relief, what I needed to hear and in so doing free him from my badgering. This would ideally happen before the Press Association filed the story for every national newspaper in the country and we'd publish first, making up for the fact that the paper on whose patch these crimes happened couldn't have a reporter at every day of the trial. These deaths had scared our community, from the dog-walker who stumbled across two bodies to the neighbour who'd found out his friend was most likely a serial killer. Having moved from Bennett's Castle Lane in Dagenham, a road not unlike the estate on which Stephen had grown up, to Suffolk Road in Barking, just 11 minutes' walk from his Cooke Street flat, I'd been deeply disturbed by the danger that had been allowed to flourish unfettered in a particularly poor part of east London. The days passed and there was no verdict. In the end, it wasn't John who gave me the news.

On the morning of November 23, I was at the Barking Enterprise Centre covering the unbelievably dull launch of the borough's Business Awards. As the council championed local firms in the borough, *BBC News* was playing in the background. I glanced at the screen and saw that Stephen's verdicts were rolling in. He had been found guilty of three murders – those of Gabriel Kovari, Daniel Whitworth and Jack Taylor. I ran back to the office. It took until the afternoon for the jury to deliver its verdict on the death of Anthony Walgate. Stephen Port was convicted of all four murder charges.[175]

Of the total 29 charges, jurors found Stephen guilty on 22 counts relating to 11 victims. In addition to the four murders, he was convicted of four rapes – those of Victim A, 19, in 2012; Victim D, 22, in 2015; Victim F in the same year; and Victim H, on an October weekend, just days before he was arrested.[176]

He was convicted of 10 counts of administering a substance against Victim A in 2012; Victim B, 20, June 2014; Anthony Walgate in June 2014; Gabriel Kovari in August 2014; Daniel Whitworth in September 2014; Victim D in January 2015; Victim F, in August 2015; Victim G, in September 2015; Jack Taylor in September 2015 and Victim H on an earlier October weekend in 2015.[177]

Jurors found Stephen guilty of four sexual assaults against Victim E, 35, July 2015; Victim F, August 2015; Victim G, just two days before he met Jack Taylor and Victim H on the same weekend he'd raped the man.[178]

The jury cleared him on three counts of rape.[179] He was, of course, not guilty of the four manslaughter charges, but only because he'd been proven, beyond a reasonable doubt, to have committed murder in each of those cases.[180] Stephen was never charged with the rapes of Anthony, Gabriel, Daniel and Jack. Yet a cursory Google search of his name will turn up stories from well-regarded news organisations that say he did just that. It's worth taking a moment to clarify why this seeming contradiction is understandable. When the Crown Prosecution Service decides whether or not to pursue a case it has to consider whether or not the charges in question will be provable in court. Built into this decision are considerations of physical evidence and witness testimony.

Regarding the physical evidence, it's clear that the police were able to prove that Stephen's DNA had been found not just on the bodies, but in places that point to a sexual component in the interaction that deposited it there. It's also clear that he drugged the victims with GHB, a drug favoured by date-rapists. But even knowing this, a charge of rape in relation to each of the murder victims would be less easily proved beyond a reasonable doubt than it would be were these men able to give evidence in court. Though he was not technically found guilty of raping his four murder victims, it would be generous to say the least were we to assume that he did not commit such an appalling act upon them, especially given his form for doing precisely that when he'd finished administering drugs to the survivors who were able to give testimony and secure convictions. Though we can never be certain of the precise nature of every second of what went on in Cooke Street, it would be foolish to assume that, upon rendering four of his victims unconscious, Stephen took a moment to reflect on what he was doing and decided against doing the very thing for which he had lured them there in the first place.

Peter Hirons had also been jailed, earlier that month, for dealing drugs to Stephen. The *Post's* sister paper, the *Newham Recorder*, reported that police suspected him to have unwittingly supplied the drugs used to murder Jack Taylor. The paper reported that, during Stephen's trial, the prosecution said that Peter had sold drugs to Stephen hours before. We also know that Stephen went to Peter's after meeting Jack, before which he was seen withdrawing cash, which could have been money he owed for the drugs that killed Jack. However, we also know that Stephen had another dealer and kept quite the stash at home, all intermingled in the chaotic mess that was the floor of his apartment, and so we most likely will never know for certain who sold the drugs which killed Jack.[181]

Peter was jailed for 30 months after admitting three counts of possession of Class A drugs with intent to supply; possession of Class B drugs with intent to supply; possession of Class C drugs with intent to supply and possession of criminal property.[182] In the six months leading up to his trial, he'd been effectively homeless. He moved from sofa to sofa while the police investigated his flat in East Ham, rendering it out of bounds.

I spoke to Peter after his release, meeting him at his new apartment. He was filled with horror at the notion that drugs he'd sold for what he believed were recreational purposes could have been used in such a sinister plot. But Stephen was a prolific user. One only has to recall the amount of drugs Ryan Edwards saw in his flat to wonder whether it's possible to pin down the origin of each of his bottles, especially given that he also had at least one other dealer, named Gerald Matovu.[183] It's also worth bearing in mind that Peter, who was nowhere near a gangland kingpin, never would have gone to prison if the man he'd sold drugs to hadn't turned out to be a serial rapist and murderer. In his words: "If it wasn't for Stephen Port, I would never have gone to prison for social drugs."

As previously stated, Peter was in total agreement with the Taylors' conviction that Jack had not willingly taken the drugs, whatever their origin. And he was deeply upset that somebody who hadn't consented to taking drugs had his life cut short by them. When I met him, he asked if I could put him in touch with the Taylors. I contacted Donna who, dignified as ever, provided her email address after Peter had expressed an urge to write to the family, perhaps to try and make sense of this tragedy. In the meantime, he was rebuilding his life, having started a business following his release, the details of which he'd rather not be included in this book lest it be associated with murders beyond his control. When I visited, a small sign hung on one of the walls at his modest east London home. It read: 'Everyone needs a little sparkle in their lives.'

14

SENTENCING

November 25, 2016

Stephen appeared as casually detached on his final day at the Old Bailey as when he had first faced the court. While shattered families and incredulous journalists gathered to hear his sentence, no doubt pondering the severity with which his crimes would be met, he appeared unnervingly bland for Britain's biggest serial killer of the decade. Proceedings opened with Mr Rees reminding the judge of the fact that Stephen had already been found guilty of lying before he'd even set foot in the Old Bailey.[184] This fact thrust to the fore the pain that Anthony's family had to feel when they heard that the man who'd deceived police over the student's death had originally evaded a murder charge. Today was for them, and everyone else who Stephen had wounded on his destructive path. And it was to the families that Mr Rees now turned, reading statements from each.

The death of Anthony was said to have destroyed his family. A statement from his mother, Sarah, said his relatives were left 'broken' and his two best friends were devastated. In a touch of humanity that it's difficult to overstate, the writer also castigated Stephen for destroying the lives of his own family – Albert, Joan and Sharon – with his crimes. Though they were not present in court, the Kovaris had also submitted a summary, if such a thing can be possible, of the profound effect Gabriel's death had on them. His brother was suffering a pain that "could hardly be described in words". His mother said that "there is no pain greater than losing a child."

Whatever custodial term was awaiting Stephen, the unde-served punishment wrought on Daniel's family was now revealed to the judge. Adam Whitworth's existence after his son's death constituted a 'life-sentence of grief'. 'The pain from his hour of grief spills into his everyday life,' the statement read. 'The light has gone out of his eyes.' There can be no better description of the same trauma that hung about his face like a fog when I briefly met him at the inquest into his son's death the previous year. Daniel's stepmother, Amanda Pearson, said that her deceased child was her first and final waking thought every day.

'We had a rich and fulfilling life ahead of us with Daniel,' she'd written. 'It's been stolen from us – I can't possibly describe the hell it's left with us but we will always be proud to have been part of his life.'

Next came a statement from Daniel's grandmother, Barbara, who said that he was the kindest, most considerate boy you could ever meet. She would miss him more than words can say.

The Taylors described totally falling apart as a family and said that nothing will ever fill the black hole that has been left, sucking out the exuberance that Jack had always radiated. Grief had forced a reliance on anti-depressants. They knew that they would have to face this loss for the rest of their lives. Throughout all of this, these same families, whose sores were opened in full view of the nation's media, remained as they had always been: composed, dignified, decent.

Now it was the defence's turn for closing remarks. The only refuge they could seek for their client was to say that he had not intended to kill his victims. They said that Stephen had spiralled into a 'vortex' characterised by pumping drugs into his body at an alarming rate. His fetish for sex with unconscious men grew into a fixation. That fixation became a compulsion.[185]

Judge Openshaw turned to Stephen and asked him to stand. He condemned him not only for luring the victims to his flat and raping them while unconscious, but for abandoning their bodies in public places. This, he said, robbed them of their dignity and left them to be discovered with drugs in a grim tableaux designed to appear sordid and accidental. He accepted that Stephen had not intended to kill, but to cause serious harm. However, he added that he must have known and foreseen there was a high risk of death, especially after killing Anthony.[186] These murders, he said, demanded a whole-life sentence. "The defendant will die in prison."

Cheering broke out in the court from what sounded like the public gallery as one man shouted "scum bag" at Stephen.

As he was also given a life-sentence for each of the four rapes, I noticed the Taylors crying. Stephen was then sentenced to a year for each time he'd administered a substance with intent, totalling a decade. He skulked out of the dock, still giving the impression that he just didn't get it.

What happened as he walked down to the cells is difficult to describe. A surge of emotion I'd struggle to define poured down on the courtroom. It was a hybrid of anguish, grief, hatred and relief, which couldn't be constrained or neatly resolved with the case's end. It exploded, somehow slowly, as a gruff male voice called out "I hope you die a long, slow death you piece of shit"[187] to the unresponsive back of Stephen's balding head.

The speaker said it carefully. I remember having the impression of it being prepared, perhaps even rehearsed night after sleepless night. This, coupled with the fragility of the almost breaking voice that delivered it, summed up the confused emotional state of those gathered in the room. The court teemed with a sickening exhilaration, frustrated and retarded by the stunted closure the sentence represented. I cannot, for one second, claim to know – or even comprehend – what those bereaved were feeling.

On the very same day, Stephen's distraught parents – Albert and Joan – declared their son was innocent. As journalists continued to wonder how the police had been blind to so much evidence, Joan told reporters her softly spoken son could not possibly have murdered anyone. He was a kind boy. She had even told him "I didn't murder anyone, Mum" the previous Sunday on the telephone.[188]

As Stephen began his new life inside, I waited outside the Old Bailey rehearsing how to approach the Taylors as they lived within the *Post*'s news patch. I'd written down the key points I wanted to get across to them and was wary of the fact I'd probably be asking these questions to people understandably eager to get home and be together as a family. Either side of me, television correspondents were summarising what had just happened into cameras as an LBC radio journalist talked emphatically into a microphone while she marched up and down the pavement.

As I was trying to figure out how best to tell the Taylors I wanted to help them secure accountability from the police and get some kind of justice for Jack over the officers who'd neglected to protect him, a presenter sprayed an ungodly amount of hairspray about her head, flooding my throat. It had been at least half an hour since the sentencing and there was still no sign of the Taylors, who I was beginning to think had snuck out of a secret exit separate to the one on which my eyes had been trained all this time.

I saw some agency reporters standing next to yet more cameras across the road, next to the exit, so I made my way over. A polite police press officer told me the Taylors would be making a short statement for the assembled scrum, but they wouldn't talk to anyone individually. Fair enough, I thought.

Shortly after, the Taylors emerged. Donna was holding a prepared statement in her hand. To her right was Jack's mum Jeanette, who looked distraught, defiant and scared all at once. Jack's other sister, Jenny, was also there. Donna spoke into a mass of microphones: "Jack was a loving son, a brother, uncle and grandson and brother-in-law, and nephew, and a true inspiration to everyone that knew him. He was the life and soul of our family, our lives will never be the same and we'd like to thank you all for showing an interest in our Jack because he meant the world to us." She said that the family finally had justice for the four young men, to whom she affectionately referred to as boys, after the appalling months through which they'd battled. "Our Jack can finally rest in peace," she added, describing his killer as a "sick, sadistic scumbag".

15

APPEAL

July 2017, Dagenham

While Stephen was in prison, life carried on in somewhat of an odd fashion for his parents, Albert and Joan. For one thing, they had to put up with me knocking on their door. I first went to their home more than eight months after their son had been jailed for life. After tracking them down, I'd written two letters asking them if they could help me understand their son's crimes. I'd left the first letter at 62 Cooke Street, having learned they were planning to sell their son's former flat and were still stopping by. I didn't receive a reply, which was to be expected given the embarrassment they must have suffered, along with the tedium and upset of journalists bothering them during the case. But I still felt it was worth a shot, so I was off to post a second letter at their address in Dagenham.

Cycling from the *Post*'s office in Barking town centre, I considered the picture I'd built of Albert in my mind. Having never spoken to him, these were entirely based upon his cursory statement quoted in the press. In one interview, his response to questions about his son's sexuality was: "Don't get me wrong – I'm against it."[189]

This formed a brutish image in my mind, one of a homophobe – probably as tall as his son. The road on which he lived was modest, giving off a quiet, almost pastoral quality. Approaching the door, I imagined a man who'd reluctantly given an interview only to focus on the urgent matter of renouncing his son's homosexuality. I prepared myself for being told to fuck off and quite possibly shoved about a bit.

Having not absorbed the age gap between Port and his parents, it was conceivable his dad would still be able to throw a decent punch, so I hoped it'd be Joan I'd find at home, if anyone at all. A sign beside their front door reading 'Beware the dog – enter at your own risk' was the first of its kind to achieve its purpose and made me mildly anxious as I paused before pressing the bell. I heard a rattling on the other side of the door.

An elderly, yet somehow childlike man in his mid-70s opened the door and I immediately went from feeling like an underdog to an aggressor. He wore a grey, loose shirt and smart but comfortable trousers. Standing at around 5ft 10ins, he was bald in the same place as his son, leaving a ring of white hair circling around the sides of his head. He wore brown spectacles of the kind you'd expect a university lecturer to wear and they gave him the air of a stylish wordsmith in retirement. I softly explained who I was, why I was there and that I wanted to help people understand what his son had done. His face seemed to flinch while I was talking, expressing a polite discomfort, and I was surprised when he didn't close the door. Through a gravelly Essex accent, he softly said that he'd talk to me in a couple of months' time, once he and Joan had managed to 'get rid of' Stephen's flat.

The baffling and nonchalant gentleness I'd seen Stephen display in court seemed obviously inherited from Albert, whose curt assurances would have felt dismissive were they spoken by anyone else. Wishing him well for the holiday he was taking to Clacton-on-Sea the following week, I gave him the letter and said he could call me any time. Though he assured me he'd call, he didn't make much eye contact and seemed to struggle with either my northern accent or his hearing so, unsure as to the success of my trip, I said goodbye and left.

* * *

Prior to my visit, Albert and Joan had been sending money to Stephen in prison as they struggled to cope with media attention and the reasons behind it. They were having difficulty processing what had happened but, like most parents, thought it a good idea to send him some home comforts, such as books and a magazine about space. More than anything, they wanted it all to go away and to enjoy what remained of their lives. The police, thankfully, hadn't burdened them with too much knowledge of Stephen's crimes. And Albert firmly believed that he and his wife couldn't have done anything about whatever had gone on. Understandably, they didn't feel responsible for whatever destruction he'd wrought. They couldn't control him.

The less they knew, the better. Even if he had done something wrong, he'd most likely been led astray.[190]

Still, I hoped they'd be able to give a valuable insight into what their son was like as a child. Were there any warning signs? Did something happen to him? Hoping Albert's apparent openness with me was genuine, I made a note to contact him in a couple of months, by which time he assured me he'd be okay to talk. I'd told him that, if I didn't hear from him, I'd be back around that time just in case he'd forgotten to call, which he seemed to be okay about. For now, I waited.

* * *

"Right, I don't agree with what you're doing and neither will he. Be careful what you're saying."

That's how my second meeting with Albert started, on his doorstep, on a sunny and humid day. I'd come a different way this time and the side of the road I'd walked down had already smashed the almost pastoral impression I'd had of his neighbourhood when I'd first visited. Unimpressive, crumbly cubes with square post-war gardens that delineated the space in which working classes could reasonably be expected to be left alone shoved themselves rudely round a road that looked like the set of a British kitchen sink drama set in the '70s.

I nodded politely as Albert grew more exasperated with my presence. He muttered something about having just sat down to work; his blue shirt under a mauve jumper once again giving him the appearance of some sort of writer. But this time, he projected less the gentle academic and more the pained conspiracy theorist who just doesn't understand why nobody gets where he's coming from. He bent forward with his hands on his knees and shook his head vigorously as he proclaimed Stephen's innocence.

"He wouldn't even kill a bloody spider," he said, adding in a friendly tone: "He's *terrified* of spiders."

"He was just a *normal* boy, just like you and me," he continued. "He had a *normal* childhood. He wasn't bullied, I know he said he was, but he wasn't."

Albert was growing ever more frustrated. He said he didn't have the time, energy or inclination to sit down and talk because he was busy caring for Joan, who was unwell. "I'm just trying to live my own life," he said. "That's all."

Nonetheless, we had a brief chat as he grew more congenial. I was hoping my visit might lead to acquiring some pictures of Stephen from his childhood. But Albert, remembering his annoyance a few seconds before, preempted my request and told me: "No photos. He never did like them. He'd hate it." Albert then issued a warning that I took to be quite sinister: "Be very careful. He could get very nasty." This was followed by a baffling attempt at pacification as he once more wore a kindly smile and suggested it was the facts I should be careful with, as opposed to my personal safety. "He don't want to get nasty or nothing," he insisted. "But be careful."

I shook his hand and, in an attempt to convince myself this hadn't been a waste of both our time, I asked if he could pass my number on to Stephen's sister. "Keep out of her way," he said. "She will tell you where to go."

He closed the door.

* * *

While Albert was protesting Stephen's innocence, however quietly, their son was baffling anyone else familiar with the case by issuing an appeal against his sentence.[191] His case is probably the only one I've ever seen in which the actual trial appeared to constitute a mere formality. From day one it seemed obvious that the police finally, after much bungling, had got their man. And everyone was baffled as to how such an odd creature had evaded them for so long. There was no chance of acquittal and it spoke only to his delusion that he'd pleaded not guilty to the 29 charges. But issuing an appeal demonstrated a level of either idiocy or desperation that would elicit in the most patient of people an exasperated sigh. He lodged his appeal in August 2018, almost two years since his sentencing. Stephen wasn't quite so stupid as to deny every charge this time, just the most serious. He was still denying the murders of Anthony, Gabriel, Daniel and Jack. Albert's insistence that he was innocent suggested that Stephen either thought he could convince others like he'd convinced his parents, or that he genuinely doesn't understand the legal definition of murder and believes that, because he did not necessarily invite young men to his flat for the sole intention of killing them, he's not guilty. Unfortunately for Stephen, the law classifies murder as the ending of another person's life through a premeditated act in which the killer intended to cause death or serious harm.

It seems most likely that this appeal was an act of idiocy as opposed to desperation. The crucial evidence that suggests this action was the behaviour of an incompetent half-wit is the date of application – nearly two years after he was convicted. Appeals are supposed to be lodged within 28 days. A spokeswoman for the families of the victims said of the appeal at the time: "This changes nothing."[192]

Two-and-a-half months later, a judge dismissed the appeal, which Mandy Pearson branded an "insult to us and to Daniel's memory". She was "overjoyed" that appeal was "seen for what it was", calling it a "futile attempt" to "excuse himself" and "drag our boys' names through the mud in the process".[193] Still, Stephen had apparently convinced those closest to him that he was innocent, placing a family-shaped barrier in between the killer and me. I wanted to know more about the man, to present a fuller picture. But the most likely options were exhausted.

16

LUKE

I had, of course, also written to Stephen himself. Shockingly, he didn't respond to my high-minded note suggesting that he should help me piece together a history of his seedy crimes in the hope that society could better understand his perversion. Nor was he moved by a journalist's desire to prevent a rapist just like him from brazenly destroying lives under the not-so-watchful eye of law enforcement. I knew he'd written to Cody Lachey. What had he done that I hadn't? He'd lied. So I ditched my lofty illusions of a killer playing fair and invented Luke Banes.

I took the first name from *Star Wars* hero Luke Skywalker and the surname from Mikaela Banes in *Transformers*, both franchises being favourites of Stephen's. I started scrawling a note pathetic and reverential in tone. Luke had crap handwriting, dropped misspelled words on the page and was bullied in school. His classmates had called him Harry Potter due to the glasses he wore (okay, that bit was true) and had mocked him as a very young child for donning *Lion King* spectacles (also true). He felt bad for Stephen being in prison because he'd once been spoken to rudely by a homophobic police officer (he was obviously gay). Luke was 28, scrawny and looking for fitness tips from Stephen, who he hoped could help him with his cripplingly low self-esteem. His lack of confidence, of course, meant that he'd never had a boyfriend and could do with a few tips. Leaving an email, phone number and my address in south London, I told him to contact me if there was anything at all that I could do to make his time inside easier. Before posting, I sprayed the illegible dirge of monotonous banality with Old Spice deodorant and Hugo Boss aftershave, hoping the dimwit would be too randy to realise how utterly clichéd and contrived this act was, should the prison officers bother to pass on the letter, which is reproduced in full below, complete with spelling errors.

Hi Stephen,

I hope you dont mind me writing to you. I wanted to send a letter because I though it must be horrible in jale and might be nice to have a friend in this situation. I was only in trubble with police once and it was terrible because I dont have many friends or family and I am not good in crowds! I hope however things are there mad easier with my letter. Sorry about handwriting but my computer is at the shop being repaired and I did not want to wait any longer to write to you. Hope this is okay. I think we probably have a lot in common as I also like sciencefiction like Star Trek and stuff. I like watching all of the films and have quite a lot of action figers. I wanted to know what things are like for you in there and if I can help.

My name is Luke Banes and I live in London and I am 28. I have read a lot about you and like I said even though I have not been in jale I have been in touch with Police before and it was very scary so maybe I know a bit how you feel? I got arrested because of a date gone wrong with a man who turned out to be an escort and hit me wen I could not give him money because he said I needed to even though I did not know and even had bought him ticket for the cinema and MacDonalds.

Police were horrible in the way they spoke to me and laughed at me because I was dating a boy. It reminded me of school when I got laughed at during PE. I red somewere that you got bullied but I dont know if it was just lies in the media. They put a picture of you in big glasses. I had glasses at school with Simba from The Lion King on them and everyone called me Simba. Then when Harry Potter came out they called me that. I also wanted your help, if that is OK. I've allways been skinny and was hoping to get in better shape and saw some pictures of you and you seem very muscly. I think if I am a bit bigger it might help my confidense. If I can help you I dont know if you use the internet but here are my detail.

* * *

He replied within two weeks, which was a fairly quick turn-around considering I'd sent it to the wrong prison and it had to be forwarded to HMP Frankland in Durham, a facility once dubbed the Jihadi Jail owing to a special unit set up for Islamic extremists.[194] Its inmates have included Moors Murderer Ian Brady as well as Charles Bronson, one of Britain's most notorious prisoners who, at the time of writing, has served more than

45 years, much of which is the result of hostage-taking and bad behaviour inside after being admitted under a seven-year sentence for armed robbery in 1974. Clearly, Stephen was deemed among our greatest living threats to civilised society.

Before exploring what it was like speaking to Stephen, a note on his spelling and grammar is necessary. His letters featured some of the worst writing I've ever seen, both in handwriting and errors. He would spell the word 'quite' as 'quit' and rather than writing 'he's' would say 'his', among other basic mistakes. I don't say this to pluck at the low-hanging fruit of mocking his severely limited abilities, but to give you a window into the mind of the man described in this book. I also think it's worth noting because it, if any further proof were needed, attests to the fact that the man who evaded police for so long was by no means a genius. Finally, it's worth pointing out that you wouldn't know how bad his writing is based on the information that follows. This is because legal and ethical advice prevents me from quoting directly from the notes, or showing pictures of them, due to the fact that Stephen believed that he was corresponding in private from within the walls of HMP Frankland. Were you able to see the full, unedited letters, you would likely be stunned at the incomprehensibility of certain passages, the messiness of his handwriting and the childlike manner in which he addresses his supposed penpal. The reader may at this point be wondering why I cannot quote directly from the notes when content from Cody Lachey's correspondence have appeared in the tabloid press and elsewhere online. When I submitted the original manuscript, two ghastly possibilities presented themselves courtesy of the publisher's lawyers – what if Stephen Port took legal action based on me invading his privacy? What if he brought forward a copyright complaint on the grounds that he owned the material therein? The unseemly outcome of such an action, however unlikely, would be that Stephen would once again get his face in the paper – but this time playing the victim. In the worst possible outcome, some of the money that readers parted with to buy this book could actually end up benefiting the very man who has wrought devastation on innocent people. Thankfully, the lack of direct quotes from his letters does not block any great insight into his mind. Stephen's letters were less than surprising, confirming that he was of low intelligence and still interested in flirtations with the type of man he could no longer rape.

His first reply began by warning Luke that he'd stop replying if any of his letters ended up in the press. He also wasn't able to discuss his case and would in later notes add his own custom version of a misspelled copyright notice claiming the material to be his own. Stephen seemed in good spirits considering his circumstances and he didn't seem overly down or depressed about life in the high-security prison. He kept the note short, saying that he'd answer more questions once we had become better acquainted. Stephen did want *one* thing from Luke – a picture. Of course.

* * *

Port asking for a picture was a problem. Not one that I hadn't anticipated on some level – I'd often thought that the surest

Killer: One of the images of Stephen Port that was shown to the jury

Picture of innocence: A school snap of Port. He is on the back row, wearing a claret and blue top. **Below:** Port used dating apps to contact his victims

Murder scene: Port's flat in Cooke Street, Barking

Victims: (Clockwise from top left): Daniel Whitworth (21), Jack Taylor (25), Gabriel Kovari (22) and Anthony Walgate (23)

Grim discoveries: St Margaret's graveyard in Barking

Tragic final footsteps: CCTV footage of Port walking with Jack Taylor

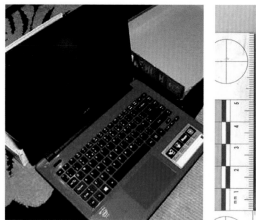

Evidence: A laptop belonging to Port that was seized by police and a bottle containing the drug GBL recovered during the investigation

I am Sorry to everyone, mainly my family but I can't go on anymore, I took the life of my friend Gabriel Kline, we was just having some fun at a mates place and I got carried away and gave him another shot of G I didn't notice while we was having sex that he had stopped breathing; I tried everything to get him to breath again but it was too late, it was an accident but I blame myself for what happened and I didn't tell my family I work etc, I know I would go to prison if I go to police and I can't do that to my family and at least this way I can at least be with Gabriel again, I hope he will forgive me.

BTW. Please do not blame the guy I was with last night, we only had Sex then I left, he knows nothing of what I have done. I have taken what g I had left with sleeping pills so if does kill me its what I deserve. feeling dizey now as took 10 min ago so hoping you understand my writing.

I dropped my phone on way here so should be in the grass somewhere

Sorry to everyone

Love always

'Don't blame the guy I was with last night':
A fake suicide note found on the body of Daniel Whitworth

Police interview: Port was evasive, denying the killings during questioning

Inquest: Deputy Assistant Commissioner for the Metropolitan Police, Stuart Cundy, arrives to give evidence at Barking Town Hall in November 2021

Guilty: An artist's impression of Port during the court case. There were cheers from the public gallery when he was given a whole-life sentence

way of opening him up would be to appeal to his base urges with a photograph. The issue was that his first letter already indicated a degree of scepticism about who I was and what I'd do with our correspondence. And then there was the small matter that sending a picture of myself could result in his father identifying me as the same person who'd knocked on his door, or in anybody sympathetic to Stephen at all alerting him to my appearance in three documentaries about the case. Stephen might not have the internet, but his sister could still find me online. And, given that I'd been understandably derisive about the man on film, sending a picture that was obviously me seemed like a bad move. I decided to buy time without losing momentum. I told him that I'd be happy to send a picture – but only if I could trust him. I warned him that I didn't want him to share it with too many inmates or prison officers just in case it ended up being a focus of ridicule in the press. Knowing that he'd had a difficult time at work while at West Ham Bus Garage, Luke expressed frustrations about his own job in a west London call centre. I portrayed him as something of a shy man who struggled to get on with colleagues and asked to know more about his friends inside. I posted the letter and hoped it would buy me a couple of weeks to figure out which – and whose – picture I'd send.

* * *

My mirroring worked. Stephen sent a second letter. It was difficult to know which among his words were purely inventions, as he came across as far more confrontational than I would have expected for an intensely shy man. Then again, his well-documented aversion to interactions had always seemed to relate to interpersonal, sexual relationships with a person who was actually in the room. There was nothing, it seemed to me, to prevent him from cultivating a more confident persona while his actual self was shielded from scrutiny courtesy of prison walls. He was at this point well-versed in using his correspondence to create alter egos preferable to his wretched self, just as he had done on social media when he was a free man. The one thing that I could be sure of was that he relished these opportunities to show his dominance, whether factual or imagined, and no doubt hoped that I would be the submissive of the two during whatever bizarre relationship was forming through these letters.

At this point, I had the awful realisation that Stephen might actually have bought my story. He had made friends with Luke Banes and invested in him, even if just to the extent that he believed him to be a real person to whom it was worth writing. I began to feel guilty. I was manipulating somebody, treating him not as an end in and of himself, but using him for a particular end that would certainly be detrimental to him. This realisation was a thoroughly unpleasant one. The alternative was that he hadn't bought it at all and would write any old bollocks in the hope of securing a picture over which he could masturbate in his cell. Regardless, I still needed a picture with which to complete this deception.

I'd already had one refusal. My 23-year-old brother wasn't keen on having his picture hanging in the cell of a serial murderer and rapist. I thought he'd work as a candidate given his skinny structure and was confident he'd be safe, but, in his words: "The thought of him looking at me and getting off on it is too much." Fair enough. I went for plan B and started scouring through old pictures of myself, ones in which I didn't resemble the me who might have been identified in connection with the case. I found one of myself sitting on a park bench in central Manchester, wearing tight skinny jeans, Dr Martens and a cardigan over an Oxford shirt. I looked nothing like my current self and it was the closest I'd ever looked to a 'twink', so it'd have to do. Then again it was still me, it bore my name and it was on the internet. Maybe it *did* look like me, but I'd noticed slight changes and interpreted them as significant. Too risky.

Onto Plan C. I made a last-ditch attempt and messaged a friend of a very slight frame who fit the bill of a twink. He happened to be straight, but, like me, could pass as gay to a killer who obviously favoured a stereotypical look. Johnny, as we'll refer to him, hadn't replied to my Facebook message. So I called him. The conversation went something like this:

Me: "You seen my message mate?"

Johnny: "No what's up? What message?"

Me: "The one about sending a picture of you to a serial killer."

Johnny: "Eh?"

Me: "Right, well you're going to think I'm mental, but just hear me out and you'll understand why it's not a big deal. I'm writing a book about that serial killer from Barking. I've been writing to him in prison under a fake name and he's asked for a picture of me. I can't use one of me, because I've knocked on his dad's door and been on telly, so I don't want to risk sinking the whole thing.

"I thought you'd be a good option because you're skinny and quite effeminate and he goes for younger, smaller guys. Before you tell me to fuck off, just bear these facts in mind: He's never getting out of prison. If he does, he doesn't have your name or any way of tracking you down. I'll delete you on social media. Even if he could identify you just from a picture of your face, he's jailed for life. And, if he ever does get out, you'll look totally different by then. So what do you reckon?"

Johnny: "Mate, look no further."

I told him to keep it quiet, deleted him from my Facebook and posted three pictures of him dressed in a ridiculous Hawaiian shirt and sipping cocktails from a coconut to HMP Frankland.

* * *

The interval in which I found myself hoping for a reply seemed to be dragging on longer than the ones in between my so far successful correspondence with Stephen. I figured he'd either sussed out that Luke wasn't real, found my friend online through Sharon or decided that he didn't fancy the person to whom he imagined he was writing. I decided there was nothing to lose from firing off another note, checking if everything was okay given the sort of people he probably had to deal with inside. That letter must have crossed with his reply, because in just a few days I received a three-page note closely followed by another one expressing dismay that the first hadn't been received. Stephen didn't seem to clock the fact that I'd taken the highly cautious step of cutting around my friend's figure so that his girlfriend and others were not included in the picture, something that surely reeks of a writer being very careful not to identify unwilling parties. I'd used the excuse that I was worried about their safety, citing the possibility that not everyone at HMP Frankland could be trusted with identifiable features of innocents on the outside. I don't understand why he didn't question this further – what could the man, or anyone else in there, do with a picture of a few pissed-up students at a party when they're in one of the most high-security prisons in the country? By the time they'd be out, their faces would have warped into middle, if not old, age. But he didn't ask, he was just happy to have something to look at. I'd tried to relate to Port as something of a loner, but I didn't want to go too far because there'd be nothing attractive to him in somebody as strange as he was. Instead, I played it as though I was quiet, maintaining I preferred a close circle around me rather than being the centre of attention, writing: 'I don't have lots of friends but I think it is better to have a few good ones than having loads of average ones!'

* * *

Stephen talked throughout his letters as though he was a confident intellectual, despite all available audio recordings of his voice portraying a bumbling man incapable of conveying the most basic of facts. Though it's true that I'm referring to unusual circumstances – his 999 call, his police interviews – those recordings are exactly what I'd expect from the descriptions of people who knew him, his father included. It's conceivable that in some circumstances he managed to sound relatively well-spoken, but that's clearly not a defining characteristic of by all accounts an inarticulate mumbler as opposed to an erudite orator. But despite his surprisingly talkative nature on the pages that found their way into my home, weeks now went by without a letter from Stephen. The delay was so unusual it got me thinking that he'd grown bored of our correspondence, or that a note had gone missing somehow. I fired off a quick letter, expressing the usual concerns about his situation in prison. There was no need for the nights I spent worrying about a letter in which he exposed me for the journalist I was, as his letters began arriving with greater regularity around the middle of August. His next note came about a week after I'd sent mine. I put this down to his pleasure at having received a half-naked picture of Justin Bieber that I had sent him after he'd expressed an interest.

* * *

I stopped writing to Stephen for two reasons. The first was the discomfort that I previously expressed. The second was that he was continuously evasive. There was a reason that I'd been asking about his fellow inmates and it was probably the same reason that was behind his vague responses.

As a high-profile sex offender, Stephen's stay in Belmarsh prior to Frankland was confined to a maximum-security part of the jail, with other rapists who were deemed to be at risk of attacks from inmates who disapproved of their perversions. While he was serving time at Belmarsh, Stephen took his sexual energies out on somebody even more notorious than he was. Together with their records of atrocious sex crimes, they formed one of the most grotesque consensual relationships of which I've ever heard. Stephen's prison boyfriend was Britain's most prolific paedophile – Richard Huckle.[195]

Richard, a scrawny figure topped with long, lank hair and sporting a wispy goatee, was 30 years old when he was handed a life sentence for abusing as many as 200 Malaysian children. Richard had molested children aged between six months and 12 years old while posing as a devout Christian English teacher in Kuala Lumpur. He masqueraded there for nine years, sharing sickening images and videos of him raping children for the pleasure of other paedophiles on an encrypted website. He and fellow high-risk prisoners were able to mix in the maximum-security area of Belmarsh, where cell doors were often left open and he and Stephen started a sexual relationship. This ended when he and Stephen were split up and sent to different prisons, but a source told *Mirror Online* that their sexual liaisons were an open secret at Belmarsh. Their guess was that Stephen and Richard probably carried on writing to one another once separated.

According to the prison's rules, sex acts between inmates are not specifically prohibited and disciplinary charges 'may not be appropriate' when 'they have a reasonable expectation of privacy'.[196]

17

TRAUMA

The coverage of Stephen's trial understandably centred on his actions and those who died as a result. But the proceedings also gave an insight into what it was like to survive one of his attacks, and living testimony to the confusing inadequacies of Barking and Dagenham Metropolitan Police officers. Two years after the trial, I made contact with one such survivor, and a sentence that he relayed to me after he heard them leave an officer's lips, stuck out: "You should be careful who you meet online." Words to this effect were spoken by a police officer as he addressed a young man who could barely stand. Stephen had drugged him and was at the scene of the interaction with police. He was then allowed to walk away. The young man in question was the person referred to as Victim B in court papers. I met with Victim B in November 2018. In a south London pub, he spoke to me about his experiences with the serial killer and its impact on his life afterwards. He was a living example of the damage that Stephen inflicted – a survivor, yes, but one who was still battling for every inch that had been taken from him.

When he bravely agreed to speak to me in the frantic hinterland of Elephant and Castle, he told me that he didn't want his real name to be printed. This is because any involvement with homosexuality will, in his estimation, ruin his life due him and his family being Muslims. He sat uneasily in the bar, not drinking, as he told me he'd met with Stephen a few times, having first made contact on the website Fitlads. On June 20, 2014, he woke up at 62 Cooke Street on the bedroom floor and wondered why he was banging on the closed door in a frenzy.

"I was on the floor screaming and shouting," he said. "It was like something was inside my body trying to get out. I was telling him: 'I need to go home! Let me go home!' As I was on the floor, he was holding me."

How long had he been at the apartment? He couldn't be sure. Victim B had gone to Stephen's at about 1pm and told him that he was tired. Stephen, who the young man had come to consider a friend, had given his shoulders a rub and a glass of what looked like water. He also suggested they take poppers. Victim B wasn't into drugs, but his host insisted.

"He said it will calm my body down and help me relax," Victim B told me. "It really hit me."

About eight hours later he awoke in darkness, begging to be taken home. "There were so many things going through my head – I was going crazy," he said. "I was in panic mode."

As he worried about what his parents, especially his protective mother, would be thinking about his whereabouts, an intoxicated Stephen dressed him and began to haul him to the station.

"He was basically walking for me," he said. "My legs felt like jelly and I had no control of my body. I was screaming and shouting, hoping that someone would see me. I saw a pub on my left-hand side and saw these three girls looking at me. My head was all over the place and I was thinking: 'Please, someone, just *help* me.' It was like amnesia – I didn't know how I'd got there."

They made it to the station and, once inside, Stephen tried to get Victim B's address out of him. Wanting at all costs to hide this episode – and especially his gay friend – from his parents, he refused. Stephen started going through his bag for more information, only for Victim B to collapse. He woke up to find a group of between three and five (he still couldn't be sure) police officers stood over him. They had sat Stephen down opposite. Station staff had called them to the scene when they saw what they believed to be a mugging in progress. But after regaining consciousness, Victim B wouldn't tell them anything. They watched as his pleas to let Stephen go home were interrupted with green vomit. The young man looked in dread at the missed calls mounting on his mobile phone. They were from his mother. He refused to go to hospital in an ambulance waiting outside and continued to insist that police let Stephen go home. The strange man sat opposite had, after all, brought him to the station. Stephen had admitted to taking crystal meth, but that's hardly an arrestable offence. I might have absolved the police for not detaining him on this occasion, were it not for what one officer said as Victim B was about to board his train.

"I was on the platform and the officer said 'you should be careful who you meet online', something along those lines," he told me. Notice what the officer did not say. The officer did not say: 'You should be careful with what drugs you're taking.' There was, in other words, a suspicion of foul play. At some point, the police had probably learned that the pair had met on social media. And this particular officer was concerned about the nature of the meeting. Even if police were blind to the situation, the scene was replete with witnesses who had seen Victim B being dragged to the station. And they'd been called to a suspected crime. Nothing was done.

After negotiating his way home through numerous concerned passengers asking him what had happened, Victim B spent the night vomiting. He didn't know he'd been drugged and researched whether or not poppers – a legal high – could have had such a bad effect. He contacted Stephen, who told him the amyl nitrate was 'very strong', 'from Amsterdam' and had knocked him out. But he still knew something wasn't right. One day, he called Stephen's phone and his boyfriend's brother-in-law – who had been in the house during Victim B's disastrous visit – picked up. They were acquainted and Victim B described what had happened, at which point the man mentioned that Stephen used illegal drugs for sexual purposes.

Before Victim B next journeyed to Cooke Street, he had decided it'd be the last time he saw Stephen. In previous visits he'd found him shy – to the point of being antisocial – but was relieved as a young man confused about his sexuality that Stephen said he just wanted to watch TV and talk. He was happy that his new friend didn't seem interested in sex. But he seemed obsessed with alcohol and drugs, which uninitiated Victim B had not at the time associated with sex. Nonetheless, these predilections had put him off hanging out. And this latest revelation, that Stephen's drug-taking and sex life were intertwined, left him needing answers about his ordeal. He decided to confront him by turning up to his house unannounced and recording whatever conversation occurred.

Pushing through his front door, Victim B told Stephen that he could have died. Though Stephen did apologise, he also, for reasons only too clear in retrospect, began mumbling about a male rape victim he knew and how the police did nothing.

"I recorded him saying sorry," he said. "I left and never saw him again."

But the horror of anybody hearing that conversation overwhelmed him. Fearing his life as he knew it would be over, he deleted the recording. As time passed, the trauma seemed less potent. That was until Stephen's bald head and off-centre eyes inflicted themselves on the British press.

"I remember going on the computer and his picture came up," he said. "That picture haunted me. He looked like a monster. Whenever I thought his picture was out of my head, I would see the picture again and the same thing would happen."

After speaking to a lawyer friend about the drugging episode, he decided to give evidence from behind a screen in court. Because of his family's religious beliefs, he was forced to relive the horrific experience alone, with only an LGBT support worker to provide solidarity.

"It was probably the hardest thing of my life," he said. "In some respects it was worse than the incident. You're transported back into that mindset and his lawyer is trying to tell you you're a liar, which was really hurtful. I was shaking. I remember thinking that throughout my whole life my family and friends have supported me and now I don't have anyone. I can't call anyone."

Victim B had never had a long-term gay relationship. And in the aftermath of the court case, when he had the chance to find himself, a plunging libido conspired with post-traumatic stress to snatch this opportunity away. The encounter destroyed his trust to the extent that even going on a date with a man called Stephen triggered a desperate anxiety.

"I became very scared of people," he said. "I remember his name going round in my head – I felt scared of the name Stephen, or even Steve."

This mental abrasion was made all the more galling by the fact that he'd turned to Stephen Port in an effort to understand himself better. He had initially been pleasantly surprised by a lack of pestering.

"Usually, online the gay life is very promiscuous. Everyone is after the next best thing – it's more about sex than in the straight life," he said. "He wasn't touching me or forcing me to have sex or anything. He wasn't coming onto me."

Stephen had further snared him by bonding with him over Islam, claiming that his ex-boyfriend was a Muslim.

"That kind of gave us something in common," he told me. "Like he understood my religion."

He said "nothing rang alarm bells" until during one otherwise normal visit, when he picked up his Coca-Cola to find it smelled very strongly of vodka, despite his repeated refusal to drink on grounds of his faith. But the reaction he got from Port when he confronted him wasn't exactly terrifying.

"I was like: 'What did you put in my drink?' He got very nervous. He was like a child that had been caught red-handed. He was stuttering and trying to make out there was nothing in it, but finally he admitted it."

Stephen displayed the same childlike qualities when he confronted him about the drugging. Victim B felt that focusing on this softer presentation, as opposed to the media's, and turning to his faith was his key to moving on.

"I had to snap out of it and the only way to snap out of it was to forgive him," he said. "At least he said sorry. That's what gives me hope that he's not a monster. I don't want to see him as a monster because it gives me that calm."

But had he put this behind him? When we met, he told me he had never spoken about his experience to a counsellor. "I'm the sort of person who just wants it to go away," he said.

He has alternated between blaming himself for the police letting Stephen leave Barking station – despite him having no experience of GHB and therefore not knowing he'd been drugged – and questioning his very identity. He told me that he was considering trying to ignore his attraction to men so that he can marry a woman, cement what I believe should be an unconditional support network regardless of sexuality and appease his family. He didn't see why he should 'choose' a lifestyle associated in his mind with so much negativity and pain. Victim B even said that this might have been God's way of telling him not to have gay relationships.

"My trust in people has gone," he said. "I have realised that, in life, no-one is actually nice. You realise what kind of person a person is when they are angry and want to hurt you. When I used to meet people, I would trust them a lot. Now I don't. I have learned from my mistakes."

The shame that his family and religious community may feel could be rendering male victims of sexual assault even more vulnerable. Peter Tatchell told me that conservative social values enforced by religion are one of the reasons that some people don't speak out, and this certainly applies in Victim B's case.

"It's so obvious that young gay and bisexual men who are not 'out', live with their families and come from homophobic communities are much less likely to come forward and report sexual assaults, violence and other abuses," Peter argues. "Homophobia is an obstacle to protecting the LGBT+ community and bringing the perpetrator to justice.

"Some gay and bisexual men, such as those from Muslim communities, are very reluctant to come forward; they fear rejection by their families and mosques and that can be a contributing factor.'

If fewer people are speaking out about the predators that targeted them, albeit for understandable reasons, it can leave attackers free to assault other people. It is safer for a rapist to strike men who won't fight back by telling their own community leaders, or even the police. Despite this, Victim B bravely took the stand against Stephen. From sitting across a table with the man, hearing and seeing his pain radiate from his words and expressions, I had a brief window into how difficult that was. It makes me admire him all the more for speaking out. But how many are not?

18

JOE

Daniel Mayger, 27, opened the door to his Barking council flat. He walked into the kitchen, turned on the tap and started to wash up the bowls, plates and cutlery that had sat dirty while he'd been at work. Daniel, who was going through a break-up with his boyfriend of five years, Jamie Roberts, was alone in the flat when he saw a stranger walk in front of his window and flash a badge. The police officer told him he was from the homicide and serious crime division and Daniel wondered what he could possibly have done to warrant such a visit as he let the man in. "I'm here in connection with the murders of four people," the officer said. "Do you know anyone called Stephen Port?"

Daniel was disturbed at the mention of murder and a blend of both dread and curiosity flooded his mind. Who was Stephen Port? A victim? The killer? Either way, he didn't know him and said as much. Just to be sure, the officer showed him a picture of the man to whom he was referring. Daniel immediately recognised the image of a shady, socially awkward drug dealer he'd been patronising. He lived yards from his flat. "Do you know this man?" the officer said. "Yeah," replied Daniel. "That's Joe."

"No, that's Stephen Port and he's been arrested in connection with these murders. I'm here to talk to you because he blocked you on social media. And that's what he did to the men he killed."

Daniel met Stephen – or Joe – on Grindr when he was looking to feed his GHB and mephedrone habits. He was already an addict when he tracked Joe down, but was in need of a new dealer given the fact that his usual seller, Scott, had suggested starting a sexual relationship. Though he didn't know it at the time, Scott's real name was Peter Hirons. Joe was already in a long-term, serious and happy relationship and knew his boyfriend wouldn't be interested in this particular experiment. So he turned Scott down and began to look elsewhere.

After making contact, Joe told him that he could get drugs but that they'd still be from Peter, because that's who he bought from. Daniel told his new contact not to tell Peter who the substances were for because he was sure that he'd refuse to supply them given their history. Daniel and Joe then stopped communicating on the dating site and instead moved onto instant messenger service WhatsApp. Joe seemed like a nice bloke. He told Daniel that he was a special needs teacher for disabled children. And he was convenient, living a four-minute walk away at most.

But when it came to the matter of handing over money for drugs, Daniel found Joe was strange in person. He found him timid, yet still retaining an untrustworthiness that spoke to a sinister, unseen, component of his personality. And once, when the looming dealer started coming around to his flat, Daniel became aware that Joe was seeking a threesome with him and Jamie.

After the police officer turned up at his flat, he gave the homicide and serious crimes division a written statement. An extract is below.

'Jamie and I had discussed the possibility of a threesome with Stephen. I knew it would be an option. It was also obvious that Stephen was up for sex when he visited. I decided not to have sex with Stephen as his mannerisms were just weird. I remember the point I decided not to have sex was when Stephen touched my waist whilst we were seated on the sofa. I told him we weren't interested in sex and just wanted the drugs. I remember that Stephen told us he didn't use "G" (I offered him some and he declined) but he did snort some mephedrone with us.'

"The whole point of moving away from Scott was we didn't want that," he later told me. "We kind of fooled around, but with people our own age, and normally when we were high. We were together for five years."

During the occasions that Stephen visited Daniel, and the one on which Daniel went to his flat, he never told his customer his real name. This was as bodies were turning up around the corner from Daniel's flat, overdosed on the same substance

– GHB – he was buying from the killer himself. When Daniel learned his real identity, he was shaken into a state of paranoia.

"The most scary part, and it still scares me today, was everyone he killed he had blocked," he told me in January 2020. That was the time Jamie and I were breaking up. I was on my own in this area, I couldn't move, and I'd just found out there was a murderer living yards away from me.

"I was completely shocked. I was paranoid. I was like who the hell else does he know? Are they murderers? The slightest bang or knock and I was jumping out of my skin."

It was in the throes of this rabid insecurity that Daniel remembered a deeply disturbing detail. Before the police had arrested Port, before his relationship with Jamie had expired, Daniel and his then-boyfriend had been having sex in the living room when Daniel noticed a figure at his window, peering in. The person ran away before he could get an accurate description of who it might be. He now wondered if that was Stephen. After all, here was a man who knew where he lived, dealt him drugs associated with chemsex and was clearly interested in more than a cash transaction.

The fact that he may well have been in a rapist and serial killer's sights prior to his arrest hit particularly close to home because Daniel had survived a rape in strikingly similar circumstances to those that Stephen's victims did not. Back when he was 17, Daniel was single and heavily into drugs, and a friend he nicknamed Birmingham John took him to meet a man called Peter. Peter lived in south London and the trio were taking drugs at Peter's apartment when Daniel was rendered unconscious by the GHB. John left for his job at a sauna, leaving the pair alone. Peter force-fed Daniel methamphetamine, which made Daniel's penis erect despite his state. Peter then raped Daniel, who awoke to another man, a drug dealer, asking if he was okay.

"You were shouting for your mum," the man explained as Daniel wondered why his backside was wet. He would later find out that he was HIV positive.

Daniel had only started using drugs by dint of a strange accident at a mansion party.

"I was a young gay person and I ended up at the house having sex," he said. "I was given a shot and thought it was booze, but it turned out to be G. I was sick and spinning – but I was intrigued. From there it just spiralled."

While living with Jamie in Barking, he would escape the drudgery of working life by getting high in the evening with his first serious boyfriend. Mephedrone and GHB were their most common choices, but they also took cocaine, meth and ketamine. In Daniel's words: "It was whatever we could get our hands on." The five-month stint of paranoia in which he found himself when he was told who Joe really was did accomplish one thing. It got him off drugs, which he'd been using on an almost daily basis until each transaction brought with it the fear of sexual assault or death.

Following their break-up, Jamie died aged 27 in April 2019 when a train hit him close to Theydon Bois in Essex. The coroner recorded an open verdict. Daniel managed to swap his council home in Barking for one closer to his family, who live in Hounslow, west London, where he grew up. His medication prevents him from passing on his HIV and allows him to live a normal, happy life with his new boyfriend and their dog. But he still feels – like so many people involved in the Stephen Port case – let down by the Met Police.

"I was told that I could call for support by the police officer who came to question me," he said. "When I did call that [victim support] number, I was explaining that I was scared and paranoid. I will never forget that the lady said: 'Okay... what do you want us to do?'

"I never got that support. They never came to check on me. It was really bad – you'd think you would at least check in."

19

REPEAT

August 18, 2018, south-west London

Police officers pull up to the detached, two-storey home of part-time actor and HR director Eric Michels. The bespectacled father of two has had minor parts in *James Bond: Skyfall* and *Jack Ryan: Shadow Recruit*. Divorced from his wife, the energy company executive had popped into town for some drinks on Thursday night before heading back home to Chessington – a far-flung London suburb – where the American lives. Or rather lived. He is dead, aged 54, the attending officers confirm. In the weeks following his death, GHB intoxication is found to be the cause of his death.[197]

A scrawny 25-year-old black male with an effeminate, lank look that doesn't seem to match his profession of drug dealer faces magistrates on November 21 charged with his murder. Gerald Matovu, from Southwark, south London, isn't just said to have poisoned Eric.[198] He's allegedly used a needle to sexually assault a boy aged 13 or over in east London too. Gerald is also accused of administering GHB without consent to another man and stealing his phone the day after Eric's body was found. Other charges include possession of 5ml of GHB at an address in east London and possession with intent to supply 500ml of the Class C substance at a St Mungo's Hostel. The pettier end of accusations feature fraud by false representation and stealing an iPhone 10 from a person in Stratford, east London. He met some of these men through the dating app Grindr. Not that he's single – his boyfriend, a 24-year-old named Brandon Dunbar, from Forest Gate, east London is said to have been his accomplice.

* * *

Gerald and Brandon had been on a 19-month rampage, with Eric being just one of the 12 men targeted. Eric had divorced from his wife of 23 years, Diane, after telling her that he was gay. They remained on good terms and worked together, despite the collapse of their marriage, to raise their children.[199]

Living as an officially 'out' gay man in the cosmopolitan capital, Eric started frequenting gay bars in Soho, finally free from the constraints of pretence. He'd been out in the district's gay bars on August 17 when he spoke with Gerald on Grindr and invited him home for sex. Eric arranged to pick Gerald up on the way to his home. Once inside, Gerald drugged Eric with GHB. He then stole his MacBook, bottles of alcoholic drinks, his phone, bank cards, driver's licence, some photographs and a suitcase before fleeing the scene in a cab.[200]

It was while he was carrying the phone that Eric's daughter tried to get in touch with her father. The 14-year-old just wanted to check whether or not he'd like to go out for dinner before she headed away on holiday. Gerald did not respond. When she messaged again, Gerald decided to act, replying: 'Hello hun I'm a little busy talk soon.' That did *not* sound like her father. It was short, non-committal, superficial. She needed to know what was going on. So she called her father's phone. Gerald picked up. Idiotically, he actually spoke to the caller, who told him she was Eric's daughter. He hung up. This confirmed her fears that something was wrong and she asked her mother to take her to Chessington where they found his body.[201]

Gerald and Brandon, meanwhile, continued about their business as normal. Using £300 stolen from Eric, they bought some GBL (which metabolises into GHB in the human body) with which to drug their next victim at a flat in east London. Spiking his drink the day after Eric was found dead, Gerald stood by as his boyfriend sexually assaulted the man with a syringe. They dumped his unconscious body in the street. Passers-by found him lying, naked, in rubble near Dunbar's flat with cuts, bruises and a broken nose. When the police turned up, they found Gerald inside the flat, surrounded by items he'd stolen from his victims.[202]

* * *

Gerald denied giving the fatal dose to Eric. He'd taken it of his own volition, he claimed in court. His conduct throughout the case was by all accounts even more appalling than his friend Stephen's. Rather than *suggesting* that he could have been a victim of rape, Gerald outright *accused* his own victim, not alive to argue back, of this vile crime. This was obviously totally untrue, but Eric's children had to sit and watch as the man who killed their father told horrific lies about him in open court. Not only that, but he developed a sadistic habit of turning to grin at them during hearings. And when they weren't there, Gerald and Brandon would await their return before greeting them with laughter from the dock.[203]

Jurors found Gerald guilty on every charge, relating to every victim. They were: the murder of Mr Michels, six counts of administering a noxious substance, seven thefts, assault by penetration, assault by occasioning actual bodily harm, possession of GBL and six counts of possessing articles for fraud. He was jailed for life with a minimum term of 31 years.

During his trial, Gerald had asked to be tried as a woman and for any custodial sentence to send him to a female prison. The killer identified as female and does to this day. The judge rejected his request[204] and it is partly for this reason that in this book Gerald is referred to as a male. But it is also for another reason. Gerald was a person who used his biological sex, that of a male, to target gay men with sexual violence. I fear that to downplay his biological masculinity would be to erase a vital component of his crimes – namely, their maleness. It cannot be seriously said that, however he identified, he was acting as a female while preying on men who would be attracted to his biological sex. He weaponised his masculinity in a profoundly vile manner and referring to him as her would only muddy the understanding of his disgraceful conduct.

Brandon was convicted of three counts administering a noxious substance, one of assault by penetration, one of assault occasioning actual bodily harm, five counts of theft, six of having articles for fraud, two counts of fraud and one count of dishonestly retaining wrongful credit.[205]

* * *

Gerald's dealings with drugs had landed him on the wrong end of the law before. In fact, in 2017, he was handed 12 months' community service, 150 hours of unpaid work and 40 days of drug rehabilitation for supplying drugs. His customer? Stephen Port.[206] In fact, Gerald had dealt drugs to Stephen before Jack Taylor's death. Gerald would often claim to be a nurse when dealing with clients. It seems plausible, at the very least, to conclude that he and Dunbar were the two men who delivered drugs to Cooke Street before one of them shoved his penis into the mouth of his drugged student guest.[207] The pair were never charged in relation to this sexual assault, but given that Stephen was terrible at covering his communications with victims, I find it hard to believe that the police wouldn't have identified another drug dealer once the case was taken out of the hands of Barking and Dagenham's officers. The only two people to have been convicted of dealing to Stephen were Gerald and Peter Hirons. And Peter doesn't exactly fit the description of a black male offered by Victim F.

20

HOMOPHOBIA

Stephen's murders, rapes, sexual assaults and the sentence in which they resulted, put him in a rare category of prisoners in Britain. He became the 60th person to be serving a sentence of a life behind bars. It shows the severity of his crimes when we consider that in the same week a terrorist called Thomas Mair was also handed a life sentence. Mair was the far-right lunatic who murdered Labour MP Jo Cox by shooting and stabbing her multiple times in Birstall, West Yorkshire.[208] The previous month, Arthur Simpson-Kent was also told he'd die in prison after he murdered 43-year-old former soap star Sian Blake – along with her sons, aged eight and four, at their home in Erith, Kent.[209] Others who had made it into the category include paedophile Mark Bridger, the alcoholic who murdered five-year-old April Jones; cop killer Dale Cregan and Michael Adebolajo, one of the two Islamist terrorists who murdered soldier Lee Rigby in Woolwich, south-east London.[210]

When Stephen began his sentence, there were around 85,000 people serving time in England and Wales.[211] So Stephen was among just 0.07 per cent of inmates serving life.

When this highly dangerous individual had murdered his last victim, Barking and Dagenham police officers were working under Borough Commander Sultan Taylor. He had previously worked in Camden, north-west London, and Kensington and Chelsea, west London. By the time he retired in April 2016, he was London's most experienced borough commander, notching up more than 32 years of service in that high-power role. And yet it was his officers who still couldn't see what was going on, even after the fourth body turned up in the same grounds as the previous two.[212]

It might be tempting at this point to once again consider that the police were put off the cases by a fundamental lack of understanding. The victims were gay and Barking and Dagenham was not known for a vibrant gay scene, or any scene for that matter. Perhaps it could be said that a lack of interaction, or a particularly small community of non-heterosexuals could have fostered an environment in which officers were understandably thrown off the truth when they discovered the bodies of young gay men. It's just that the statistics of the time don't quite bear this out.

The Office for National Statistics (ONS) split England into 31 regions, organising them by the percentage of gay and lesbian people known to be living in those areas. Such is the social and economic diversity of the sprawling capital that the ONS split it into 'inner London' and 'outer London' to put a figure on the gay and lesbian population from 2013 to 2015. Of the 31 English regions, inner London came first, with about 3.1 per cent of its population identifying as homosexual. Next came Cambridgeshire, Greater Manchester, Devon, West Yorkshire, Lancashire, East Sussex, Dorset, Tyne and Wear and South Yorkshire. Outer London – incorporating Barking and Dagenham – sat at number 11 in a tie with Derbyshire, with its homosexual population sitting at one per cent. So, outer London was just below the top third in the country in terms of the percentage of its homosexual population.[213] And even if Barking and Dagenham had the most dwindling of the outer London populations of gay people, it's surely inconceivable that its officers shouldn't learn from their counterparts in Soho and other inner London areas as the whole point of the Metropolitan Police is that it's a countywide force serving Greater London. It's at the very least not clear that the appearance of a dead gay man should have thrown police off to the extent that they ignored what was actually going on and believed a stranger interpretation of events due to their exceptional ignorance of homosexuality.

And yet the murders of gay, young men were missed. A surface-level reading of the situation spoke to a lack of engagement with, or outright refusal to consider, the borough's gay residents. This perception did not bloom in a vacuum. Notions of anti-homosexual bigotry weren't restricted to the police in the minds of outside observers. The local authority, Barking and Dagenham Council, had also suffered a reputational blow thanks to its deputy leader, Liam Smith, six years before Stephen had murdered his first victim.

Councillor Smith was a short-haired, portly Labour representative who became known for a nasty exchange at a council by-election in Chadwell Heath. It was 2008 and, in a Labour stronghold, Conservative candidate Neil Connelly won himself a seat in what was a frustrating shock for the borough's political left-wing. His 60-year-old mother, Sue Connelly, was elated and couldn't risk what she thought would be a good-humoured jibe at Smith, saying: "All right Liam, that's 4-0!"[214]

Hardly inflammatory, it's surely the kind of mild gloating that one must expect in the jubilance of a win. But Smith was incensed. "Shut up you fat fucking dyke," he spat. "Go back to the farmyard."[215] Aside from being baffled as to why a heterosexual, married grandmother of eight was being called a lesbian, Sue was shocked by the outburst.

This wasn't Neil's first encounter with Smith. He told me that in their previous dealings Smith would engage in 'nasty' and 'arrogant' displays in the council chamber.

"Every time I ever met him he was, for want of a better word, a knob," he said. But this latest conduct caught him off-guard.

"I couldn't believe what I actually heard," he said. "We'd done about 14 hours of campaigning that day and I was tired and not quite processing things properly – but I should've lamped him right there and then. I was just in a state of complete disbelief."

Neil had himself been the victim of a homophobic stabbing in nearby Romford the previous year. Attackers knifed him in the face and leg after one of the gang called him a 'poof' for wearing shiny shoes while walking home from the pub. He told me that the five or six councillors who witnessed Smith insult his mother were equally shocked and described the display as "aggressive".[216] For Neil it was clear. Smith had simply snapped, ditching all pretence of decorum. This incident wouldn't stay within the walls of the local by-election count. It hit the press. Rather than accept responsibility, Smith engaged in a bizarre defence which involved alleging a Tory conspiracy. He'd been the victim of a smear campaign, he insisted. It must have been a particularly attractive initiative, for the disapproval now hitting the web pages of *Pink News* wasn't just restricted to Conservative voices. Independent candidate Dee McIlroy had been there too. She said the use of the word dyke was "unnecessary", "irrelevant" and "homophobic".[217] Was she, too, part of a conspiracy?

Smith even denied using the word at all, despite the fact that he was later cautioned by police and forced to write a letter of apology to Sue. The Crown Prosecution Service (CPS) confirmed that he'd used the slur, but a spokeswoman said "it was not being used in a homophobic way against Mrs Connelly".[218] It may well be hard to be homophobic to a straight woman, but this doesn't address the seriousness of the matter. Smith knew the connotations of such a word. And at the very least, even considering that it may have a different significance or meaning to him, he should have realised the implications of somebody holding elective office barking this insult out at an election count. But perhaps, after all, he didn't mean it as a lesbian slur. Perhaps he was using it in its semi-ironic context of referring to women who make a virtue of their butchness. The writer Christopher Hitchens, by no means a homophobe, once referred to 'dykes' in an article referencing female comedians who behave in a butch manner on stage, as opposed to lesbians.[219] Or perhaps Smith was attempting to 'take the word back', slipping it into the banalities of standard usage in the hope of robbing it of its power. Sadly, I'm not prepared to grant him the benefit of the doubt. Why? Because this was not an isolated incident for Barking and Dagenham's council.

Neil recalled an incident concerning Richard Barnbrook, who was one of the 12 councillors for the racist British National Party and secured a seat in 2006, lasting four years and crossing over with Smith's role as deputy council leader. That year, Labour dominated the authority and Neil was its sole Conservative. He says that he was surprised to turn up to Barking Town Hall one evening to find A4 sheets of paper scattered across the chamber's desks detailing how Barnbrook had appeared in gay pornography. Barnbrook denied that he'd appeared in a porn film, describing *HMS Discovery: A Love Story* as an art film. He said that the only nudity in it is a couple of guys running into a river and even the national press couched any claims that it was porn in quote marks.[220]

Neil decided he'd engage in some awareness-raising of his own, leaving print-outs of articles chronicling the abuse his mother had suffered at the hands of Smith. But when he distributed the papers, he was told that he was not allowed to litter the chamber with the pieces of paper. To be clear, Smith, while in a leadership role, oversaw the ridicule of a rival based not on his vile politics, but based solely on the fact that he'd appeared in a film depicting homosexuality. Meanwhile, a councillor who enjoyed the least power in the authority was not able to use precisely the same method to draw attention to an actual homophobic slur. Again, it's possible that the leafleter had more of a problem with an elected official appearing in what he perceived to be pornography as opposed to him intending to ridicule homosexuality. But I am once more reluctant to take this kind view when this was a council whose deputy leader would hurl the word 'dyke' about a public place with such abandon. Neil had expected politics to be a nasty business, but nothing had prepared him for the reality of working with Smith. He quit, claiming the viperous tactics on display left him disillusioned and hopeless.

"It's one of the nastiest games you can get into," he said. "People who are supposed to be on your side, knife you in the back. I think [Smith calling my mother a dyke] was one of the straws that broke the camel's back. You take one knock, shake it off, take another and shake that off and when you get another you just can't be arsed."

The fact that a figure with such authority as Smith's would resort to shouting 'dyke' at a political rival's mother and still manage to advance, raised concerns about the powerful's perceptions of gay and bisexual people in the borough. I also could not find a single example of him apologising to lesbians in general despite being an elected official. He obviously didn't think that the incident warranted a remark to his public, other than his crazed denials, of course. Residents responded by protesting at Barking Town Hall, calling for Smith to stand down.

At the very least, now was the time at which he should apologise. He didn't. He became council leader in 2009. While I was writing this book, a spokesperson for the council acknowledged that the authority back then was different to the relatively amicable one at which I'd sat in on meetings as a reporter, saying that "Barking and Dagenham is a very different place to 15 years ago."

The way in which the powerful treat or interact with particular elements of their communities inevitably sows doubt about what those people can expect from public servants. But a flashpoint, such as the Stephen Port case, should surely give public servants of all varieties the perfect excuse to identify the points at which they went awry. Sadly, this didn't seem to be the case for the police, at least not in the estimation of Ryan Edwards. Ryan said that, even in the aftermath of such obvious failings, the police were unwilling to reach out to people left feeling vulnerable and unprotected. It's worth bearing in mind that Stephen's offending wasn't a freak occurrence restricted to one victim. He'd been convicted of 25 charges relating to the murder, rape, sexual assault and drugging. And these weren't behaviour traits that ended with this particular individual. His network, including Gerald Matovu, had engaged in similar criminal behaviour. Though it would be hysterical for every gay man in London to be feeling scared, it was reasonable that homosexuals who lived in the very borough that was the scene of Stephen's depravity had outstanding concerns. Ryan was certainly one of them, but he felt shunned in the aftermath of Stephen's arrest. He'd already been in touch with Barking and Dagenham Police as part of the investigation, which culminated in his court testimony. Aside from this, he'd also worked as a 'secret shopper' snuffing out the mistreatment of gay people in various workplaces. This meant he had links that could prove beneficial in building bonds of understanding between the police and those who might be feeling overlooked or neglected. He even put together a report for the borough's police. Not only did the force not reach out to Ryan, even as its members were shamed into submitting to Independent Police Complaints Commission (IPCC) scrutiny, he said that they dismissed his efforts to collaborate on a safer future for gay people in the borough.

"I was known to the police," he said. "There was a real resistance from the police to constructively engage with me. I certainly should've been on their radar."

Prior to this wall of silence, the police had met with Ryan. He found the three outreach sessions they held 'extremely frustrating' as officers insisted they were doing everything that they could and denied that any real changes needed to be made. Not that he'd expected much. He recalled their lack of action when they'd discovered the bodies. The same police force that lines roads with notices asking for witnesses to car crashes didn't put out one such notice outside St Margaret's Church, though they did issue appeals online that the *Barking and Dagenham Post* ran.[221] Still, Ryan insisted that there was a general lack of urgency and that this inaction was something specific to the Barking and Dagenham unit compared with his other experiences in the capital. When he lost his phone in Soho, for example, he said Westminster officers were incredibly helpful. He also attested to good service from officers in Redbridge, a borough that borders Barking and Dagenham.

Ryan was left with the impression that Barking and Dagenham was an unwelcoming place for men like him – and this was at a time when the local force had an LGBT liaison officer[222], which makes you wonder what the point of such a role was.

Ryan's experiences in Barking and Dagenham, and his positive interactions with other forces, shouldn't be taken as evidence that these problems existed nowhere else in London. They are one man's subjective experiences and thus cannot claim to present a complete picture from which we can diagnose all relevant problems. But his interpretation of these events complements evidence of various failings across the capital to protect sexual minorities from violence.

Human rights campaigner Peter Tatchell echoed his point, referring to other killers of gay men after Stephen's sentencing: "The police mishandling of the Stephen Port murders echo their previous failings in serial killings of gay men, including those by Dennis Nilsen, Michael Lupo and Colin Ireland. The lessons from those sub-standard investigations have still not been learned.

"If four young middle-class women had been murdered in Mayfair, I believe the police would have made a public appeal much sooner and mounted a far more comprehensive investigation. The killing of low-income gay men in working-class Barking was treated very differently. Police officers stand accused of class, gender and sexuality bias."

21

WARNINGS

There exists an almost perfect test case for Peter's suggestion. On March 14, 2008, a 23-year-old Norwegian student was raped and murdered at 220 Great Portland Street. The apartment block stood in the Fitzrovia district of central London. Martine Magnussen's 5ft 4ins body was discovered under a pile of rubble in the block's basement two days later. The London Metropolitan Police have only ever had one suspect. He was the Regent's Business School classmate with whom Martine left the exclusive Mayfair nightclub Maddox. His name is Farouk Abdulhak and he was seen taking a cab with Martine at around 2am. The then 21-year-old son of Yemeni billionaire Shaher Abdulhak, he fled to his home country by private jet in the hours after allegedly killing Martine, before her body had been discovered. There being no extradition treaty between the UK and Yemen, he has never faced trial. But it wasn't for a lack of trying on the part of the police.[223]

Farouk's goateed chin and entitled expression would become a mainstay on Scotland Yard's Most Wanted list while he sat safely in Yemen. When Martine's family flew to London upon hearing of their missing daughter, police arranged to pick them up from the airport and brought them to Belgravia police station. No brush-off for *this* grieving family. Just the one death was enough to jolt these officers into action. Swift to identify their suspect, the primary reason that he has remained free is a diplomatic technicality. Whereas the reason that Stephen stayed free after his first kill was because of a lack of diligence in the investigation surrounding Anthony Walgate's death. Where Stephen slipped through officers' fingers because of their lack of action, Farouk evades them in spite of it. And it wasn't a pursuit that stayed in London in the form of a Most Wanted list. This manhunt went global when the police issued a European Arrest Warrant.[224] Foreign Secretary David Miliband responded to the killing by personally intervening and submitting a one-off extradition request to Yemen. Even Queen Elizabeth II herself got involved in 2010 when Martine's father, Odd Petter Magnussen, wrote to her to ask for assistance in his fight for justice. Anybody who remembers the attention that the Queen's tears garnered when Princess Diana died knows that it is rare, almost to the point of being unprecedented, for the Royals to let their stoicism slip. But the monarch responded to the letter expressing her 'sorrow' at the death and the fact that the case had not been solved.[225]

Of course, the reply was penned by assistant private secretary Doug King, but it still conveyed profound condolences and constitutes an extraordinary reply, the rarity of which is not diluted by the fact that, like many other correspondences, it was penned by someone else's hand.

It read: 'Her Majesty was deeply sorry to read of the terrible loss that you and your family have suffered, and the continuing distress caused by the fact that your daughter's killer remains at liberty.

'She has asked me to convey her sincerest condolences to you and your family. With regard to your request for Mr Farouk Abdulhak to be extradited from Yemen to the UK to stand trial, I'm afraid that this is not a matter on which Her Majesty can personally intervene.

'However, she has asked me to refer the matter to the Home Secretary, The Rt Hon Alan Johnson MP, whose department is responsible for government extradition policy and who I hope will be able to advise you further.'[226]

At the time of writing, it is 13 years since Martine's body turned up in a pile of rubble. As recently as March 2021, the Met Police said they were still demanding that Farouk give himself up[227]. But why? Why did police do their job in this case and not the Port case? Could it be, as Peter's interpretation suggests, because she was found in a block of flats where second-floor apartments cost around £2,600 a month in rent[228] as opposed to being ditched in a graveyard? Or was it because she was a woman? We may never know whether it was the location or the sex of the victim that inspired such a response, but one thing is clear: The police, government and even the Queen did *something*.

Defenders of the police might point to the fact that Anthony, Gabriel, Daniel and Jack were found slumped in the street, a conceivable portrait of a tragic overdose, whereas a woman found under rubble has clearly been hidden by a killer. True, but this doesn't escape the fact that in all five cases (Stephen's four murders, and Martine's death), there were clear, observable signs that someone had placed the bodies. Of course, rubble is more obvious than clothing that has been pulled up, or bruising under the arms consistent with being dragged. But police are not lay people. They aren't supposed to look at a crime scene in the way you or I do. They are meant to notice these things. And we know that they did in the Barking murders. They saw the 'rubble', if you will. They just didn't push the matter further. Not even on the fourth go.

As alluded to by Peter Tatchell, the Stephen Port case was not the first in which London's police officers had failed to protect gay men. In fact, part of what makes the failings of Barking and Dagenham's unit so baffling is that an even more notorious killer had terrorised homosexuals in the capital more than 30 years prior.

1983:

The most infamous case in which a serial murderer targeted gay men in 20th century Britain was undoubtedly that of Dennis Nilsen. He operated unmolested for five years, killing at least 12 victims. During that time, the Metropolitan Police Service had no idea that Nilsen, who was sexually attracted to males, had been plucking young men and boys from London's gay scene. His story is interesting to compare to that of Stephen Port, for reasons that shall be discussed once his crimes have here been explored.

On February 3, 1983, Nilsen's neighbour Jim Allcock noticed that there was a blockage in the sewage system at Cranley Gardens in Muswell Hill, north London. The apartment block's residents were suffering unpleasant failures when attempting to flush waste down their toilets. Fearing an overflow, Jim used acid bought from an ironmongers to try and clear the mysterious blockage. Twice he failed. Two days later, plumber Mike Welch was on the scene and found that even his trusty tools wouldn't do the job. Returning with a ladder, he peered through the wall into the intersection where accumulated waste from the various flats merged and finally managed to clear it. But the system remained blocked. Dyno-rod engineer Michael Cattran arrived three days later and lifted the manhole leading directly to the sewers. A revolting smell greeted him and Jim, who he told: "I may not have been in the game for that long, but I know that isn't shit." The smell was rotting flesh. He was sure of it. The sight of up to 40 chunks of greyish-white matter lined the sewer floor. The next day, Fiona Bridges said she'd heard someone rooting around in the sewer during the night. Meanwhile, Michael had retrieved four pieces of bone and a six-inch chunk of flesh redolent of a chicken's. They called the police and a pathologist confirmed the remains were human.[229]

When the polite, almost retiring, figure of 37-year-old Dennis Nilsen returned home from his job at the civil service on February 9, three police officers were waiting. They told him they wanted to speak about human remains found in the sewer. Nilsen feigned surprise and the officers told him to drop the act. They wanted to know where the rest of the body was. Nilsen said: "In two plastic bags in the wardrobe next door. I'll show you." He added: "It's a long story. It goes back a long time. I'll tell you everything. I want to get it all off my chest."[230]

Riding in the car to the station, he was asked whether there was just the one victim, or a few. He horrified police by declaring his relief at finally being able to tell somebody that he'd murdered "15 or 16" since 1978. There were the remains of three men in his flat, the only one whose name he knew being Stephen Sinclair. Another he knew as John the Guardsman. Of the third's identity, he had no clue.[231]

On November 4, Nilsen was convicted of six counts of murder and two counts of attempted murder. He was handed life imprisonment.[232] Nilsen was off the streets for good. But how had he, like Port, been missed in the first place?

Nilsen was far from hopeless at school, by no means stupid. Though he struggled with mathematics, he excelled in art and did well in English literature. While serving in the Army, he passed five O Levels in maths, English, catering science, map reading and current affairs. He also attained a professional qualification in catering.[233]

Unlike Port, Nilsen was also resourceful and averse neither to risk nor fighting if necessary. Aged 21, he was posted to Aden where he worked with the military in charge of terrorists held in Al Mansoura Prison. He hitch-hiked through terrorist territory to get back to Al Mansoura and emerged unscathed, arriving back at the jail on the back of an Arab vegetable lorry. It's worth comparing this reckless daring with Port, who couldn't so much as look a man in the eye and had to rely on drugs to incapacitate somebody in preparation for rape. Nilsen was also skilled, particularly with regards to cutting up corpses due to his experience as a butcher.[234]

Rather than dumping corpses in the open, he dug up the floorboards at his home in Melrose Avenue, where he'd lived before Cranley Gardens, to hide the body of an Irish youth he'd murdered after they met at the Cricklewood Arms. After seven-and-a-half months, he had brought up the body for burning. Nilsen lit a bonfire in his back garden, knowing nobody would be watching next door, where a derelict house stood. Had anybody passing suspected anything, the seven-foot-high fence would shield him. And, just to be sure, he threw rubber onto the fire to hide the smell of burning flesh.[235] When disposing of internal organs, Nilsen would sometimes cut them out and place them carefully in the gap in fencing between his house and the next. Nestled in there, they'd be gone in a day thanks to the diligence of various cooperative diners living in the dirt.[236] Notice that at no point did it occur to him to dump a body outside his flat. Nor did it appear an attractive prospect to take his victim 400 yards across London and pose it in a public space. Three times.

It wasn't just the killer that was different in this case. It was his victims. Barring one person – Canadian tourist Kenneth Ockenden – each of Nilsen's targets had the attraction of being able to disappear without much notice. They were homeless, drug addicts, unemployed, or in trouble with the law. Many were in London not because they were from the capital, but because they had so few ties that they could drop everything and head there in the hope of finding a better life. Once there, they became even more anonymous as the bustling indifference of city life swelled about them.

Take Martyn Duffey, from Merseyside. A troubled child, he'd told his parents that he was off to the local library aged 15. He hitch-hiked to London, slept rough for a week then returned courtesy of the Soho Project charity. He saw psychiatrists as a child and his school specialised in educating maladjusted children. He struggled with valium addiction and after a run-in with the law over an evaded train fare, he told his parents he was off to New Brighton, also in Merseyside. Instead he turned up in London. He slept in train stations and a few days into this vagabond lifestyle he met Nilsen, aged 16, in 1980. Back at his home, he drank a couple of cans of lager, then went to bed – only for Nilsen to strangle him. His corpse, too, was stuffed under the floorboards.[237]

Or consider Billy Sutherland. Sutherland was a heavy drinker from Edinburgh who'd also had a troubled childhood and migrated to London where he stole and prostituted himself as seemed necessary. When he vanished, his mother secured his place on a missing persons list. As though he wasn't difficult enough to track, there were already 39 other Billy Sutherlands on the list. He was killed aged 27 at Melrose Avenue.[238]

Malcolm Barlow, meanwhile, had spent most of his life in the care home system and hospitals for the mentally disabled.

By 1981, the Sheffield-born 24-year-old's parents were dead and he was living off social security payments in London. Nilsen found him on the pavement close to his home, and learned that epilepsy medication had caused his legs to give way. He got the young man an ambulance, only to find he'd returned the next day and was standing outside the wrong house. He took in his acquaintance, cooked them both a meal and murdered him.[239]

The first Cranley Gardens victim was John Howlett, a habitual liar regularly in trouble with the police. His family kicked him out when he was 13. He'd been imprisoned for stealing. The third, the aforementioned Stephen Sinclair, was a punk who hung around Leicester Square in central London. He had serious personality problems and took any drug he could get hold of. He injected speed, cut his arms and had a habit of injuring himself on purpose. His homes were squats and hostels.[240] Not one of these victims correspond to the well-adjusted, aspiring and family-oriented personalities seen in Anthony Walgate, Gabriel Kovari, Daniel Whitworth and Jack Taylor. This is not said in order to disparage Nilsen's victims. But the fewer connections one has, the easier it is to disappear without so much as a raised eyebrow.

When the Nilsen case broke into the public consciousness, no longer restricted to the killer's mind, floorboards, back garden, and plumbing, ire was focused on police. He hadn't even seen out his trial when *The Sun* published an article declaring 'POLICE BLUNDERS'. A *Sunday People* comment piece said 'a cynic might say, on recent form, that the more people a man kills, the longer the police will take to catch him'.

Of particular interest to detractors were three reports left to rot in the police's filing system.

One related to Andrew Ho, who reported that Nilsen attacked him. He contacted police in 1979. But the police were unable to accuse Nilsen, because Ho declined to make a written statement. He also ruled out appearing in court. With no other witnesses, there was nothing the police could do.[241]

Another concerned Douglas Stewart, who would go on to be a witness for the prosecution against Nilsen. Stewart also reported an attack, but he'd turned up to Kilburn Police Station after drinking alcohol. It was a common rule that officers not take statements from a claimant who has been drinking. So they told him they'd take a statement once he'd sobered up the next day. Two attempts to reach Douglas failed. And neighbours even told police that no Douglas lived at the given address. Only a man called Tommy and his wife had resided there. Stewart did not contact the police to make the statement.

Finally, journalists reported that Robert Wilson found a bag that the biology student knew for a fact contained human remains just half a mile from Nilsen's address. But the truth is that, although he did find a bag and turned it over to police, he neither told them that he had a specialism in biology nor that the items within were human in origin. What's more is that the bag in question could not have led to Nilsen's arrest. It contained animal remains, the handiwork of a local butcher.[242]

It is important to cut through these allegations of police failings not simply to absolve the officers involved of any wrongdoing, but for the same reason that it is important to point out the relative skill of Nilsen's operation when contrasted with Port's. In the former, police faced a killer who deliberately operated under their radar, knew how to dispose of bodies and whose day job and public persona betrayed none of the signs of a serial murderer. In the latter, police faced an operational idiot so clueless that he not only failed to properly dispose of the bodies of men he'd murdered, but positioned them publicly for anybody to find. And in the one case, in which a member of the public did not stumble across a body, he'd already called the police to incriminate himself. True, there was a reason, aside from savvy, that Nilsen was able to operate so freely. Something clearly needed to be done about the fact that certain gay men in London could so easily find themselves exiled from the thoughts of mainstream society and the institutions tasked with protecting its members. But the failings in this case speak to a wider problem, potentially more intangible in nature, than the clearly identifiable instances in which individual officers repeatedly failed to apprehend Port.

Another factor worth bearing in mind is that the officers who arrested Nilsen in 1980s Britain also had nothing like the power of their modern counterparts to establish guilt. Nilsen's death toll is only known because of his detailed admissions – remember he was only *convicted* of six murders when the real number looks likely to be as high as 15. His conversations with these men prior to their deaths were not written down as they happened and stored in a format easily accessible to police. The police who eventually nailed Nilsen could not hack into his brain and replay the conversations he'd had with his victims even if they'd suspected him. Whereas the police who should have been investigating Port had the opportunity of checking his devices from the day he flagged his first victim. There, they would have found messages, fake profiles and a predilection for pornography centred on rape. They had the option. They just failed to act.

Another reason that the Nilsen case is worth bearing in mind regarding the conduct of police when dealing with another serial killer who targeted gay men decades later is because of the red flag such a prolific murderer should have thrown up. I'm not here to suggest that officers involved with Nilsen operated spotlessly, but it would seem evident from extensive writings on the case that police failings were not the key factor. That said, up to 15 men died needlessly in London. Even for a guiltless police force, this should have acted as a warning. A warning that predators who exclusively target gay people exist. A warning that they will take advantage of people who exist outside the mainstream, outside of acceptability and some of the protections that life offers. The lesson to be learned here was that the Met needed to be on guard against comparable threats in the future. But what was surely unthinkable is not just that something similar would happen again, in the same city, but that this time it would have been far easier to stop the killer.

No law enforcement agency can guard all the people all of the time. And were a 21st century equivalent of the resourceful Nilsen to present himself, officers would have a problem on their hands, even with the considerable breakthroughs in crime detection technology. But Port was not Nilsen's equivalent. He wasn't even close. Three of his transparent murders could have been thwarted. Or at least immediately investigated. Especially when his victims weren't loners with few familial ties. The fact that basic lessons were not passed down from a tougher case to one that, even without those lessons in mind, would have been easier to solve, is incredibly worrying.

Not only was Port not Nilsen, but his world, his England, was not that of Nilsen. Being gay in the late '70s and early '80s, even in London, was far more novel than it was in 2014 and 2015, two years after the Marriage (Same-Sex Couples) Act was introduced. Though gay people still face prejudice from assorted morons even in the cosmopolitan capital, there are far fewer barriers to acceptability. Declaring yourself gay in 21st century Britain is not to cut yourself off or render yourself beyond the pale, if anything it's those that are prejudiced against homosexuals who are regarded as odd. The majority of people across the country still believe gay people matter. In 2017, the government conducted the largest national survey on sexual minorities ever recorded. Respondents were lesbian, gay, bisexual, trans or intersex, and of that mixed cohort, homosexuals reported the highest 'life satisfaction' at 6.9 out of 10.[243]

1988:

We live in a country in which a *Conservative* Prime Minister of recent memory, David Cameron, considers it a flagship achievement that, under his leadership, gay marriage was legalised. Whereas in the late '80s, Tory Prime Minister Margaret Thatcher pushed through a piece of legislation that would be held in contempt by sections of the UK's non-heterosexual population. Section 28 of the Local Government Act 1988 prohibited local authorities from promoting homosexuality by teaching or publication.[244] Supporters of Section 28 argued that the legislation only banned the *promotion* of homosexuality in schools and other facilities or groups run by councils. Its critics, including Peter Tatchell, said that it translated into a very different reality and legitimised homophobia not just in the classroom, but outside too.[245] For them, this wasn't a straightforward ban on the promotion of certain sexual orientations to children, but represented a politely worded green light to wider homophobia. Were I looking to either absolve or condemn Section 28, I'd focus on the specific wording of the legislation. However, assigning blame isn't really the concern here. The key fact is that opponents of the ban had a perception of it which, whether valid or mistaken, claimed there was inequality before the law based upon one's sexual orientation. This contributed to a gulf between those people and the servants assigned to protect them. Such perceptions meant the fostering of mistrust as opposed to a flourishing of cooperation. Whether one thinks that Section 28 was correct or incorrect, it is this perception, and its potential consequences, that mattered for Britain in the years preceding the Stephen Port case.

It would also be unfair to dismiss concerns about Section 28 itself, given the context in which the legislation appeared. I find it credible that supporters of the law may well have only voted for the enforcement of the precise wording. Any legal penalties applied outside the wording of the law are therefore the responsibility not of the law itself, but of the people involved in misapplying it. But the suspicion and hostility with which Section

28 met was understandable given Thatcher's outspoken views on homosexuality. Before she enacted Section 28, Thatcher addressed its introduction at the Tory Party Conference of 1987 in words which today would be unthinkable, even for an ostensibly right-wing party.

She said: "Too often, our children don't get the education they need, the education they deserve. And in the inner cities, where youngsters must have a decent education if they are to have a better future, that opportunity is all too often snatched from them by hard-left education authorities and extremist teachers.

She continued: "Children who need to be taught to respect traditional moral values are being taught that they have an inalienable right to be gay... all of those children are being cheated of a sound start in life, yes *cheated*."[246]

The legislation passed against a backdrop of police officers arresting gay men for 'gross indecency'. This, whether the fault of Section 28 or not, left gay men feeling forced underground. When scenes and people go underground, they risk not having the same access to necessary protections from the police that they would enjoy while occupying a more acceptable corner of civilised society. Peter Tatchell argued that this legislation, bolstered by a speech implying that children shouldn't be taught they have the right to be gay in a free society, contributed to pushing homosexuals into the firing line of state authority. This was also happening in the context of a ban on gay people being allowed to serve in the Army. And an era in which plain clothes police officers would go undercover at London's Victoria station to entice men into sexual activity before arresting them[247], when they probably should have been dealing with 'queer-bashing' campaigners described as 'rife'.[248] This worsening of relations between segments of the gay community coincided with some particularly notorious violent crimes targeting homosexuals in the capital.

1988:

Barrister Christopher Schliach was knifed to death in his west London home, where his attacker stabbed him more than 40 times. Just three months later, gay hotelier Henry Bright was stabbed to death in his home, which was also in west London. Hotel porter William Dalziel, also a homosexual, was found unconscious on an Acton roadside three months later. He later died of head injuries.[249]

1990:

The murder of gay actor Michael Boothe in 1990 was supposed to be a game-changer for policing in London. Mr Boothe, 49, was murdered in Elthorne Park, which lies in the west London borough of Ealing. On Saturday, April 29, the jobbing actor was drinking in Earl's Court with some gay friends, before they went home to one of the group's Ealing homes. At about 12.15am on Sunday, Michael decided to walk the short distance home from his friend's address. He passed public toilets well-known for cottaging, at the edge of Elthorne Park. Police were familiar with the site as they spent the early months of that year arresting gay men after staking out the location. But they weren't there that night, when a group of thugs attacked Michael.[250]

Clinging to the park's railings after the group had left him, Michael called out to a passer-by at 12:40am: "Please help me. I've been beaten up and I think my leg's broken." The man called an ambulance, whose crew Michael told he'd been beaten by a group of about six males. After managing a brief description, Michael died hours later of massive internal bleeding. His attackers had stamped on him with such enthusiasm that one of Michael's feet was all but severed from his leg. Ealing CID's Detective Inspector Richard Woodman described the attack as "an extraordinarily severe beating, of a merciless and savage nature".[251]

And yet the best the police managed was to arrest and question a gang of youths known for making homophobic comments. Reviewing the case at the time, the Met concluded Mr Boothe's lifestyle was "destined to bring him into contact with his murderers". The case remains unsolved to this day.[252]

1993:

Colin Ireland killed five men in 1993. He was far from careful, picking out each one of his victims and meeting them in the same pub, The Coleherne in west London. The 2007 review conducted by the police's LGBT advisory group said that he'd evaded officers due to their "lack of knowledge of the gay scene in London". This meant that they were initially unaware that Ireland met his victims at the same venue. Just as in the Stephen Port case, officers also failed to investigate similarities in the way the bodies were found. These vital links – just as in the Stephen Port case – were only spotted after the death of the fourth victim. When Ireland was finally caught, he told officers that he targeted homosexuals because "they keep their mouths shut and don't tell the police things".[253]

2002:

Geoffrey Windsor was murdered in Beaulieu Heights, a park in Croydon, south London, that had already experienced homophobic attacks. The park lies between South and Upper Norwood and was a well-known 'cruising' spot at which gay men could engage in casual sex.[254]

2003:

Section 28 lasted 15 years before it was finally repealed under Tony Blair's New Labour government in 2003. But by that point it loomed in the psyche of those concerned with affording equal rights to sexual minorities. The protests of the 1980s, coupled with the legislation's long lingering into the '90s, had ensured its infamy. People who'd never read Section 28 – myself included – assumed by default that the state and its various organs were naturally hostile to homosexuals. It seemed, to me at least, that the proper position was one of suspicion and vigilance in these matters, whatever progress appeared to have been made.

2007:

The voices of sexual minorities enjoyed a greater clout in the new millennium than they had in the 1980s. Whereas the popular view of advocacy work in the Thatcher years calls to mind noisy protest and arrests, it now encompassed advisory groups scrutinizing officers in mainstream publications. One such outfit was the Lesbian Gay Bisexual Transgender Advisory Group, who in 2007 commissioned a report into crimes against sexual minorities in previous years. Its members wanted to find out why these attacks had happened, but looked beyond the obvious violence of the perpetrators and examined the attitudes of the men and women assigned to stand in their way.[255]

The investigation concluded that gay men had died needlessly not because of random attacks, but because of the environment in which the perpetrators were allowed to flourish. It argued that the police had failed to investigate attacks on homosexuals seriously.[256] If correct, this could mean that thugs capable of murder matured with the understanding that attacks on gay people wasn't taken as seriously as attacks on straight people. If one believes that, then the obstacle of punishment, which might otherwise stand in the way of violent impulses, is at least somewhat removed.

The review concluded inquiries were marred by a reliance on stereotypes and the prejudices of investigators, all of which contributed to a knowledge gap. Alarmingly, 40 per cent of the cases were unsolved at the time of the review. The report also claimed that mainstream media coverage had either mirrored or worsened these problems.[257]

One key problem identified in the report was the notion that sexuality is a choice. A senior officer is quoted explaining why being beaten on the grounds of sexual orientation is not comparable to being beaten over the colour of one's skin.

"A person born with any sort of colour doesn't have a choice in the matter," he said. "I would suggest that sexual preferences, however, are a matter of individual choice."[258]

Addressing the murder of Geoffrey Windsor, the report's authors concluded that there was "insufficient communication of the level of risk associated with the cruising ground to the very wide range of people using it". It recommended better intelligence-sharing between officers. The final diagnosis was that "institutional homophobia" had fuelled failings.[259] In short, better relations were still needed between potentially vulnerable homosexuals and the police.

* * *

Leaving aside accusations of institutional homophobia, one factor that marred any hope of an investigation into the crimes of Stephen Port was a general dismissiveness. Barking and Dagenham's experts in law enforcement demonstrated on a number of occasions that they weren't interested in chasing up the concerns of bereaved relatives. Be it in their refusal to release CCTV, their lack of equipment as basic as a notepad[260] or their resignation that they might never be able to find out what had happened, this was a theme throughout each of the four tragic deaths.

Sadly, the Barking murders weren't the only high-profile crimes that resulted in the Metropolitan Police Service rolling its eyes with a superior sigh. Nor was this something restricted to gay victims. John Worboys was a black cab driver who raped, sexually assaulted and drugged women he'd lured into his car. In 2009, he was finally jailed with an indeterminate sentence, the minimum of which was set at eight years. Though he was only convicted for attacks on 12 women[261], police believed that he could be the rapist behind more than 100 reported assaults.[262]

Women had been coming forward as early as 2002 to claim that Worboys had attacked them. Reliving such trauma comes at an intimate cost to the victim, but it is endured in the hope that justice be served. These women didn't get justice when they made the reports. What they got was *laughter*.[263]

The specific account that elicited such a response is as follows. A 19-year-old student told officers that Worboys had persuaded her to have a drink in 2007. He then forced a pill down her throat, knocking her unconscious. When she awoke, her tampon had been ripped from her vagina. She was bruised. It's this last detail that seemed particularly amusing, as officers laughed and told her that she must have fallen over while drunk. More than that, they knew that any intoxicants in her system were probably her own. The detective constable dealing with her wrote in a police report: 'The victim cannot remember anything past getting in the cab.'[264]

It's perfectly reasonable that she wouldn't, given that Worboys drugged his victims to satisfy his sexual deviancy. But, just like Anthony, Gabriel, Daniel and Jack, police reckoned it more likely the intoxication was the fault of the victim, remarking: 'It would seem unlikely that a cab driver would have alcohol in his vehicle, let alone drug substances.'[265]

Nonetheless, they did arrest Worboys. But, upon questioning, they believed his version of events. Such was his credibility, they didn't even bother to search his home for evidence, nor did they attempt to corroborate victims' accounts. He remained free.[266]

This was despite the student's story echoing that of a victim who came forward in May, 2003.[267] But then, the police couldn't check her account against the similar one from five years previous. Why? An officer had lost the file.[268] Even if they had kept them, they contained no witness statements nor photographs of the injuries that she had reported.[269]

As the victims mounted, Worboys was finally charged in 2008. For its part, the Met claimed in 2010 that the Crown Prosecution Service had advised them not to take further action on up to 40 cases.[270] A rapist, and a brazen one at that, so confident as to pile women into his car in one of the world's busiest cities, had been believed over surviving victims.

* * *

Less prolific than Worboys, but potentially more embarrassing to the Met, was sex attacker Kirk Reid. He evaded police for 23 years, during which time he carried out at least 71 offences. He was only convicted of 28 sexual assaults in 2009, but police later linked him to many more cases stretching back to 1984, when he was accused of raping a 17-year-old girl in Battersea, south-west London. Eleven years later, Reid was acquitted of indecent assault after a woman claimed he assaulted her in an alleyway in central London. It wasn't until 2008 that police linked him with a separate rape, also in 1984. He attacked seven women in 2002 alone, including one whom he raped, leaving DNA on her skirt. The same year, offences from December 2001 were linked with that rape. An intelligence report was compiled after he was stopped due to reports he was following a woman. Still he walked free.[271]

In January 2004, Reid's car was reported to police in connection with an assault. Police did not follow up on the report. Officers logged an incident with Reid the following month and identified him as a 'person of interest' because he tooted his horn at a woman *in front of patrolling police looking for a sex attacker.* He attacked three more women. One of those women gave evidence to officers, another identified him in an identity parade. He remained free.[272]

Reid continued to assault women before police finally arrested him in February 2008. He received a life sentence, with a minimum of seven-and-a-half years, in June 2009, for two rapes and 26 sexual assaults with police fearing that he'd committed far more attacks stretching back to 1984.[273]

It's important to pause for a moment and consider that the Reid and Worboys rape trials were chronologically close to Stephen's first murder. One might not expect embarrassment to last from the 1980s to the 2010s. They might be allowed to fade into obscurity and, if unacted upon, mean that progress is sacrificed at the altar of complacency. But to have two high-profile rape cases in which the police dropped the ball so comprehensively in the same year should shock a system into action. That action, however short-lived, could surely manage to last a few years. The memory of that action, and the shame that birthed it, would surely be on the minds of serving police officers six short years later when the body of Anthony Walgate turned up outside the flat of a man who'd hired him for sex. Apparently, it wasn't.

22

PROMISES

Stephen Port's sentencing, the assurance that he'd never again freely walk the streets of Britain, meant that attention could now be focused entirely on the police. They'd obviously been central to the story throughout the trial, the details of which made it obvious that grave errors had blighted capture. But with Stephen and his drug dealers inside, there was only one direction left in which to shine the light of accountability. The Independent Office for Police Conduct (IOPC) was tasked with guiding its glare. This did not, however, seem to be a cause for optimism, especially once it emerged in 2019 that not one officer had been disciplined as a result of its report.[274] To understand why, it's worth digging into the history of police watchdogs in Britain. Their failings soon become apparent and any hope of improvement diminishes.

The IOPC traces its roots back to the Police Complaints Board (PCB) of 1977, since when multiple rebrandings have been necessitated by the public's plunging confidence in the watchdog. Botched investigations, failures to secure evidence and the perceived favouring of police officers over and above the victims of the force's behaviour all rank among the reasons.

Prior to the forming of the PCB, the police force that was the subject of a complaint would actually handle their own allegation. This is about as stupid as allowing a criminal to investigate himself, trusting whichever conclusion he then presents. The exception to this rule concerned complaints which the Home Secretary considered serious enough to take out of the force's hands. But even in those cases, the investigation wouldn't be handled by a body independent of the police. It would simply be shunted to another force, allowing for a general brotherhood of police solidarity to take priority, as opposed to an independent investigation.

Scandals in the mid to late-70s included Met Police involvement in a £175,000 robbery at the *Daily Express'* offices, a £225,000 robbery outside Willans & Glyn's Bank's headquarters and a £200,000 armed robbery of the *Daily Mirror's* offices which ended in the fatal shooting of 38-year-old guard Antonio Castro[275]. Operation Countryman, which probed allegations of corruption within the police force, found that corruption was 'historically and currently endemic' as opposed to being the result of a 'few bad apples'.[276]

Never since its founding in 1829 has the Met faced pressure like this. This corruption was exposed during the infancy of the PCB, with Operation Countryman spanning from 1978 to 1982. The idea behind the PCB was that the body would be independent from the forces under investigation. But it failed to inspire confidence in its supposed aim – the regulation of a police force with a view to making necessary improvements. But the perception of the police from certain sections of the community with which they frequently interacted remained negative. The Brixton riots of 1981 provided a flashpoint and rallying cry for black residents of south London who perceived the police to be institutionally racist. Three years later, Margaret Thatcher's Conservative government scrapped the PCB as it became evident that public confidence in the police was shaky at the very least.

Its successor was the Police Complaints Authority (PCA). Sweeping onto the scene in 1985 with a whole word to distinguish it from its failed predecessor, it brought with it increased powers of supervision over the police forces investigating other squads. But at a time when it was important to swiftly improve confidence in the police, the publishing of investigations could take years. A West Yorkshire Police probe into the West Midlands Serious Crime Squad took six years to surface after its 1989 commissioning.

The racist murder of 18-year-old Stephen Lawrence at a south London bus stop in 1993 changed everything. The lack of arrests sparked a fight for justice, with the Met accused of failing to investigate properly due to the deceased being black. Sir William Macpherson led a public inquiry into the police's actions following the killing and, in 1999, the Macpherson Report concluded that institutional racism was at play within the Met. Its 70 recommendations included the Home Secretary considering what steps should be taken to ensure serious complaints against officers are investigated.

And so it was decided that the UK's police watchdog should be independent of the forces it was investigating. It also became independent from government, political parties and pressure groups as the Independent Police Complaints Commission (IPCC) replaced the PCA in 2004.[277] But it was funded by the Home Office. And the Home Secretary appointed its seven operational commissioners, as well as its three non-operational commissioners. It wasn't just the funding of the IPCC that pointed to the sheer inefficacy of the PCA, but the fact that one of the new body's investigations would be a probe into the PCA's handling of the Hillsborough enquiry. The enquiry had investigated police action at a 1989 FA Cup semi-final match between Liverpool and Nottingham Forest in 1989, when a crowd crush at Hillsborough Stadium in South Yorkshire resulted in 97 people dying. The tragedy leaves a legacy of bitterness between those who were being policed on that day and those responsible for enforcing law and order. Catalysts for this resentment included the false claims of an officer, as published in *The Sun*, that Liverpudlians were seen robbing their dead counterparts in the crush and attacking police.[278] In short, a police investigation into a police force suspected of having a hand in the deaths of 97 people through negligence was so dissatisfactory that the IPPC not only took over the investigation, but investigated the original investigation. That's how low public confidence, especially among Liverpudlians, was in the police and its watchdog.

Unsurprisingly, the IPCC's brief was to be even more independent from the police than its predecessors. This was emphasised by the fact that it was illegal to become a commissioner for the watchdog if you had worked for the police at any point. The IPCC was a considerably beefed-up take on its predecessors, with four types of investigation:

1. Independent – Conducted by IPCC investigators and overseen by a commissioner with the same powers police enjoy;
2. Managed – Directed by the IPCC but undertaken by local forces' Professional Standards Departments (PSDs);
3. Supervised – Directed by local PSDs under terms of references set by IPCC. The IPCC was sent the final investigation report and complainants not happy with the outcome were able to appeal to the IPCC;
4. Local – Carried out entirely by local PSDs or officers working on their behalf. Dissatisfied complainants can appeal to the IPCC after a local investigation.

So, after hundreds of independent investigations, hundreds of managed probes and thousands of cases tackling complaints about outcomes and the way complaints were handled, did this body win public confidence? No. At least not according to the UK Government, which set out a series of damning blows to the reputation of various police forces during the IPCC's tenure.

The Hillsborough disaster was the largest probe into police misconduct in British history. The investigation, paired with criminal investigation Operation Resolve, involved the interviewing of tens of thousands of people. The interviews cost at least £80million.[279]

The IPCC announced in 2012 it would investigate the police's failure to declare a major incident, their failure to close the tunnel to the stadium's stands, which led to overcrowded pens, the alteration of police officers' statements, and the shortcomings of previous probes. The IPCC looked at at least 10,000 lines of enquiry, took 120 survivor complaints and at least 4,000 statements, of which 400 were from police officers. Charges were brought against three former South Yorkshire Police officers.

Former Chief Inspector and Superintendent Sir Norman Bettison was charged with misconduct in public office related to alleged lies concerning his involvement in the aftermath of Hillsborough and the culpability of Liverpool fans. Former Chief Superintendent Donald Denton was charged with intent to pervert the course of justice relating to changes made to witness statements, as was former Detective Chief Inspector Alan Foster. Their solicitor, Peter Metcalf, was charged with committing acts with intent to pervert the course of justice relating to changes made to witness statements.[280]

Operation Resolve also saw David Duckenfield, the most senior officer in charge of match safety on the day, charged with 95 counts of manslaughter by gross negligence. The case against Bettison was dropped in 2018.[281] Duckenfield was cleared in 2019.[282] Denton, Foster and Metcalf were acquitted in 2021.[283] The IPCC either seemed inept at assigning blame correctly, or it was a paper tiger.

The sad reality is that even if the IPCC was perfect, it still wouldn't necessarily win over public support. There is a tension at the heart of its remit, in that in order to prove itself trustworthy and win trust in law enforcement, it must also be honest about the failings of police forces. In its quest to produce accountable policing, it must in the short term highlight the unaccountability with which some forces had operated. But it wasn't just police forces of days gone by that suffered reputational damage during the IPCC's tenure, it was the IPCC itself.

In 2008, the Police Action Lawyers Group – comprising 100 legal professionals specialising in police complaints – accused the IPCC of displaying favouritism toward officers.[284] This was most evident, they said, in the way the body handled cases of deaths in custody. They also alleged indifference and rudeness toward complainants and the rejection of complaints despite powerful supporting evidence.[285] The group expressed 'increasing dismay and disillusionment' over 'the consistently poor quality of decision-making at all levels of the IPCC'.

A former member of the watchdog spoke out about how ineffective the IPCC was, writing an opinion piece for *The Guardian* in which he accused it of favouring the very people it was supposed to hold accountable. In essence, the whole point of having a watchdog was being undermined by the watchdog itself.

Former commissioner John Rawley pointed out that just 11 per cent of complaints were upheld. Of the serious assault allegations, one per cent were substantiated. The watchdog viewed itself as part of the family of police agencies, as opposed to an independent body of accountability, he argued. Rawley said that from 2007-2008, the chances of complaints being upheld depended largely on which force you were expressing a grievance against. If you complained in West Yorkshire or

Humberside, you'd most likely be one of the 96 per cent who were dismissed. In Bedfordshire, you'd have slightly better odds, with 80 per cent dismissed.[286]

* * *

Perhaps most relevant to the Stephen Port case was the IPCC's investigation of the Met's handling of the afore-mentioned black cab rapist John Worboys in 2010. It identified 'individual and systematic' issues, including the failure to secure forensic swabs and prompt blood and urine testing. The watchdog found that officers were insensitive to victims of sexual violence, upholding complaints against five out of eight officers investigated. It recommended the dismissal of none. Instead, the IPCC suggested written warnings for two officers and words of advice for three. This was in spite of the probe revealing that if 'crucial investigative opportunities' had not been missed, Worboys could have been stopped sooner. Deputy chair of the IPCC Deborah Glass hailed written warnings as 'a serious sanction' and 'wake-up call', but conceded the public may ask: 'If you cannot sack them, what's the point?'[287] The victim who police ridiculed in 2007 was totally unsatisfied and said that 'jobs should have been lost'.[288]

Just like the grieving relatives who lost family members to Stephen's crimes, Worboys' victims were not kept updated on the case, and after the IPCC probe the regulator recommended that information be made available for victims online so as to provide them with regular case updates. Keep in mind that this was five years before Jen and Donna Taylor had to hound

Barking and Dagenham Police into action. The sharing of intelligence with local agencies where there is a high risk to the community, as well as working with the voluntary sector to encourage women to report attacks to third parties was also recommended.[289]

When a parole board decided to release Worboys in 2018, one of his victims received the news when she saw her rapist's face in the media as she cooked tea for her children. There was no warning and solicitors representing 11 of the victims said they were "devastated". They challenged the decision and the decision was overturned in the High Court that same year.[290]

* * *

Perhaps the strangest headache for the IPCC was what became known as Plebgate in 2012. A seemingly trivial exchange between Tory MP Andrew Mitchell and police officers guarding Downing Street spiralled out of all expected proportions. Mitchell was accused of calling an officer a 'pleb' for not letting him through a gate immediately. The controversy centred on a simple narrative about the member of a party seen as posh and elitist abusing the very people protecting him while his government unleashed cuts to police funding.

The exchange at the centre of the row had spanned a grand total of 15 seconds between Mitchell and PC Toby Rowland. *The Sun* newspaper, in September of that year, reported that the Conservative chief whip had unleashed the underused, archaic and classist term 'pleb' in the direction of PC Toby Rowland. And he'd thrown in a 'fucking' for good measure. He was said to have insulted the officer after being refused permission to cycle through the main gates. In the face of calls to resign, Mitchell admitted swearing, but did not admit to using the P word. His refusal to specify precisely what he did say was seized upon as evidence against him by Detective Sergeant Stuart Hinton, who spoke with him weeks after the argument. The litigious cyclist wasn't happy about this and pursued the tabloid in a libel case. He was determined to prove that he hadn't called an officer a 'fucking pleb'. But he lost. Two years after the row, a judge ruled that Mitchell had probably branded Rowland a pleb. Having earned the reputation of a true hater of the great unwashed, Mitchell was ordered to fork out damages. And *The Sun*'s legal costs. Just when we thought that the squabble might finally fade into obscurity, the IPCC got involved.[291]

In 2015, West Mercia Inspector Ken Mackaill was found to have given misleading accounts of a meeting between him and Mitchell following the row. He was found to have breached standards of professional behaviour after calling for Mitchell to resign. In 2012, he'd told the media that Mitchell had not given a full account of the row during the meeting.[292] But then a recording emerged. The tape indeed featured Mitchell offering an account to the officers in his Sutton Coldfield constituency office. The transcript recorded Mitchell as saying: "I did say under my breath but audibly, in frustration: 'I thought you lot were supposed to fucking help us', and it is for that I apologise. I am grateful to that officer for accepting my apology and I should never have said it and I will never do it again."[293]

The IPCC said no further action would be taken against Mackaill. And what should have been a minor spat ended with the impression that certain officers look after their own to the detriment of outsiders.[294] The expected drop in public confidence was compounded by the fact that the IPCC *supervised* the investigation, rather than actually *conducting* one of its own. This meant that police officers under considerable strain were interviewing others who were claiming that one of the politicians associated with their pay cuts regarded them as lower on the social strata. This might not have been the best decision in the pursuit of impartiality. What followed was a scathing report on the IPCC in 2013, seven months after the Home Affairs Committee announced an inquiry into the body's effectiveness and independence. It found the IPCC to be 'woefully under-equipped and hamstrung in achieving its original objectives'. The Home Office conceded that the watchdog did not have the powers necessary in order to ensure meaningful reform.[295]

* * *

Change was once again in order. The Stephen Port case might have been referred to the IPCC, but the eventual report would issue from the IOPC – the Independent Office for Police Conduct – whenever it actually surfaced. This latest incarnation had the power to initiate investigations without relying on a force to refer itself, as Barking and Dagenham Met had to do to its predecessor in 2015.

It also had the power to determine appeals and recommend remedies, with a shortened process for deciding whether or not a case should go to a disciplinary hearing. In addition, the IOPC could reopen probes if new evidence had emerged and investigate all disciplinary claims against chief officers. The IOPC came into force in 2018, two years after the country had witnessed the catastrophe that was Stephen's case play out in court. It had been a mere matter of months since allegations of police ineptitude in relation to the case had decorated news pages. Surely, the IPCC would have been swift to act in light of the coverage, and the IOPC would now take decisive action.

* * *

But, yet again, reasons to be hopeful were scarce. We'd already seen that not one officer had been questioned in relation to the Stephen Port case by May 2017. The regulator's commissioner, Cindy Butts, said that the watchdog had not been able to absorb the 7,000 pages necessary to meet pre-interview disclosure requirements. She insisted that at that stage investigators had analysed more than 700 documents and analysed about 200 statements. Branded 'impotent' in the press, the latest incarnation of the watchdog was once again accused of failing. Daniel Whitworth's step-mother, Mandy Pearson, said that the lack of progress was "insulting and distressing".[296] Failure to begin interviews was made all the more serious by the fact that seven of the police officers under investigation had been served with gross misconduct notices. Ten others were facing charges of misconduct.[297]

It took months for the 17 police officers to see through the interview phase. But that didn't mean they actually sat down to be interviewed in any meaningful way. In fact, all but one of the

17 officers being investigated had refused to answer questions in their interviews. Sixteen officers gave 'no comment' interviews, preferring to submit prepared statements.[298] The fact that the watchdog only secured spoken answers to specific questions from one officer is all the more galling when one considers that in May 2017 investigators explained away their impotence by claiming interviews had not started because they were keen to ensure the evidence collected at the interview stage was 'as robust and comprehensive as possible'.[299] At the time, the watchdog claimed to be doing this by giving the officers the time they requested to digest a large amount of evidence before questioning began. They required time to reflect upon and absorb the information that would confront them in the interview. Sixteen presumably needed that huge stretch of time to knock together a written statement. The one officer who did submit to an interview was not one of the seven facing a gross misconduct notice. After the interview and before the investigation's conclusion, that officer resigned.[300]

The IOPC concluded its inquiry in August 2018, passing the resulting report to the Metropolitan Police. The watchdog announced on the 14th that it had written to solicitors representing the families of Stephen's victims and police pledged to respond 'shortly' to the report, which included opinions on whether or not officers should face disciplinary proceedings. Crucially, the IOPC staved off media scrutiny by saying that the findings would not be published for journalists until the new inquests had concluded and accurately assessed the cause of death for each of Stephen's victims. At the time, the inquests were set for 2019.[301]

This was the first IOPC investigation I'd ever watched unfold in real-time from the very start. It was difficult not to conclude that the seemingly pointless gaps in progress were designed to minimise the impact of the final publication. It seemed excusable that, in the beginning, with the amassing of documents and the arrangement of interviews, the process would hit snags. But once the report had been shown to the families, what could possibly take so many months to get it out to the public? It's possible that I'm ignorant of a vital reason that it's kept from the press for what morphed from months into years. But the toothlessness of how the police were treated, combined with keeping it out of public scrutiny, is bound to raise suspicion. It felt like being fed small chunks of bad news bit by bit, which had they hit all at once would confirm that the IOPC was all but pointless. Even if these suspicions were unfounded, it baffled me as to why an institution that is designed to at least present a veneer of transparency would behave in such a way, especially when those most likely to be hurt by its findings – the families – had already seen the result. A key component of the IOPC's mission is to ensure public confidence. How can it claim to be living up to this noble aim by severely limiting the availability of its findings?

These suspicions were compounded when, before the report was even out, it was revealed that not one of the wordsmith officers who'd taken the time to pen what they should have said in an interview would face penalties over the case. Despite admitting it had found 'systemic failings' in the Metropolitan Police, the watchdog said not one of the officers would face any sort of discipline. There was no need to worry, though, they'd told nine of the officers that they would be required to do better in future.[302] This watchdog, this protector of people, this voice of yours and mine against incompetence, corruption and institutional failings within the police, also asked that the Taylors, the Walgates, the Whitworths and the Kovaris not to comment on the report in the press.[303]

After securing this pledge, the IOPC put out an understatement so insubstantial it appeared to dissolve upon reading. It said: 'While we agreed none of the officers involved in these investigations may have breached professional standards justifying disciplinary proceedings, we will be making a number of recommendations to the Metropolitan Police to address some of the systemic failings our investigation identified. We have advised the families of Stephen Port's victims and the officers involved that the performance of nine officers fell below the standard required. They will now be required to improve their performance.'[304]

Peter Tatchell had been following the IOPC investigation closely. He told me that he was deeply worried by its opacity.

"The fact that they let any of the officers decline to be interviewed suggests that they have something to hide," he said. "That means there's a big fear that some of those officers got together to check each other's [written] statements before submitting them. Certainly it's a widespread suspicion.

"All but one officer refused to be interviewed. The rest merely submitted statements. We don't know to what extent those officers colluded and collaborated to make sure their statements were non-contradictory."

* * *

Understandably sceptical about the capability of Walthamstow Coroner's Court to hold the new inquests, Jack Taylor's family were pushing for the fresh inquests to be heard in the High Court or Old Bailey. Donna Taylor said the scale, complexity and implications of the Stephen Port case demanded the highest level of legal scrutiny. She said she couldn't understand why it would not be heard in the High Court. Jack had been dead for almost three years at this point and Donna had still not been able to grieve due to the demands of the fallout from her brother's murder, from her and Jen's investigation in 2015 through to the IOPC finishing its report. In the end, it was decided that the inquests would be held at Barking Town Hall.[305]

23

AFTERMATH

Following the total hash that was made of the police investigation and, as a result, the inquests into the deaths of his victims, the grieving families understandably wanted as robust a process as possible in regards to the fresh inquests. The original findings were quashed and a joint inquest ordered into the deaths of all four murder victims, with the press reporting on 'new information' that had been unearthed since Port's sentencing.

Puzzling as this was given the amount of damning evidence available not just before Port's November 2016 sentencing, but before he'd even got around to murdering Jack Taylor, the news was welcomed by the grieving families. Daniel Whitworth's step-mother, Mandy Pearson, said it was an important step in correcting the record of his death.

"This is an important start to getting some of the many wrongs concerning Daniel's death corrected," she said. "The very least we can do for Daniel is to get the facts about his death recorded correctly and, with a new inquest, we are hopeful we can do that for him and for Gabriel, Anthony and Jack."[306]

Following the trial's end, the families were represented in the media and legally by Hudgell Solicitors, whose civil liberties legal executive said: "Holding all four inquests together for Gabriel, Daniel, Anthony and Jack will help identify if institutional failings and discrimination within the Metropolitan Police played any roles in their deaths. This is another important step in the families' fight for justice."

Both the inquests and the publishing of the IOPC report were set to take place in 2019, four years after Jack's death. In October 2018, Chief Coroner Mark Lucraft QC agreed that a judge would be appointed to conduct the inquests, as opposed to a standard coroner. Dr Shirley Radcliffe, a coroner working in east London, had asked for the case to be moved out of the area, which was still overseen by senior coroner Nadia Persaud, who had presided over the original inquests into the deaths of Gabriel Kovari and Daniel Whitworth.[307] Dr Radcliffe wanted the hearing to be held in a different jurisdiction due to concerns from the grieving families' legal team over 'whether enough questions were asked' the previous time around. Solicitor Paul Clark said: "One example is that there was a series of questions about a fake suicide note."[308]

At the time of writing – October 2021 – the inquest is finally in motion, having started earlier this month. The coroner will not reach conclusions about Barking and Dagenham officers in relation to the deaths of the four men. It will determine the direct cause of the deaths, which were drug overdoses. It is unclear how the release of the IOPC report to the media could prejudice these proceedings any more than the high-profile murder trial five years ago.

* * *

Once the inquests were underway, journalists had an idea as to how long they'd last. Between eight and ten weeks was the ballpark figure. This meant that hearings would conclude before my publishing date and I hoped that this would give me a way in to finally getting a comment from the Met Police's press bureau. Statements up until this point had been vague and I was hoping for something proper, side-stepping the worry about them commenting before the inquests had concluded by assuring them that whatever they gave me wouldn't be published until after the fact.

In the hope of securing something specific, I laid out some of the key points that the book makes about police conduct, so that they had the opportunity to put their side across.

The main points were:
- Barking and Dagenham MPS refused to check Stephen Port's electronic devices after they found a young man named Anthony Walgate, whom they knew he'd hired as an escort, dead outside his flat. They instead arrested him for perverting the course of justice. Despite him being found guilty of that offence, he then dropped off their radar.
- Police then failed to investigate as murder an almost identical death when the body of Gabriel Kovari was found about 400 yards away from Stephen's flat.

- About three weeks later, police refused to DNA test a blanket covered in Port's semen which was later found under the body of his third victim Daniel Whitworth. They also did not investigate a suspicious suicide note in Daniel's hand which would later turn out to be faked by Port.

- Port's fourth murder victim, Jack Taylor, was found in almost the exact same spot as the second and third victims. Not only did the police not spot the pattern, they refused to treat his death as suspicious. This included telling Jack's sisters that releasing CCTV wasn't something they'd usually do. Only after concerted pressure from the sisters did they release vital CCTV to the media, which showed Jack with his killer. Port was identified within hours, showing the importance of releasing the footage.

- The families and friends of the victims believe that homophobia was an element in the lack of investigation. They believe this homophobia manifested itself in an attitude that gay people simply take drugs and overdose despite obvious evidence that could have pointed to foul play from the start, including the fact that all the bodies had clearly been dragged (evidenced by bruises on their limbs, and their clothes either having ridden up or being inside out).

- Not one of the police officers involved in the mishandling of the Stephen Port case has been disciplined.

I stressed that this was a brief overview, and not a comprehensive list of every single complaint. I offered to provide more specifics and additional complaints should they feel that I wasn't giving them enough information to comment properly.

The Press Bureau responded the following day, stating that it might not be possible to comment until the inquests were over. The press officer asked whether I was looking for a general comment or responses to each individual complaint. I responded that I was looking for a general statement, as opposed to lots of individual comments, which would ideally express the key concerns raised. I also offered to take lots of individual comments if that would be preferable and give the force more scope to defend itself. They responded to ask for a deadline. I gave them the deadline of September 10, when I'd begin rounding off and tidying up the book. These conversations took place from August 17-19, 2021.

On September 8, I received this statement from the Met Police: 'While we can't comment in detail as we await inquests into the deaths of the four young men who died at the hands of Stephen Port, we have already apologised to the families affected for missed opportunities to catch Port sooner. We reiterate those apologies now and understand what a devastating impact Port's crimes have had. Our thoughts and sympathies are with the families as always.

'In October 2015, we voluntarily referred ourselves to the Independent Office for Police Conduct (IOPC). The IOPC investigation focused on the Met's handling of the deaths before they were deemed suspicious and formally linked.

'We have fully cooperated with the investigation and await the final IOPC report. We have been informed by the IOPC that no officer has a case to answer for gross misconduct, however the performance of nine officers fell below the standard required and this has been addressed by way of formal learning for the future.

'We have already worked hard to improve how we respond to unexplained and suspicious deaths and our officers' understanding of drug-facilitated sexual assaults. In developing our investigative practices, we have worked closely with LGBT+ communities to enhance awareness and training of our frontline officers. We are sincere in our desire to learn and respond better.'

It appeared that, until the hearings were concluded, comments on the specifics of the case would be unattainable. It's worth remembering that this was five years after Stephen's sentencing and seven since the Met had botched the investigation into Anthony Walgate's death. And there certainly would be questions to answer, as the inquests proved when they began to unfold.

Jurors sitting at Barking Town Hall heard that, although the police weren't particularly suspicious about Anthony Walgate's death, a paramedic was. Antony Neil's first clue was the temperature of the body. Its coldness showed that the young man had been dead for some time and it seemed unlikely that a young man would collapse in the street only for nobody to see him and show concern, possibly saving his life. It would surely make more sense that he had died elsewhere then been dragged to that spot. And then there was the body's positioning. Anthony was sat cross-legged, appearing posed. He didn't look like he'd suffered a seizure and fallen down as a result, as Stephen had implied when he'd called 999. Neil told the jury that never in his career had he seen a seizure victim crumple neatly to the floor in a cross-legged pose. Police forensic medical examiner Dr Mark Munro, meanwhile, said the death was "probably non-suspicious". However, he did acknowledge in his official form, to which the police of course had access, that the body appeared to have been moved.[309]

But what was truly puzzling was the fact that, with a dead body before them, the police acknowledged that Stephen was also a suspected rapist from a previous case. The rape was alleged to have occurred in Stephen's flat. Of course, we now know that he had drugged Anthony to knock him unconscious and sexually abuse the escort at that very site. And we know that is what killed him. For some reason, the same officers that believed it credible enough that Stephen may have sexually assaulted Anthony, did not take the next logical step when they saw that the young man had died of a GHB overdose and arrest him over the death. It would seem at the very least prudent to do so. Inspector Gary Learmonth gave evidence too, saying that a mark on Anthony's torso bore a mark that looked like a "possible footprint". He understandably believed that the death was "potentially suspicious".[310]

Another officer, Mike Hamer, also had his suspicions about the case. When Daniel Whitworth turned up dead at St Margaret's, he firmly believed that it was a case of 'if and when' Stephen would be arrested on suspicion of murder. He flagged the case to the Metropolitan Police's Murder Investigation Team (MIT), believing they would be better suited to investigate than Barking and Dagenham's borough police. But was shocked when the MIT turned down the case, in spite of suspicions that had existed since the aforementioned rape case of 2012 (of which he was later convicted, just in case you don't recall). It seems that a lack of suspicion wasn't restricted to certain Barking and Dagenham officers. The MIT turned down Hamer's request because they too did not believe that there was enough evidence to suggest homicide.[311]

The next revelation is shocking for two reasons. Stephen's laptop was not inspected until after the death of Daniel. In part, this is shocking because of the amount of credible suspicion that already existed about him long before that death. Why did it take this long? But it's also baffling because that inspection should have stopped him from killing Jack Taylor. The Met Police's homicide command had instructed Barking and Dagenham officers to submit the laptop after the death of Anthony Walgate, for reasons that are now only too obvious. But despite the advice, offered in June 2014, the laptop and phone were not submitted until the following April. Trainee Detective David Parish was the officer who submitted the laptop and phone, receiving a USB with downloaded material a few weeks later. He claimed that the only thing of note appeared to be access to gay pornography. But he didn't notice the drug rape sites or social media accounts – and their messages. He acknowledged that this was a mistake on his part, possibly due to his inexperience at the time.[312]

China Dunning, the friend of Anthony who originally reported him missing, also revealed the wall she hit when trying to get the laptop analysed in June 2014. Police told her it would be too expensive, that only two people would ever know what had happened in that room and one of them was dead.

DS Martin O'Donnell allegedly told her: "You need to let it go. You're not going to find out."[313]

Had it not been for the original inquest into Anthony's death, it would not have been sent for examination. Once it was, it offered a grim insight into Stephen's depraved predilections as he boasted about sex with a drugged man who was 'like a rag doll'.[314] We now also know that Stephen sent hundreds of thousands of lines in messages about sex and drugs to men on gay dating sites from those very devices. The pornography he watched was also featured heavily in these conversations, providing an ample source of concern if only it had been spotted at the time. The messages were "absolutely incessant", with Stephen sending them "all day, every day", Detective Inspector Mark Richards told Barking Town Hall. In fact, the only time Stephen seemed to stop sending these disturbing messages and watching the pornography seemed to be when he went to Barking train station to meet a hook-up and bring them back to his flat, where pornography would resume. Richards became heavily involved in the case when he worked with Operation Lilford. But that operation only came into being after the four murders were finally linked.[315]

And it emerged that Stephen's guilty verdict relating to a slew of charges might not even be the whole story of the damage he wrought on men he brought back to his flat. The police identified six living victims who neglected to join the prosecution's cases against him.

It wasn't just the police's inactivity that came under scrutiny at the inquests, it was their actions too. Anthony Walgate's parents described the investigation as a "travesty" and said that detectives "smiled" and seemed to be "almost joking" throughout their grief. Anthony's dad, Thomas Walgate, said the officers broke the news to him by telling him that his brother Anthony had died. When Thomas told them he didn't have a brother called Anthony, they told him it must be his son. He originally found family liaison officer Detective Constable Paul Slaymaker to be amicable, but was struck by his strange demeanour at a later meeting. He said that the situation at hand seemed to the officers to be "almost some sort of a joke".[316]

Sarah Sak was struck by how quickly her son's supposed drug habits were taken as read. Slaymaker had noted that she told him Anthony enjoyed a drink and dabbled in drugs – possibly cocaine. She told jurors that was "an absolute lie" and that her impression was that death by consensual chemsex was already being taken for granted as the cause of her son's demise. Her next claim was key. Sarah told Slaymaker that she believed her son had been murdered. He is then alleged to have told her flat-out that Anthony was not murdered and that his death was unexplained. So here we have an officer who not only wasn't convinced that a murder had taken place, but was actively convinced of the precise opposite. This was, as we now know, before the laptop of the man who should have been the prime murder suspect was analysed. It's puzzling to me how any officer could come across Anthony's body and not be strongly suspicious that a murder had taken place. But it boggles the mind to consider coming across such a scene and being utterly convinced that a murder had not taken place.[317]

It would be damning enough if this conviction had stopped there. But Slaymaker appears to have doubled-down on his belief. Frustrated with the lack of a police investigation, Sarah thought it might help to get her local MP involved. Perhaps the publicity would force the police into action. Sarah said that a perturbed Slaymaker spoke to her after she made the approach, saying: "How many times do I need to tell you? Anthony was not murdered."[318] This left her wondering how many times she would have to say the precise opposite.

Relations worsened with the deaths of Daniel and Gabriel. Just as Donna and Jenny would begin to once Jack Taylor turned up dead, Sarah had been keeping an eye on Barking. She couldn't believe the proximity of Daniel and Gabriel's bodies and was convinced they were linked. The obvious similarities with her own son's death could mean that his case was looked at properly. But when she pointed this out to Slaymaker, she claims he snapped at her and told her that the two young men had nothing to do with one another. He described Gabriel as homeless – a fact that would have easily been disproven if he'd bothered to reach out to the few London contacts Gabriel had, which included Ryan Edwards, who had followed his move-in with Stephen. Daniel, meanwhile, couldn't possibly be linked to any criminal behaviour in Barking – because he didn't live in the area.[319]

Police also failed to include key details that could have led to the swift apprehension of Stephen, stopping him from killing again. Detective Sergeant Martin O'Donnell did not share intelligence about the aforementioned 2012 allegation of rape against Stephen when Anthony died. He also did not order a search on the police's national database to see if Stephen Port's name turned anything up. Then, when Stephen lied 'multiple times' about his interactions with Anthony, and his reason for being at the flat, before he finally caved and admitted hiring him as an escort, those lies weren't put on the report. He admitted these were terrible mistakes on his part.[320] If he had not made these mistakes, just think how unbelievably guilty Stephen would have appeared to anyone reading the police report. He surely would have been arrested. Three lives would have been saved.

One particularly strange detail to emerge from the inquests was provided by Barbara Denham, the dog walker who stumbled across the bodies of Gabriel and, later, Daniel. It called to mind the police reaction in the immediate aftermath of Anthony's death, when they questioned Cooke Street residents and showed a visible presence even though they weren't regarding the matter as suspicious. Barbara said that upon finding Daniel's body, she called the police and told them that she was the same woman who'd phoned in identical circumstances just a few weeks before. She was impressed by the sheer number of officers who came to St Margaret's. "They all came flying over there," she told the inquest. "There were lots that day." And yet, just as Stephen's neighbours reported a heavy police presence following Anthony's murder, nothing came of it. This is a confusing picture: officers whose immediate reaction was akin to those swooping on a suspicious crime, only to make no arrests or even treat the scene that warranted such a response as suspicious.[321]

Perhaps a clue to this response lies in the testimony of Detective Constable Nainesh Desai. He admitted that he failed to spot a link between the deaths of Anthony and Gabriel, who were, of course, found in different places but whose deaths bore key hallmarks in common. Desai attended both crime scenes and even interviewed Stephen one week after Anthony's death. Yet despite having this experience with Stephen before he saw Gabriel's dead body, he told the inquests that he simply could not make the link between the two. "For the life of me I couldn't put the two scenes together," he said. "I didn't think the two were linked. I wish I had."[322]

Is it possible that he was in line with the majority opinion? Is it possible that most of the officers who attended those crime scenes simply could not make that link? If this was the case, then the Met faces a far more serious problem than officers unwilling to investigate these types of deaths. Because the problem it faces in that nightmarish scenario is one in which unwilling officers are forced to investigate by their superiors – and just cannot see the link.

* * *

It's important to consider the voices of the police officers under fire during the inquests, not just to give them their say, but because any external pressures that could have marred the investigation must also be flagged if correction is to take place. Detective Chief Inspector Chris Jones said that he "cannot accept for one minute there is any bias in the approach to the investigation". He was referring specifically to the death of Anthony Walgate. And though he claimed to have reflected and challenged himself on whether 'unconscious bias' may have played a role in his approach, he said that he was "absolutely content" that it did not interfere with his job.[323] Without peering into his mind and replaying his thoughts, it's difficult to know. But it seems reasonable to assert that there was bias in the investigation. What other word is there for an investigation that prejudicially leans in one direction and not the other, despite there being clear reasons to correct course? Jones wasn't aware of the 2012 rape allegation against Stephen, nor was he aware that the 999 caller had reported Anthony "gurgling" at a time medics later deduced he must have been dead. However, the fact remains that officers presented with a crime scene which bore key hallmarks of interference with the body leant towards one theory and turned from another.[324]

Another factor to consider is the pressure that London's high crime rate places on its serving officers. Sarah Sak recalled a particularly difficult conversation with Slaymaker in which she told him that if Anthony had been killed in Hull, things would be moving faster. She felt that he'd become a number in the capital, swallowed up into its violent crime statistics. He responded by telling her: "We get more deaths in a week here than you get in Hull in a year."[325]

O'Donnell, too, spoke of a police force struggling to keep on top of its case load because it was overworked. He spoke of enormous pressure in the office. This might have something to do with the model under which officers are now expected to operate. Long gone are the so-called 'Bobbies on the beat' who patrolled local communities in the hope that their presence would deter would-be criminals for illegal activity. Now, police are expected to race to the scene of a crime after it has already happened. The best case scenario of a stabbing is that the victim is wounded and traumatised, but doesn't die and the perpetrator is sent to prison. But somebody has still been stabbed, and perhaps that would not occur under the watchful gaze of a trusted police officer with whom locals were familiar. O'Donnell used an analogy to describe working in Barking and Dagenham while Stephen was on the loose. He said it was like spinning plates, rushing to one that had crashed onto the floor and quickly racing off to another that had fallen. In such an environment, he said, it was easy to miss things.[326]

Officers' levels of training also became the focus of concern when Detective Constable David Parish offered his evidence to jurors. He apologised for the late date at which Stephen's laptop was analysed, before the questioning turned to whether or not he was personally responsible for failings in the investigation. Parish replied that "some of the things I was asked to do [on the investigation], I wasn't trained in," adding: "I could have had more training." It's a worrying state of affairs to consider that a police officer in the capital city of England felt under-equipped to deal with what was an incredibly solvable case. It is, in a way, more worrying than the notion of police officers just not bothering to investigate. For those officers in any police force can be purged, with new blood being brought in and trained with the existing infrastructure. But how is a police force supposed to improve if that infrastructure isn't satisfactory in the first place?[327]

Though some officers were contrite and seemed genuine in their will to explain and understand what had befallen the Met, others were not. Andy Ewing, who was the borough commander during the case, denied that there had been systemic failings within the investigation that were his responsibility. This was in spite of the fact that, when Detective Chief Inspector Tony Kirk told him that Anthony had probably "died at the hands of another", Ewing told him that there weren't any suitable detectives to investigate within the borough. Such a lack of qualifications would seem to most to be a systemic failing, but Ewing also told the inquest that Barking and Dagenham's CID was generally fit for purpose. He told the inquests that he accepted errors were made but "I am struggling to see how that is a systemic failure which was part of my responsibility and statement of expectation."[328]

Gabriel's former flatmate, John Pape, once again found himself at an inquest into the death of his friend. And he wasn't so keen to allow that the police could blame being overstretched and underfunded for their lack of action as Stephen unleashed his sexual depravity on Barking. His response might be seen by some officers as unforgiving, but I regard it as containing an astute observation. He said: "I think it's been said here that the police were underfunded and under emotional strain. But I think, when grieving families, [a] boyfriend and friends are getting close to the truth and trying to raise the alarm 10 months before the Met are even willing to acknowledge the deaths are suspicious, it can't be a funding issue. What resources did the families and friends have? What emotional strain were we under at that time?"[329]

His conclusion was the flourishing of a suspicion that had germinated back when Gabriel died. Prejudice was the only explanation for this incompetence.

24

CONCLUSIONS

Despite years having passed since Stephen faced justice, questions still remain. These questions relate to his crimes, the behaviour of police officers and where the Met goes from here. I should first address what may have been identified as an open question by those who followed the trial closely – that of whether or not Stephen raped the four men he drugged to death. We will never know for certain. Only he knows what happened, he made sure of that. Death, though a clue to charges of murder, does cover other tracks. Without witnesses to call to the stand, given the fact that Stephen murdered them, charges of rape would be incredibly difficult and perhaps even impossible to prove, hence the rape charges that surfaced related to the living. Even if the prosecution had been able to prove anal penetration, which it did not, ascertaining that Stephen had sexual intercourse with the victims against their consent is a tall order given that there was only one side alive to tell the story of what happened in each case between two men at 62 Cooke Street.

The fact that the men were given enough date-rape drugs to render them unconscious and kill them proves an intent to commit a sexual assault, but it does not prove beyond reasonable doubt that Stephen penetrated them with his penis against their consent. It would also have fallen to the prosecution to prove beyond a reasonable doubt a timeline that simply cannot be established due to the privacy of the murders. The lawyers would have had to prove that the victims were rendered unconscious before Stephen penetrated them against their will. Or that the victims had rejected the idea of sexual intercourse, then been drugged. This simply cannot be proven beyond a reasonable doubt. We don't have the ability to replay those final hours or hack into the mind of the one living witness. And so Stephen was not convicted of these four rapes. These facts, however, do not stand in the way of reasonably believing that he did rape these four young men.

To that end, it's worth reviewing what we *do* know, in order that Stephen doesn't get to wriggle away from vile crimes that I believe he committed. We know, for example, that Stephen was found to have drugged these men because of his convictions. We also know that he targeted other young men in this fashion for sexual purposes because there are living witnesses who convinced jurors of this at the Old Bailey. We know that Stephen's internet search history, and homemade videos, evidenced a fetish for sex with unconscious men who were younger and smaller than he. Finally, Stephen is now a convicted rapist on four counts other than the charges relating to the men he murdered.

It's also worth looking at each of his murder victims, to determine whether they were the sort of people who would take GHB willingly before Stephen forced onto them an additional dose to which they did not consent. I don't see any evidence that the four victims would have consented to taking any GHB.

Anthony was working as an escort. He was careful enough to tell his friends what he was doing that evening. It seems unlikely, therefore, that he would accept voluntarily a dose of GHB, notorious for knocking out even the most willing of participants, and elevating the potential for danger in that situation he'd hitherto been so cautious about. He'd also explicitly discussed GHB with a friend and told her that he'd never take the substance.

Gabriel showed no definite signs of recreational drug use. But even if he had, it would seem incredibly unlikely that he would willingly partake in them with a man who had made him nervous. A man who had shown sexual interest and had left Gabriel with the impression that he was 'bad'. A man who Gabriel was so desperate not to be in bed with that he'd cautiously exiled himself to the sofa.

The only reason to think that Daniel could have willingly taken a dose is the ever unreliable word of Stephen, when he was desperately and inadequately trying to wriggle off the charges. Ever keen to smear the young man, he told arresting officers Daniel would hand out drugs at parties they attended. These were the same parties at which Daniel and Gabriel supposedly met before their relationship took a tragic turn as attested to in the fake suicide note. We know this to be nonsense. And, even for somebody without a deep knowledge of the case, Stephen's lies are made all the more obvious by another falsehood, in which he told the same officers: "I don't administer drugs to anyone."[330]

Jack, according not only to his sisters but to an actual drug dealer with whom he briefly spent time, did not take drugs. In fact, he outright refused them when he met Peter Hirons. It therefore seems like a leap to suggest that he'd do so randomly with a stranger.

Given these facts, and given the fact that Stephen was found to have drugged these men, we should consider what could have motivated him. I'll leave it to the reader to determine which of the following is more likely: Stephen drugged these men for the simple amusement of seeing their inhibitions unwillingly lowered and did not act. Stephen drugged them in order to rape them. If you're in any doubt at all, here is what Judge Openshaw said in his closing remarks: Regarding Anthony Walgate, he said: "I think that the inevitable and irresistible inference is that the defendant deliberately administered a drugs overdose to Anthony Walgate, with the intention of penetrating him whilst he was unconscious, which I have no doubt that he did."

Referring to Gabriel Kovari, he said: "… I draw the inevitable inference that shortly after that call was made, the defendant surreptitiously administered drugs to Gabriel Kovari, intending then to penetrate him when he was unconscious; the overdose that he administered proved fatal."

On the murder of Daniel Whitworth, he said: "He and the defendant made contact through a gay dating website, called Fitlads. After very many exchanges they agreed to meet on the afternoon of the 18th September; Daniel left work early and texted his partner to say that he would be late back, but he clearly contemplated only a short visit to the defendant's flat in Barking. As to what happened after he arrived, only the defendant now knows, but at half past 10 the next morning, 19th September, he deleted his Fitlads account, the obvious and inevitable inference is that he did so because Daniel Whitworth was already dead and he was attempting to delete traces of their contact."

On Jack Taylor, he said: "There is evidence that he had accessed gay dating websites before, but he was not 'out'; there were strong indications that he did not voluntarily take *drugs*. After an evening of modest social drinking at a local club, he went home and accessed Grindr. He contacted the defendant and they agreed to meet at Barking railway station, which they did at about a quarter past three on the morning of 13th September. He then went back with the defendant to his flat. Again as to what happened there the defendant is now the only living witness."

It seems extremely unlikely that Stephen wouldn't follow through on a desire that was well-established at trial, during which jurors also heard key DNA evidence showing a sexual interaction. In fact, the only alternatives of which I can conceive are absurd and incredible:

1. He drugged the boys during consensual sex, then stopped himself from partaking in his favourite fetish because he suddenly had an attack of conscience.
2. He gave them a measure of GHB he thought they would enjoy, but would not knock them out, contradictory to his perversion.
3. He reasonably believed that they consented to him carrying on despite them having no control over the unwelcome drugs that were coursing through their limp bodies.
4. He violated their consent with a clear goal of sexual assault by administering the drugs, but couldn't quite go through with raping them, despite having done it to four other men before his arrest.
5. He drugged the men, they died in front of him, quickly, and he had necrophilic sex with them despite never expressing an interest in such activity.

Rapists aren't known for their attacks of conscience. And Stephen's conduct after each of the deaths shows that he viewed these young men not as people with hopes and ambitions, but as tools to facilitate his desires. If they died in the process, so be it. Once they were dead, the killer's concern was not repentance or the guilt he might feel at a family without answers. It was to do his best in erasing evidence that they'd spoken through gay networking sites. Then it was onto the next 'twink' who could satisfy his needs[331]. An otherwise uninteresting text message seems particularly poignant to this point. Having already murdered Anthony Walgate, Stephen boasted of Gabriel moving onto his sofa. He invited him around to come and look at his new 'twink' flatmate. There wasn't a hint of fear evident that what had happened to Anthony could also happen to Gabriel. Gabriel was nothing but a sexual type, a twink, to be gazed upon, abused and then dumped once he was no longer capable of being raped while asleep.

* * *

When Stephen was arrested, the specificity of his sexual crimes were impossible to miss. This was not a sex offender who chose targets indiscriminate of sex or orientation. He targeted men attracted to other men. Those men had been comprehensively let down. Before allegations of homophobia made headlines, before the sentencing raised key questions about the police, John Pape, Gabriel's former flatmate, had his own, private suspicions.

John believed that prejudice borne from ignorance was a factor in the gross negligence that followed the killings, as evidenced by his remarks that the police greeted the news of four young gay men dying with little suspicion, as though they expected them to drop dead in graveyards. Perhaps the officers involved might only have come into close contact with homosexuals through their police work. The logic that follows from this is that if you only see gay people as criminals or victims, it could impact on the way in which a straight officer views gay people in general. Perhaps a lack of diversity or awareness was the problem and whether it would help to have more openly gay officers in the Met, so that straight people who didn't hang out with gay people by choice would at least have positive interactions with them at work. The camaraderie that arose from such interactions could then spill out as a general solidarity with gay people unfortunate enough to find themselves the victims of a crime. It might also guard against a one-dimensional view of gay people as vacuous hedonists partying to pounding music in between drug-fuelled orgies. Being gay might not be seen as a dangerous, drug-centred phenomenon if officers of the law were open about such things.

Ryan Edwards was similarly perplexed at the police's response to the deaths. He described the Met's reaction to the murders as a "shut down of any kind of communication with the local community". It's possible that the mere fact that he noticed this is evidence that the police had a different way of dealing with crimes against gay men, especially if he only noticed it as a result of its abnormality when compared with outreach following crimes against heterosexuals. And Ryan was in something of a position to be taken seriously on these matters. As previously addressed, he'd worked as a researcher and 'secret shopper' to assess the quality of services gay people could expect. Part of this work was assessing support services offered to LGBT victims of crime by Barking and Dagenham police officers. Working undercover, he wrote a report in 2012 revealing what he felt were unacceptable failings. Recalling his report to me five years after its writing, he said he'd found it impossible to be allocated an LGBT liaison officer by borough police. Viewing the case through an experienced eye of gay rights activism, Peter Tatchell thinks homophobia could have played a role, but also allows for ineptitude and negligence. He also offers another explanation.

"A more benign view would be that some officers have the view that when a section of the gay community does chemsex, it sometimes ends in tragedy and that's just a fact," he said. "It's almost as if some officers seem to think gay men engaging in a hedonistic lifestyle should expect that they will face dangers, including potential harm."

In other words, what was expected of gay men was an altogether riskier lifestyle than that of straight men. This could explain the lack of outreach after the fact. It's possible that officers thought that warning gay men familiar with the dangers of their lifestyle would have been pointless.

Peter Hirons found himself dealing with the police from a very different perspective to those of John and Ryan. He wasn't a family member or friend of the bereaved, though he felt profound sadness about Jack's death. He was a criminal. And the impression that he had of the officers with whom he dealt – remember this is after the case had been taken out of Barking and Dagenham Met's hands – was one of cluelessness. When we met, he recalled with exasperation having to explain what Grindr was to officers during questioning. It seems, to put it kindly, odd that police in a metropolitan capital city wouldn't know the basics of a dating app, especially given how prevalent social media are in the communications of the public, and therefore its criminals. What he was most disturbed by, though, was his vulnerability in prison as a gay man. He'd been to prison staff about his cellmate, who had made plain the disdain with which he viewed homosexuals. It's important to realise how scary this would have been. It's tolerable when you meet somebody like that on the outside, where they probably obey the law and there's no reason to think that their views will translate into violence. But for a man experiencing his first, and only, stint in jail, that assumption of safety was not the same. This was a potentially dangerous man, an individual who may well have felt vulnerable himself on the inside. Concerned about how his cellmate's views might manifest, he tried to get help. Once he'd moved to another cell, and made it clear that there was at least one problem prisoner, he was surprised by what happened next. "We had a gay rights meeting held by one of the officers," Peter told me. "The thing that struck me was that to invite me to it, they slipped a note under my shared cell door. They didn't know who I had as a cellmate, it wasn't very discreet. I don't think they understand at all."

The officers clearly knew of Peter's concerns at this point, yet they risked the note falling into the hands of another homophobe. Having met Peter, it's clear within about five minutes where his sexual proclivities lie, and presumably even if his cellmate was an intolerant bigot, he'd have been aware. But this shouldn't be taken for granted, especially regarding someone who may now be trying to conceal clues to his sexuality given his experiences inside. And what if the cellmate deduced from the note that Peter had 'grassed' on another inmate? That's an incredibly dangerous place in which to find oneself.

As depressing as the recollections of John, Ryan and Peter are, things would be so much easier to fix if the problem was plain ignorance. But, even lacking in metropolis trappings as Barking and Dagenham is, it's near-impossible to believe that its police force only ever dealt with gay people during the execution of their duties, not encountering them anywhere else in 21st century London.

It's tempting to diagnose homophobia as the central factor in police negligence after each of Stephen's murders. To do so identifies a simple, unlikeable enemy in the form of hostility to homosexuals. It would also give a clear way of moving forward to a safer London, one in which it is not so easy to murder gay men undetected. And though I'm not saying that it was not a factor, focusing entirely on the perceived homophobia of certain police officers ignores complexities in this case that I believe are vital to our understanding and the prevention of anything like this happening again.

The elements of police conduct that could be attributed to homophobia in the Barking murders were not, I believe, instances of officers not caring about these men because they happened to be gay. What we had here were officers perfectly capable of comprehending that fatal drug use is not a logical consequence of being same-sex attracted. They were perfectly capable of empathising with gay men and understanding the profundity of their lives being taken. However, what certain officers in this case did was to readily believe a narrative that fit with a particular gay scene. The horrifying thing to comprehend is that the notion of prevalent drug-taking in certain quarters of the gay community rings true – and for good reason. Numerous people I've spoken to in the course of writing this book, as covered throughout its pages, and in my day-to-day life, have attested to a side of gay culture in which drug-taking is a major factor. In the year preceding Stephen's first murder, *Pink News* produced numerous articles suggesting that drug use is a very real concern for gay communities, especially in London, citing a rise in crystal meth[332] and a worrying correlation between drug use and HIV diagnoses.[333] So it is not unheard of for gay men who, as were the victims, in their twenties, to take drugs. This type of person does exist in the more party-oriented segments of gay culture. But what the police did in this case, in repeated instances, was apply the wrong narrative. They bought the idea that the dead men in front of them had belonged to a subculture within the gay population that is frivolous, fun and naughty. Not only did they make this assumption without knowing the personalities of the victims, they persisted with it in the face of surviving relatives attesting to the personalities that did not fit that mould. To these officers, the victims' homosexuality was a particular brand of gay. These were not the kind of gays who lead a conventional life with long-term relationships and behaviour roughly the same as straight people when outside the bedroom. No, these were the kind of gays that took drugs. The kind of gays that love drugs so much that they must be taken in graveyards. The kind of gays that die young.

Nonetheless, homophobia doesn't sufficiently explain the

failings discussed in this book. There are other important factors to consider. Crossing over with the fact of sexuality was of course the sex of the victims. Each was male. Men, for good reason, are generally seen as less physically vulnerable than women. A combination of denser bones, taller average height, muscle mass and superior upper body strength make the average man more suited to combat than the average woman. This makes it reasonable to believe that they are more suited to defending themselves from violent predators. This reality is why so many people are nauseated when a man punches a woman, but will rubberneck at a pub fight between two people of the same sex. It is not such a leap that when a man turns up dead, it is less shocking than the body of a woman. Men are seen as less vulnerable. It's possible that this general impression survives even the scenario in which the attributes responsible for this perception are rendered impotent by GHB. Put simply, it is less shocking when men die. This is not said to absolve the police involved in the Stephen Port case, who are required to investigate without fear or favour. But it is a human reality.

* * *

Then there is the question of location. You may recall that, at the start of this book, I invited you to picture the local area in which you work. I did this to try and show you how absurd it would be to come upon four bodies in said town, city or village, and suspect nothing. But this doesn't give you the full picture. You may work in an affluent area, or a quiet place. The borough of Barking and Dagenham is not affluent. And the area in which

Stephen lived as an adult is certainly not quiet. This may have been an imperfect manner in which to convey how you, or any average member of society, might feel upon discovering four bodies in such a place. To try and show you what I mean, I'm going to sketch out my impression of Barking, Dagenham and its surrounding areas from living and working in the borough. I do this because we need to be honest about the way in which even people who care deeply about the area can view it.

In December 2014, I moved to Dagenham from south Wales to take up my job at the *Post*. Save for an assault as a child in which half a brick had been thrown at my face, I'd never before been a victim of crime. Within a couple of months of living down Bennett's Castle Lane, some kids had nicked my scooter. This took some doing, as it wasn't running at the time and was falling apart at the rear. Nonetheless, the determined joyriders got it working and, having restored its purpose, rendered it unusable. But moped theft was to be expected in London, given how easy they are to steal, and at least I'd settled nicely in other ways. My local pub at the time was The Cauliflower in Ilford, next to our office. One night I was walking home after a few drinks when I saw some scaffolding up ahead past Goodmayes railway station. A bulky man was walking toward me, with a taller, lank friend in tow. There wasn't enough room for all of us under the scaffolding and I thought I'd better get out of the way and let them through. Once I was clearly out of the way, I felt an enormous, sharp pain in my stomach and fell, breathless, to the floor. I turned my head to locate the two men, assuming that I'd either done something wrong or between us we'd managed to clash in a way that could have hurt them. I asked if they were all right, then realised that the bulky one must have steamed into me and punched me in the gut. He was now trying to break free from the grip of his skinny friend, who was warning me not to do anything. It had the ring of a threat and there was no way I'd be able to best one of them, let alone two. So I just went home. On another night, I took exception to the way in which a bouncer referred to my drunk female friend. He told me: "You need to control your woman." Being a mouthy shit, and not comprehending that anyone would react to words with violence, I told him not to be so rude. This huge man promptly grabbed me by the throat, lifted me slightly and walked me calmly out of the pub. I was becoming far more accustomed to violence and general crime than ever before.

The following summer, I moved to Suffolk Road in Barking. The shared house was close to the train station and an 11-minute walk from 62 Cooke Street. I didn't know much about what it'd be like to live in Barking, but I immediately preferred it to Dagenham on the basis of it having two pubs next to the Tube station: The Spotted Dog (the classy option, which kicked out around midnight) and the Barking Dog (a Wetherspoon, which stayed open for an hour longer). On an otherwise calm evening in the latter, a young man had to be dragged out of the pub by his friends as he threatened violence against me and my friend, Iain, for being 'northern cunts' imposing on his 'cockney manor'. This was because Iain supported Sunderland, not West Ham, a fact that emerged while we were talking about football. I didn't watch football at the time, but the inebriated 20-something decided I supported Bolton Wanderers and was furious about that, too.

On a considerably messier night, I left the Spotted Dog to find the lights from police cars and ambulances staining the street blue. Across the road, a large bald man was crouching over another. The large, bald man was Rob, my flatmate who'd left the pub shortly before me. He was covered in blood. Closer inspection showed that he was holding a man's ear, which had been all but severed, pressing it to his head in the hope of keeping it attached. The victim, too, was covered in blood. Rob had stumbled on the injured man after a knife attack, which judging by the wound seemed to have been sprung on him from behind. Were violent incidents such as these the sole occurence of nights on which copious amounts of alcohol had been imbibed, they would be easy to write off as part of the chaos of night life. But they weren't.

One weeknight, I was walking through Barking town centre, speaking on the phone to my mother while heading to Asda. Passing down a side street that opens up into the town centre, I saw again the now familiar presence of police. A teenager had been stabbed. I spoke to a few other people, who appeared to know the victim. They were incredibly hostile, but displayed little shock over what had happened. Not one of them appeared to be over the age of 19.

In the two years that I lived in Barking and Dagenham, one thing was inescapable: this was a high crime, violent area. So what? You may ask. You might expect these incidents throughout London, by virtue of the fact that it has more people than anywhere else in the UK and, therefore, more criminals. But the difference with Barking and Dagenham, as opposed to Islington or Hackney, is that there's no shining city landscape with which to bask in escapism when this terror rampages down your street. The other key difference, for me, was that these acts of profound violence didn't seem out of place in Barking.

By this time, Barking wasn't just the place in which I lived, I worked there too. The *Post* had moved from Ilford to a grim tower office block puzzlingly named Maritime House in the centre of town. Each morning on the way to work, I'd see poor people, angry people and men who appeared to have an almost ritualistic habit of pissing against whichever surface was at hand, usually the bridge over the train tracks. This created a sense of a place that for whatever reason did not, or could not, look after itself. In my time there, I'd gone from thinking that crime was a sad fact for unfortunate people far from my orbit to expecting its presence. Things that would look extraordinary in my hometown became banal. And the brutal fact of the matter is that I would have been far less shocked by the sight of a dead body in Barking than I would have in Mayfair. It seems to me that the police, despite being required to act in spite of such perceptions, instead suffered from the same despondency. Shrugging helplessly at the sight of a crime might be understandable from a member of the public with no tools at his disposal to tackle the problem. But it's unfathomable that the same lack of action would persist in the men and women required to step in at that very moment. Not only are police officers tasked with the job of protecting people from, and solving, crime, they are cognizant of the brutality that comes with their jobs on a regular basis. I could not necessarily blame the police for prejudices over which they have no control, or perhaps even have no awareness. What is beyond me is the fact that even the plushest of patches to them must seem disproportionately dark and compromised, because they deal with the population of those areas who bring chaos and disorder to otherwise pleasant streets. It's totally unimaginable to me that knowledge of this fact, combined with the training that they must surely receive, would not cancel out any apathy induced by the general nature of a borough. And even if it did, how many people care about every second of their job? I can think of not one that I know. And yet they perform their duties because they are paid to do so. These aren't average men and women. They aren't being handed a wage to perform menial tasks. These are men and women who are fully aware of their responsibilities. It's understandable that civilians respond to a place like Barking and Dagenham differently than they do to Richmond, Alderley Edge or Henley-on-Thames. But it's utterly ridiculous to grant this same generosity to men and women charged with investigating the most serious of crimes. These are officers entrusted with the safety of Londoners. And what makes their failure so appalling is that they had the tools to act during each and every moment that they discovered another body. They see brutality often. It's their *job* to see it. It's their job to *act*.

It's this failure to act that was the true problem. No

matter how crime-friendly an area may appear, no matter how appropriate it may appear to find a body in a certain part of London, each officer should come to the scene blocking out any mental baggage that threatens to negatively influence their conduct. There can be no excuse, for example, for failing to carry out DNA tests or for reaching conclusions about the deaths based entirely upon assumptions that contradict evidence. Even if officers had low expectations of Barking, they are tasked with, as far as possible, looking at each case with fresh eyes, free of any prejudicial perspective that may lurk beneath the surface.

One might think that the police officers' failure to carry out basic tasks was an act of gross negligence based on a lack of suspicion. However, a more disturbing scenario must be entertained: that they actively chose not to engage in crucial crime-detecting, in *spite* of their suspicions, however limited. This reading of the events struck me as possible when I came across an article in which a neighbour of Port's described the scene after officers found Anthony Walgate's body in the street outside. Kristina Piliciauskaite lived in the Cooke Street block with her husband and 11-month-old son, two floors above Stephen. She had a clear view of the street from her flat and, at the sound of police and ambulance sirens, looked outside to see what was going on. Seeing a body covered in a sheet, she noticed the legs were poking out as emergency workers descended. But this wasn't a one-stop event for Barking and Dagenham Police. They were in and out of Kristina's block of flats for 'about a week', 'checking everyone in and out of the block of flats and asking us if we saw anything'.[334] Why on Earth would a police force do such a thing if they did not suspect criminal behaviour beyond perverting the course of justice? Why question people who most likely hadn't been in their reclusive neighbour's flat about a boy who'd died of a drug overdose by his own hand in said apartment? Blind prejudice simply doesn't account for this detail; if the police believed that gay men take drugs and die, because that's what homosexuals do, why ask any questions at all? The more disturbing question is: why didn't they follow up on this with an analysis of Stephen's electronic devices, despite the pleas of Anthony's family? It's difficult not to conclude that they simply couldn't be bothered. And this seems to track with their initial obstruction toward the supposedly difficult task of releasing the CCTV footage of Jack Taylor walking through Barking, which turned out to be incredibly easy, incredibly useful and only hit the press thanks to the outside interference of Jack's determined family. Whatever the reason for this laziness, lethargy and apathy, it's clear that it was there despite the suspicions that must surely have existed in the minds of trained police officers working in London.

We've dealt with what the Met *weren't* doing while Stephen Port was free to murder people. But what about what they *were* doing, elsewhere in London? Well, in 2015 while they were refusing to investigate the death of Jack Taylor, having already refused to investigate the three previous deaths, they arrested 857 people for offensive social media posts. In 2014, when they were overlooking the deaths of Anthony Walgate, Gabriel Kovari and Daniel Whitworth, more than 1,200 people were prosecuted under the Communications Act nationally.[335] These prosecutions arose from a total of 2,315 arrests.[336] You could be forgiven for thinking that offensive tweeting is a far less serious crime than murder. But then again, it's easier to post something stupid on social media than it is to kill. You're more likely to do it and therefore people offending one another online is more common than serial killing. Therefore, we should expect more arrests for that behaviour. If you're thinking like that, your framing is deeply flawed. This is not about the general arrests of suspected serial killers, who are thankfully an aberration in our society. The point here is that the police literally went out of their way to arrest hundreds of people for *saying* something while one of its forces was refusing to investigate a far more serious matter right before their eyes. By all means, if it is to be the job of the Met to police Twitter, I understand the hundreds of arrests. What I *don't* understand is going out of your way to find and physically detain a human being after spotting something online, while failing to arrest a man for murder after he calls you to the scene himself, presenting a body that has clearly been moved. There's also a question of priorities here. The Communications Act of 2003 defines the characteristics that an illegal social media post could contain. It says people who could be arrested are those using a public electronic communications network in order to cause annoyance, inconvenience or needless anxiety[337]. That's a pretty wide scope, and must necessarily include a range of offenders from outright calls to racial violence, to somebody making a joke. And even given the fact that nasty tweeting is far more common than murder, there was a clear refocus of Met policy to target people for online behaviour where they had not before. This is why 2015 represented a 37 per cent increase in such arrests since 2010. At some point, for some reason, in the years leading up to the Stephen Port murders, Twitter had become a huge concern to the Met. The fact that their clampdown coincided with missing Britain's biggest serial killer in a decade is incredibly worrying.[338]

* * *

The one comfort people can derive from such a public catastrophe is the light it shines on the police. Under the full glare of ordinary citizens, it might be assumed that things have to get better. For things not to improve would be so bad for the Met that it is in its own interest not to be complacent. But, as we have seen, the Stephen Port case was not this force's first warning. Where it goes from here remains a concern, not only because of the murders that preceded Stephen, but because of the people in charge of the Met. When considering the fact that one officer was disciplined over the handling of the case, it's worth bearing in mind that a lack of punishment and reward of error is far too common in the Metropolitan Police Service. It's hard for the Met to argue that they have a culture of accountability given the mistakes of the woman currently in charge.

Met Police Commissioner Cressida Dick is the most senior police officer in Britain, and has been since February 2017. She made history as the force's first female and openly homosexual boss, which was excellent PR for those keen to communicate the force's modernity. London Mayor Sadiq Khan, of the Labour Party, hailed it as a "historic day". But when it comes to her actual suitability for the role of protecting lives in London, it is difficult to see why she was chosen for this flagship position. Put bluntly, Dick has failed upwards.

Twelve years before she became commissioner, she was involved in a deadly operative blunder that is in some ways worse than the police's mishandling of the Stephen Port case. The body count in the Port case was higher, but nobody actually killed those men other than Port himself. However, in 2012 Dick headed up the counter-terrorism operation that led to officers shooting dead Jean Charles de Menezes. The killing of a terrorist at Stockwell tube station would undoubtedly have been a good thing, worthy of rapid promotion. Except he wasn't a terrorist. He was wrongly identified as an attempted suicide bomber. Dick was in charge of an operation that killed an innocent 27-year-old electrician on the streets of south London. Nobody was prosecuted. But the police were fined for breaching health and safety regulations.[339] Later, it emerged that one of the officers under Dick's command had gone to the toilet when he was supposed to be monitoring Menezes. This break from surveillance contributed to the killing. In 2009, Dick headed up the arrest of Tory MP Damian Green, who was held for nine hours as he stood accused of leaking information from the Home Office. A report into the arrest found it was 'disproportionate and ill-advised'.[340]

In 2021, when she was coming up for her second term,

Khan once again offered his backing to her, calling her force "the finest police service in the world".[341] This was despite the fact that in 2019, the capital, now nicknamed Lawless London, had seen its murder toll hit the highest level in a decade.[342]

Her handling of coronavirus lockdown restrictions, meanwhile, was at best confusing and at worst selective. As the public got used to images of the police chasing away people sat on park benches in London's wide open parks, she was pictured applauding the NHS on Westminster Bridge while not obeying the social distancing rules. Not only was she supposed to be enforcing these rules, but on the off-chance she'd forgotten the restrictions, they were being promoted in shops and ground adverts on the capital's pavements that encouraged people to keep two metres apart.[343]

And then there was the confusion over the right to protest during lockdown. Whatever one thinks of the coronavirus regulations during the pandemic, it cannot be denied that lockdown rules affected basic human rights that are central to a democracy. If a government, and a police chief, are to take those away, it must be done consistently and without prejudice, otherwise the authorities are essentially granting rights for one group and taking them away from another. The removal of rights is common in wartime, when people understand that their very existence is at stake. But in peacetime, even during a pandemic, the threat is less clear, less immediate in our minds than a bomb dropping on our homes. Amid the debates about the threat of the novel coronavirus, the last thing Britain needed was more confusion. And yet that's exactly the environment Dick fostered with her policing of protests in the capital. In May 2020, officers dispersed protesters demonstrating against lockdown. They then abandoned enforcing the restrictions when Black Lives Matter supporters – far greater in number and therefore presumably more likely to be carrying the virus within their ranks – marched the very next month. Not only did the police allow these protests to go ahead, some kneeled before protesters in solidarity with those protesting the killing of George Floyd. Whatever one thinks of the death of a black man at the hands of a white police officer in the US, it is a serious departure from British policing for officers to take a political stand during protests. They're there to police everyone, by consent, and cannot be seen to be this biased – even against unpleasant individuals. Eleven months after these demonstrations, a uniformed officer was filmed chanting "free free Palestine" and hugging a protester. The rights and wrongs of Israel, Hamas, or anyone else for that matter are utterly irrelevant. This is a serious departure from what the police are supposed to do in Britain. Would this officer have been so comfortable to take a political stance had Dick not presided over this culture of bias?

* * *

You might think Dick's gravest failing – the Menezes killing – was a long time ago, and consider the possibility that she did some stellar police work in between his death and her appointment as commissioner. But before she was chief, Assistant Commissioner Dick was accused in a report of delaying its work investigating police corruption relating to the unsolved murder of private detective Daniel Morgan.[344] The Morgan affair not only offers an insight into her behaviour, but into the behaviour of the Met stretching back decades as the report was published in 2021, 34 years after the 1987 murder. In June of that year, Dick said that she had no intention of resigning over the Daniel Morgan revelations. She was re-appointed. Cressida Dick should lead the force until 2024.[345]

The question with which we are now left is this: Why should the public expect accountability, discipline or improvement in the context of this re-appointment?

For her part, Dick defended her performance in recent years. She pointed to a 'reduction' in violent crime during her time in the job. But for me, the fact that somebody whose CV is populated with substantial failings is not cause to hope that the Met will not screw up when faced with a serial killer as dangerous and stupid as Stephen Port.

* * *

The Stephen Port case is the clearest example of police inadequacy facilitating a serial killer that I have ever seen. Some murderers are smart. Not Stephen. Some cover all clues left behind. Not Stephen. Some pick their targets at random, making it hard to establish a pattern and from that build a profile of the suspect. Not Stephen. Make no mistake, Stephen Port was a dolt. He should not have been capable of getting away with murder for 15 months. The sole reason he was able to operate in this manner was the baffling response of officers, which came to almost nothing, save for notable exceptions previously discussed. They made it easy for a killer who wouldn't ordinarily find murdering undetected possible. Stephen's were easy kills.

There were many reasons for this, which I've hopefully explained sufficiently enough that they do not need repeating. Whatever was in the minds of the various officers who came into contact with the case, whatever their opinions about gay men, one fact was made plain after Stephen's sentencing. Journalist Stephen Daisley wrote in *The Spectator* an article entitled '*How to get away with murder*'. It surfaced in response to the BBC's documentary, *How Police Missed the Grindr Killer*. He concluded his article with a stark reality, writing: "It was hard to watch Thursday night's programme and not conclude that there's still one way to get away with murder in this country, or get away with it for longer: Kill a gay."[346]

This cannot happen again. There is little point in a police force that partakes in Pride parades, pins rainbow badges proudly on its officers and sprays that same pattern of unity on its cars if it can't even stop gay men being murdered. The Met has had plenty of time to change, stretching all the way back to Dennis Nilsen. Now is the time to *act*.

ACKNOWLEDGEMENTS

This book would not have happened without Richard Wyatt, a dear friend from Dagenham who told me I should set it down on paper. Thanks are also due to Chris Pleasance, my former flatmate who acted as a proof-reader when I sent it off to publishers and agents. Isabella Nikolic, my girlfriend, was the first person to read an extract from the book and convince me it was decent, providing much-needed encouragement. Special thanks are also due to the people who have granted me their time in the writing of *Easy Kills*. Peter Hirons and Ryan Edwards both invited me into their homes in the hope that they could help me make sense of the police's handling of the Stephen Port case. My friend, referred to as 'Johnny', and Stephen's former classmate, referred to as 'Liam', were also instrumental. Victim B's bravery and patience in speaking to me cannot be overstated and I sincerely hope that, wherever he now finds himself, he has put this awful episode behind him and is living a happy, fulfilling life. Daniel Mayger was similarly helpful and brave in addressing the profound difficulties he's been through in the hope of raising awareness of young men who also fall victim to predators. Peter Tatchell and Neil Connelly were also kind enough to give me their time and I extend my gratitude accordingly. Thank you to Janine Rasiah, who first put me on the Stephen Port case when she was my editor. And thanks are due to Ramzy Alwakeel, not just for agreeing to be interviewed for this book, but also for giving me my first proper job in journalism at the *Barking and Dagenham Post*. Thanks are also extended to Michael Adkins for the same reason. Finally, thank you to Paul Dove, Rick Cooke, Adam Oldfield, Roy Gilfoyle and all the team at Mirror Books for publishing my first effort.

ENDNOTES

1   *Serial killer Stephen Port jailed for rape drug murders*, BBC, London, 2016, https://www.bbc.co.uk/news/uk-england-38102454

2   S Murphy-Bates, *Stephen Port: Jurors shown pictures of alleged serial killer's Barking flat*, Barking and Dagenham Post, London, 2016, https://www.barkinganddagenhampost.co.uk/news/crime/http-www-barkinganddagenhampost-co-uk-news-crime-court-stephen-port-3338864

3   S Murphy-Bates, *Stephen Port: Watch Barking poison killer accuse murder victim of dealing drugs*, Barking and Dagenham Post, London, 2016, https://www.barkinganddagenhampost.co.uk/news/http-www-barkinganddagenhampost-co-uk-news-stephen-port-watch-barking-3340970

4   S Murphy-Bates & J Rasiah, *Stephen Port: How police told the Post there was 'nothing suspicious' about Barking churchyard deaths*, Barking and Dagenham Post, London, 2016, https://www.barkinganddagenhampost.co.uk/news/stephen-port-how-police-told-the-post-there-was-nothing-3340670

5   S Murphy-Bates, *Families of Barking killer Stephen Port's victims urge witnesses to come forward*, Barking and Dagenham Post, London, 2017, https://www.barkinganddagenhampost.co.uk/news/families-of-barking-killer-stephen-port-s-victims-urge-witnesses-3344120

6   Mr Justice Openshaw, *R v Stephen Port sentencing remarks*, Judiciary of England and Wales, Central Criminal Court, London, 2016, p1

7   P Cooke, *Barking man charged with murder to appear at Old Bailey*, Barking and Dagenham Post, London, 2015, https://www.barkinganddagenhampost.co.uk/news/barking-man-charged-with-murder-to-appear-at-old-bailey-3323378

8   M Robinson, *'I am still shaking': Stunned parents of alleged serial killer tell of their shock as their male escort son is accused of murdering four men he met on gay websites and poisoning them with party drug GHB*, MailOnline, London, 2015, https://www.dailymail.co.uk/news/article-3278793/Man-40-appear-court-charged-murdering-four-young-men-15-months-poisoning-bodies-graveyard.html

9   S Lee, *Memories of Becontree council estate 100 years on*, BBC, London, 2019, https://www.bbc.co.uk/news/uk-england-london-48462491

10   A Brookes, *Ford Dagenham plant celebrates 90th anniversary*, Barking and Dagenham Post, Archant, London, 2021 https://www.barkinganddagenhampost.co.uk/lifestyle/heritage/ford-dagenham-90th-anniversary-8394040

11   L Barton, *Barton's Britain: The Becontree estate*, Guardian, London, 2009, https://www.theguardian.com/travel/2009/oct/09/bartons-britain-becontree-estate

12   J Ryan, *PORT'S 'GAY MP ROMPS' Serial killer Stephen Port boasts of gay romps with MPs and a kids' TV presenter in letters sent to pen pal from prison*, The Sun, London, 2016, https://www.thesun.co.uk/news/2271442/serial-killer-stephen-port-boasts-of-gay-romps-with-mps-and-a-kids-tv-presenter-in-letters-sent-to-pen-pal-from-prison/

13   L Wakefield, *'Grindr killer' Stephen Port and the horrific murder spree that shocked a nation*, Pink News, London, 2021, https://www.pinknews.co.uk/2021/10/07/stephen-port-serial-grindr-killer-timeline-ghb/

14   M Robinson, *'I hope you die a long, slow death': Victims' relatives hurl abuse at 'monstrous' Grindr serial killer Stephen Port as he is told he will die behind bars for murdering four men*, MailOnline, London, 2016, https://www.dailymail.co.uk/news/article-3970924/Grindr-serial-killer-Stephen-Port-die-bars-drugged-raped-murdered-four-gay-men-dumping-bodies-street.html

15   M Robinson, *Revealed: Extraordinary moment the chef accused of poisoning and killing four gay men appeared on TV alongside Celebrity Masterchef contestants*, MailOnline, London, 2015, https://www.dailymail.co.uk/news/article-3282343/Moment-chef-accused-poisoning-killing-four-gay-men-met-online-appeared-television-alongside-Celebrity-Masterchef-contestants.html

16   R Spillett, *Listen to chilling 999 call 'made by gay serial killer after he dumped the body of his first victim outside his flat claiming he'd had a seizure or was DRUNK'*, MailOnline, London, 2016, https://www.dailymail.co.uk/news/article-3834733/Serial-killer-Stephen-Port-s-999-call-claiming-victim-drunk-seizure.html

17   C Davies, *Stephen Port convicted of murder of four men*, Guardian, London 2016, https://www.theguardian.com/uk-news/2016/nov/23/stephen-port-convicted-of-of-four-men

18   J Rasiah, *Stephen Port: 'Rape fantasy' fetish listed on Barking serial killer's social media profile*, Barking and Dagenham Post, London, 2016, https://www.barkinganddagenhampost.co.uk/news/stephen-port-rape-fantasy-fetish-listed-on-barking-serial-killer-3340644

19   Ibid

20   Ibid

21   E Wanderley, *"I lived with a man who I later discovered was a serial killer," says Brazilian*, Correio Braziliense, Brasilia, 2020, https://www.correiobraziliense.com.br/mundo/2020/08/4871235--vivi-com-um-homem-que-depois-descobri-ser-um-serial-killer---diz-brasileiro.html

22   Ibid

23   M Ridley, *'BLOOD ON THEIR HANDS' Grindr killer Stephen Port's neighbour says two of his victims would still be alive if police had properly investigated his first murder*, The Sun, London, 2019, https://www.thesun.co.uk/news/8878755/grindr-killer-stephen-ports-neighbour-says-two-of-his-victims-would-still-be-alive-if-police-had-properly-investigated-his-first-murder/

24   *Stephen Port's 999 call* (audio), BBC, London, 2016, https://www.bbc.co.uk/news/av/magazine-37973255

ENDNOTES

25   Mr Justice Openshaw, *R v Stephen Port sentencing remarks*, Judiciary of England and Wales, Central Criminal Court, London, 2016, p2

26   *Stephen Port's 999 call* (audio), BBC, London, 2016, https://www.bbc.co.uk/news/av/magazine-37973255

27   *Stephen Port trial: Alleged serial killer's 999 call played to jury*, BBC, London, 2016, https://www.bbc.co.uk/news/uk-england-london-37628639

28   *Who were Stephen Port's victims and why did it take police 15 months to catch him?*, ITV, London, 2021, https://www.itv.com/news/london/2021-10-05/who-were-stephen-ports-victims-and-what-was-he-convicted-of

29   Mr Justice Openshaw, *R v Stephen Port sentencing remarks*, Judiciary of England and Wales, Central Criminal Court, London, 2016, p2

30   D De Simone, *How did police miss Barking serial killer Stephen Port?*, BBC, London, 2016, https://www.bbc.co.uk/news/magazine-38045742

31   E Pennink, *Stephen Port: full details of dating website serial killer victims revealed in court*, Independent, London, 2016, https://www.independent.co.uk/news/uk/home-news/stephen-port-full-details-dating-website-serial-killer-victims-revealed-court-a7433721.html

32   *Stephen Port: Paramedic was suspicious about first victim's death*, BBC, London, 2021, https://www.bbc.co.uk/news/uk-england-london-58833693

33   Mr Justice Openshaw, *R v Stephen Port sentencing remarks*, Judiciary of England and Wales, Central Criminal Court, London, 2016, p3

34   K Dennett & E Tanatarova, *Retired Met Police chief denies responsibility for 'systemic' errors in probe into death of Stephen Port's first victim as inquest hears serial killer's past sex assault allegation was missed for a week*, MailOnline, London, 2021, https://www.dailymail.co.uk/news/article-10129031/Ex-Met-Police-chief-denies-responsibility-errors-probe-death-Stephen-Port-victim.html

35   L Williamson, *'I just lost it with the police': Parents of Stephen Port victim say death investigation was a 'travesty'*, MyLondon, London, 2021, https://www.mylondon.news/news/east-london-news/i-just-lost-police-parents-21945241

36   M Robinson, *'I hope you die a long, slow death': Victims' relatives hurl abuse at 'monstrous' Grindr serial killer Stephen Port as he is told he will die behind bars for murdering four men*, MailOnline, London, 2016, https://www.dailymail.co.uk/news/article-3970924/Grindr-serial-killer-Stephen-Port-die-bars-drugged-raped-murdered-four-gay-men-dumping-bodies-street.html

37   C Davies, *Stephen Port trial: timeline of his crimes*, Guardian, London, 2016, https://www.theguardian.com/uk-news/2016/nov/23/stephen-port-trial-timeline-crimes

38   *The four young murder victims of serial killer Stephen Port, ITV*, London 2016, https://www.itv.com/news/2016-11-23/the-four-young-murder-victims-of-serial-killer-stephen-port

39   Ibid

40   Mr Justice Openshaw, *R v Stephen Port sentencing remarks*, Judiciary of England and Wales, Central Criminal Court, London, 2016, p3

41   D De Simone, *How did police miss Barking serial killer Stephen Port?*, BBC, London, 2016, https://www.bbc.co.uk/news/magazine-38045742

42   Ibid

43   Mr Justice Openshaw, *R v Stephen Port sentencing remarks*, Judiciary of England and Wales, Central Criminal Court, London, 2016, pp3-4

44   C Davies, *Stephen Port told his sister of dead body in his bedroom, court hears*, Guardian, London, 2016, https://www.theguardian.com/uk-news/2016/oct/13/stephen-port-told-sister-dead-body-in-his-bedroom-court-hears

45   Ibid

46   Ibid

47   K Cain, *'WISH ME LUCK' Text message sent by 'gay serial killer' to his sister after he told her a man had died in his flat after taking drugs*, The Sun, London, 2016, https://www.thesun.co.uk/news/1970275/text-message-sent-by-gay-serial-killer-stephen-port-to-his-sister-after-he-told-her-a-man-had-died-in-his-flat-after-taking-drugs/

48   S Linning, *'Please God, not another one': Dog walker, 67, who found two victims of the Grindr serial killer in the same churchyard one month apart tells of her horror'*, MailOnline, London, 2016, https://www.dailymail.co.uk/news/article-3967246/Please-God-not-one-Dogwalker-67-two-victims-Grindr-serial-killer-describes-moment-second-body.html

49   S Grandison, *Grindr Killer*, BBC Three, London, 2016

50   C Davies, *Stephen Port victim's landlord: 'I felt I hit a brick wall with the police'*, Guardian, London, 2017, https://www.theguardian.com/uk-news/2017/jan/03/stephen-port-victims-landlord-i-felt-i-hit-a-brick-wall-with-the-police#_=_

51   Ibid

52   S Grandison, *Grindr Killer*, BBC Three, London, 2016

53   D De Simone, *How did police miss Barking serial killer Stephen Port?*, BBC, London, 2016, https://www.bbc.co.uk/news/magazine-38045742

54   S Linning, *'Please God, not another one': Dog walker, 67, who found two victims of the Grindr serial killer in the same churchyard one month apart tells of her horror'*, MailOnline, London, 2016, https://www.dailymail.co.uk/news/article-3967246/Please-God-not-one-Dogwalker-67-two-victims-Grindr-serial-killer-describes-moment-second-body.html

55   Mr Justice Openshaw, *R v Stephen Port sentencing remarks*, Judiciary of England and Wales, Central Criminal Court, London, 2016, pp3-4

56   R Spillett, *Police questioned 'gay serial killer Stephen Port over the death of his first victim - but then released him to kill three more young men'*, MailOnline, London, 2016, https://www.dailymail.co.uk/news/article-3824787/Police-questioned-gay-serial-killer-death-victim.html

57   C Davies, *Stephen Port trial: police took fake suicide note at face value, court told*, Guardian, London, 2016, https://www.theguardian.com/uk-news/2016/oct/06/stephen-port-trial-police-took-fake-suicide-note-daniel-whitworth-face-value-court-told

58   S Murphy-Bates & J Rasiah, *Stephen Port: How police told the Post there was 'nothing suspicious' about Barking churchyard deaths*, Barking and Dagenham Post, London, 2016, https://www.barkinganddagenhampost.co.uk/news/stephen-port-how-police-told-the-post-there-was-nothing-3340670

59   D De Simone, *Stephen Port case: Daniel Whitworth's family 'disgusted' with police*, BBC, London, 2016, https://www.bbc.co.uk/news/uk-38106593

60   Ibid

61   F Mayhew, *'Unusual but not suspicious' says Met detective about three Barking bodies*, Barking and Dagenham Post, London, 2014, https://www.barkinganddagenhampost.co.uk/news/unusual-but-not-suspicious-says-met-detective-about-three-barking-3308650

62   Ibid

63   C Davies, *Stephen Port victim's landlord: 'I felt I hit a brick wall with the police'*, Guardian, London, 2017, https://www.theguardian.com/uk-news/2017/jan/03/stephen-port-victims-landlord-i-felt-i-hit-a-brick-wall-with-the-police#_=_

64   Ibid

65   M Daly, *Did Police Homophobia Allow a Serial Killer to Target Gay Men for Over a Year?*, Vice, New York, 2016, https://www.vice.com/en/article/gqy9k7/did-police-homophobia-allow-a-serial-killer-to-target-gay-men-for-over-a-year-grindr-barking

66   C Davies, *Stephen Port victim's landlord: 'I felt I hit a brick wall with the police'*, Guardian, London, 2017, https://www.theguardian.com/uk-news/2017/jan/03/stephen-port-victims-landlord-i-felt-i-hit-a-brick-wall-with-the-police

67   *Stephen Port: Dog walker describes finding two of serial killer's victims*, BBC, London, 2021, https://www.bbc.co.uk/news/uk-england-london-59062956

68   S Murphy-Bates, *Double drug overdose killed Barking lovers found in church grounds*, Barking and Dagenham Post, London, 2015, https://www.barkinganddagenhampost.co.uk/news/double-drug-overdose-killed-barking-lovers-found-in-church-grounds-3318748

69   D Sandford & D De Simone, *Stephen Port case: Coroner raised concerns about police investigation*, BBC, London, 2016, https://www.bbc.co.uk/news/uk-38096318

70   S Murphy-Bates, *Drugs killed lovers found dead at Barking church*, Barking and Dagenham Post, London, 2015, https://www.barkinganddagenhampost.co.uk/news/drugs-killed-lovers-found-dead-at-barking-church-3319460

71   D Sandford & D De Simone, *Stephen Port case: Coroner raised concerns about police investigation*, BBC, London, 2016, https://www.bbc.co.uk/news/uk-38096318

72   D De Simone, *The killer the police missed*, BBC, London, 2016, https://www.bbc.co.uk/news/resources/idt-d32c5bc9-aa42-49b8-b77c-b258ea2a9205

73   S Murphy-Bates, *Double drug overdose killed Barking lovers found in*

church grounds, Barking and Dagenham Post, London, 2015, https://www.barkinganddagenhampost.co.uk/news/double-drug-overdose-killed-barking-lovers-found-in-church-grounds-3318748

74   D Sandford & D De Simone, *Stephen Port case: Coroner raised concerns about police investigation*, BBC, London, 2016, https://www.bbc.co.uk/news/uk-38096318

75   S Grandison, *Grindr Killer*, BBC Three, London, 2016

76   *Stephen Port, Crimes that shook Britain*, Sky, Title Role Productions, Manchester, 2017

77   S Grandison, *Grindr Killer*, BBC Three, London, 2016

78   Mr Justice Openshaw, *R v Stephen Port sentencing remarks*, Judiciary of England and Wales, Central Criminal Court, London, 2016, p6

79   Mr Justice Openshaw, *R v Stephen Port sentencing remarks*, Judiciary of England and Wales, Central Criminal Court, London, 2016, p6

80   C Davies, *Stephen Port trial: timeline of his crimes*, Guardian, London, 2016, https://www.theguardian.com/uk-news/2016/nov/23/stephen-port-trial-timeline-crimes

81   J Curtis, *Jury shown chilling CCTV of forklift driver walking with 'gay serial killer' to his flat just hours before he was killed with lethal dose of date-rate drug GHB*, MailOnline, London, 2016, https://www.dailymail.co.uk/news/article-3852424/Jury-shown-chilling-CCTV-forklift-driver-walking-gay-serial-killer-flat-just-hours-killed-lethal-dose-date-rate-drug-GHB.html

82   *Alleged serial killer Stephen Port 'filmed meeting victim'*, BBC, London, 2016, https://www.bbc.co.uk/news/uk-england-london-37704898

83   *Stephen Port, Crimes that shook Britain*, Sky, Title Role Productions, Manchester, 2017

84   Ibid

85   *How Police Missed the Grindr Killer*, BBC, London, 2016

86   A Lee, *Sisters who helped catch a serial killer*, Express, London, 2016, https://www.express.co.uk/life-style/life/736626/Jack-Taylor-Stephen-Port-serial-killer-sentenced-Old-Bailey-four-murders-police

87   C Davies, *Could Stephen Port have been stopped? Questions haunt victims' families*, Guardian, London, 2018, https://www.theguardian.com/uk-news/2018/aug/26/could-stephen-port-have-been-stopped-questions-haunt-victims-families

88   *How Police Missed the Grindr Killer*, BBC, London, 2016

89   *Stephen Port, Crimes that shook Britain*, Sky, Title Role Productions, Manchester, 2017

90   *P Cooke, Barking man charged with murder to appear at Old Bailey*, Barking and Dagenham Post, London, 2015, https://www.barkinganddagenhampost.co.uk/news/barking-man-charged-with-murder-to-appear-at-old-bailey-3323378

91   *Jury shown videos of alleged serial killer Stephen Port 'raping man'*, Sky, London,

2016, https://news.sky.com/story/jury-shown-videos-of-alleged-serial-killer-stephen-port-raping-man-10617128

92   T Williams, *How serial sex predator and murderer Stephen Port who killed four men then dumped their bodies in a graveyard gave himself away in police interview with SIX signs of anxiety*, MailOnline, London, 2018, https://www.dailymail.co.uk/news/article-6444551/The-moment-serial-sex-predator-murderer-Stephen-Port-gives-away.html

93   *Stephen Port, Crimes that shook Britain*, Sky, Title Role Productions, Manchester, 2017

94   S Murphy-Bates, *Stephen Port: Watch Barking poison killer accuse murder victim of dealing drugs*, Barking and Dagenham Post, London, 2016, https://www.barkinganddagenhampost.co.uk/news/http-www-barkinganddagenhampost-co-uk-news-stephen-port-watch-barking-3340970

95   P Cooke, *Barking man charged with murder to appear at Old Bailey*, Barking and Dagenham Post, London, 2015, https://www.barkinganddagenhampost.co.uk/news/barking-man-charged-with-murder-to-appear-at-old-bailey-3323378

96   S Murphy-Bates, *Stephen Port: Barking churchwarden recalls shock at finding body in graveyard*, Barking and Dagenham Post, London, 2019, https://www.barkinganddagenhampost.co.uk/news/http-www-barkinganddagenhampost-co-uk-news-stephen-port-barking-churchwarden-3340616

97   P Hill, *EXCLUSIVE: Serial killer Stephen Port boasts of bedding MPs and BBC TV star in chilling letters sent from cell*, Mirror, London, 2016, https://www.mirror.co.uk/news/uk-news/serial-killer-stephen-port-boasts-9337857

98   Ibid

99   Ibid

100   Ibid

101   J Nevett, *Grindr serial killer Stephen Port claims he modelled high street underwear for Debenhams*, Daily Star, London, 2018, https://www.dailystar.co.uk/news/latest-news/grindr-killer-stephen-port-modelled-16865883

102   C Lachey, *Reading a letter from serial killer Stephen Port aka the Grindr killer part 4*, YouTube, 2018, https://www.youtube.com/watch?v=CBCAiinEDWA

103   C Lachey, *Cody Lachey - Reading a letter from serial killer Stephen Port aka the Grindr killer part 1*, YouTube, 2018, https://www.youtube.com/watch?v=WpTjbwxujI4

104   C Lachey, *Reading a letter from serial killer Stephen Port aka the Grindr killer part 1*, YouTube, 2018, https://www.youtube.com/watch?v=WpTjbwxujI4&t=26s

105   Ibid

106   Ibid

107   C Lachey, *Reading a letter out from serial killer Stephen Port aka the Grindr killer part 2*, YouTube, 2018, https://www.youtube.com/watch?v=0YctJIzi46o&t=78s

108   Ibid

109   C Lachey, *Reading a letter from serial killer Stephen Port aka the Grindr killer part*

4, YouTube, 2018, https://www.youtube.com/watch?v=CBCAiinEDWA&t=345s

110   Ibid

111   C Lachey, *Cody Lachey - Reading another letter from serial killer Stephen Port aka the Grindr killer*, YouTube, 2018, https://www.youtube.com/watch?v=hJKSQ57A9Jg&t=515s

112   Ibid

113   C Lachey, *Reading another letter from serial killer Stephen Port aka the Grindr killer part 3*, YouTube, 2018, https://www.youtube.com/watch?v=3REy3Ua0n_o&t=611s

114   C Lachey, *Reading a letter from serial killer Stephen Port aka the Grindr killer part 4*, YouTube, 2018, https://www.youtube.com/watch?v=CBCAiinEDWA&t=345s

115   C Lachey, *Cody Lachey - Reading another letter from serial killer Stephen Port aka the Grindr killer*, YouTube, 2018, https://www.youtube.com/watch?v=hJKSQ57A9Jg&t=515s

116   Ibid

117   C Lachey, *Cody Lachey - Reading a letter from serial killer Stephen Port aka the Grindr killer part 1*, YouTube, 2018, https://www.youtube.com/watch?v=WpTjbwxujI4&t=26s

118   C Lachey, *Cody Lachey - Reading another letter from serial killer Stephen Port aka the Grindr killer*, YouTube, 2018, https://www.youtube.com/watch?v=hJKSQ57A9Jg&t=515s

119   C Lachey, *Reading a letter from serial killer Stephen Port aka the Grindr killer part 4*, YouTube, 2018, https://www.youtube.com/watch?v=CBCAiinEDWA

120   S Murphy-Bates, *Stephen Port: Jury sworn in for trial of alleged Barking serial killer*, Barking and Dagenham Post, London, 2016, https://www.barkinganddagenhampost.co.uk/news/crime/stephen-port-jury-sworn-in-for-trial-of-alleged-barking-3339588

121   S Murphy-Bates, *Stephen Port: Escort sent 'in case I get killed' message hours before death*, Barking and Dagenham Post, London, 2016, https://www.barkinganddagenhampost.co.uk/news/crime/stephen-port-escort-sent-in-case-i-get-killed-message-3339590

122   Ibid

123   Ibid

124   J Rasiah, *Stephen Port: 'Rape fantasy' fetish listed on Barking serial killer's social media profile*, Barking and Dagenham Post, London, 2016, https://www.barkinganddagenhampost.co.uk/news/stephen-port-rape-fantasy-fetish-listed-on-barking-serial-killer-3340644

125   S Murphy-Bates, *Stephen Port: Escort sent 'in case I get killed' message hours before death*, Barking and Dagenham Post, London, 2016, https://www.barkinganddagenhampost.co.uk/news/crime/stephen-port-escort-sent-in-case-i-get-killed-message-3339590

126   Ibid

127   Ibid

128   *Serial killer Stephen Port jailed for rape drug murders*, BBC, London, 2016, https://www.bbc.co.uk/news/uk-england-38102454

129   *Stephen Port: Alleged Barking serial killer 'told sister there was a dead body in his bed'*, Barking and Dagenham Post, London, 2016, https://www.barkinganddagenhampost.co.uk/news/crime/stephen-port-alleged-barking-serial-killer-told-sister-there-was-3339412

130   *Stephen Port murder trial: 'Rape' videos shown to jury*, BBC, London, 2016, https://www.bbc.co.uk/news/uk-england-london-37660034

131   *Stephen Port: Alleged Barking serial killer 'told sister there was a dead body in his bed'*, Barking and Dagenham Post, London, 2016, https://www.barkinganddagenhampost.co.uk/news/crime/stephen-port-alleged-barking-serial-killer-told-sister-there-was-3339412

132   *Stephen Port's 999 call* (audio), BBC, London, 2016, https://www.bbc.co.uk/news/av/magazine-37973255

133   Ibid

134   *How did police miss Barking serial killer Stephen Port?*, D De Simone, BBC, London, 2016, https://www.bbc.co.uk/news/magazine-38045742

135   *Stephen Port: Alleged Barking serial killer admitted moving dead body*, Barking and Dagenham Post, London, 2016, https://www.barkinganddagenhampost.co.uk/news/crime/stephen-port-alleged-barking-serial-killer-admitted-moving-dead-body-3338746

136   Ibid

137   Ibid

138   R Spillett, *'BTW don't blame the guy I was with last night': 'Fake suicide note' left by a 'serial killer to frame his third victim for killing his second'*, MailOnline, London, 2016, https://www.dailymail.co.uk/news/article-3836212/Sister-gay-serial-killer-Stephen-Port-tells-court-body-phone-call.html

139   Ibid

140   Ibid

141   Ibid

142   Ibid

143   *Jury shown videos of alleged serial killer Stephen Port 'raping man'*, Sky, London, 2016, https://news.sky.com/story/jury-shown-videos-of-alleged-serial-killer-stephen-port-raping-man-10617128

144   D O'Mahony, *'GRINDR KILLER' SEX TAPE Jury shown 18-minute video of 'gay serial killer' Stephen Port 'raping unconscious man'*, The Sun, London, 2016, https://www.thesun.co.uk/news/1978855/jury-shown-18-minute-video-of-gay-serial-killer-stephen-port-raping-unconcious-man/

145   C Stroud, *'GRINDR KILLER' VID Gay 'serial killer' filmed himself and another man 'drug raping unconscious man on New Year's Eve'*, The Sun, London, 2016, https://

www.thesun.co.uk/news/1993055/gay-serial-killer-filmed-himself-and-another-man-drug-raping-unconscious-man-on-new-years-eve/

146   D O'Mahony, *'GRINDR KILLER' SEX TAPE Jury shown 18-minute video of 'gay serial killer' Stephen Port 'raping unconscious man'*, The Sun, London, 2016, https://www.thesun.co.uk/news/1978855/jury-shown-18-minute-video-of-gay-serial-killer-stephen-port-raping-unconcious-man/

147   N Morley, *Alleged Grindr serial killer 'filmed himself drugging and raping victim'*, Metro, London, 2016, https://metro.co.uk/2016/10/17/alleged-grindr-serial-killer-filmed-himself-drugging-and-raping-victim-6198118/

148   Ibid

149   Ibid

150   Ibid

151   F Simpson, *Stephen Port: Alleged serial killer 'filmed sex with transgender man after he passed out'*, Evening Standard, London, 2016, https://www.standard.co.uk/news/crime/stephen-port-alleged-serial-killer-filmed-sex-with-transgender-man-after-he-passed-out-a3371436.html and N Morley, Alleged Grindr serial killer 'filmed himself drugging and raping victim', Metro, London, 2016, https://metro.co.uk/2016/10/17/alleged-grindr-serial-killer-filmed-himself-drugging-and-raping-victim-6198118/

152   S Murphy-Bates, *Stephen Port: Jurors shown pictures of alleged serial killer's Barking flat*, Barking and Dagenham Post, London, 2016, https://www.barkinganddagenhampost.co.uk/news/crime/http-www-barkinganddagenhampost-co-uk-news-crime-court-stephen-port-3338864

153   Ibid

154   Ibid

155   Ibid

156   J Curtis, *Jury shown chilling CCTV of forklift driver walking with 'gay serial killer' to his flat just hours before he was killed with lethal dose of date-rate drug GHB*, MailOnline, London, 2016, https://www.dailymail.co.uk/news/article-3852424/Jury-shown-chilling-CCTV-forklift-driver-walking-gay-serial-killer-flat-just-hours-killed-lethal-dose-date-rate-drug-GHB.html#ixzz5EFe5RVd7)

157   *Alleged serial killer Stephen Port describes 'hyper high' sex*, BBC, London, 2016, https://www.bbc.co.uk/news/uk-england-london-37789892

158   E Penninck, *Alleged serial killer Stephen Port tells trial party drug GHB gave him 'hyper high' during sex*, Mirror, London, 2016, https://www.mirror.co.uk/news/uk-news/alleged-serial-killer-stephen-port-9139105

159   A Joseph, *Chef, 41, accused of killing the gay lovers he met on Grindr tells jurors he would never have sex with unconscious strangers because they 'might wake up and punch me'*, MailOnline, London, 2016, https://www.dailymail.co.uk/news/article-3879390/Chef-41-accused-killing-gay-lovers-met-Grindr.html

160   *Alleged serial killer Stephen Port describes 'hyper high' sex*, BBC, London, 2016, https://www.bbc.co.uk/news/uk-england-london-37789892

ENDNOTES

161   A Joseph, *Chef, 41, accused of killing the gay lovers he met on Grindr tells jurors he would never have sex with unconscious strangers because they 'might wake up and punch me'*, MailOnline, London, 2016, https://www.dailymail.co.uk/news/article-3879390/Chef-41-accused-killing-gay-lovers-met-Grindr.html

162   Ibid

163   *Stephen Port: Alleged Barking serial killer 'wouldn't have minded being drugged and raped'*, Barking and Dagenham Post, London, 2016, https://www.barkinganddagenhampost.co.uk/news/crime/http-www-barkinganddagenhampost-co-uk-news-crime-court-stephen-port-3341286

164   *Serial killer accused Stephen Port 'last saw alleged victim at sex party'*, BBC, London, 2016, https://www.bbc.co.uk/news/uk-england-london-37798375

165   Ibid

166   *Stephen Port: Alleged Barking serial killer lied to police because 'the truth sounded like a lie'*, Barking and Dagenham Post, London, 2016, https://www.barkinganddagenhampost.co.uk/news/crime/stephen-port-alleged-barking-serial-killer-lied-to-police-because-3341766

167   Ibid

168   *Chef accused of killing lovers says he would never have sex with unconscious strangers*, Express, London, 2016, https://www.express.co.uk/news/uk/727156/chef-accused-killing-lover-stephen-port-says-never-have-sex-unconscious-high-horny-court

169   Ibid

170   Ibid

171   Ibid

172   *Stephen Port: Alleged Barking serial killer 'wouldn't have minded being drugged and raped'*, Barking and Dagenham Post, London, 2016, https://www.barkinganddagenhampost.co.uk/news/crime/http-www-barkinganddagenhampost-co-uk-news-crime-court-stephen-port-3341286

173   *Stephen Port: Alleged Barking serial killer 'selfishly' pursued fetish*, Barking and Dagenham Post, London, 2016, https://www.barkinganddagenhampost.co.uk/news/crime/stephen-port-alleged-barking-serial-killer-selfishly-pursued-fetish-3341044

174   *Serial killer accused Stephen Port a 'compulsive liar'*, BBC, London, 2016, https://www.bbc.co.uk/news/uk-england-37899399

175   S Murphy-Bates, *Stephen Port: Barking serial killer found guilty of all four murder charges*, Barking and Dagenham Post, London, 2016, https://www.barkinganddagenhampost.co.uk/news/crime/http-www-barkinganddagenhampost-co-uk-news-crime-court-stephen-port-3340620

176   Mr Justice Openshaw, *R v Stephen Port sentencing remarks*, Judiciary of England and Wales, Central Criminal Court, London, 2016, https://www.judiciary.uk/wp-content/uploads/2016/11/sentencing-remarks-r-v-stephen-port.pdf

177   Ibid

178   Ibid

179   Ibid

180   Ibid

181   *Serial killer's East Ham drug dealer jailed for 30 months*, Newham Recorder, London, 2016, https://www.newhamrecorder.co.uk/news/crime/serial-killer-s-east-ham-drug-dealer-jailed-for-30-3092048

182   Ibid

183   J Morgan, *Dealer who supplied UK gay serial killer Stephen Port with drugs to poison victims walks free*, Gay Star News, London, 2017, https://www.gaystarnews.com/article/dealer-supplied-uk-gay-serial-killer-stephen-port-drugs-poison-victims-walks-free/

184   M Robinson, *'I hope you die a long, slow death': Victims' relatives hurl abuse at 'monstrous' Grindr serial killer Stephen Port as he is told he will die behind bars for murdering four men*, MailOnline, London, 2016, https://www.dailymail.co.uk/news/article-3970924/Grindr-serial-killer-Stephen-Port-die-bars-drugged-raped-murdered-four-gay-men-dumping-bodies-street.html

185   Ibid

186   Mr Justice Openshaw, *R v Stephen Port sentencing remarks*, Judiciary of England and Wales, Central Criminal Court, London, 2016, https://www.judiciary.uk/wp-content/uploads/2016/11/sentencing-remarks-r-v-stephen-port.pdf

187   S Murphy-Bates & J Rasiah, *Stephen Port: Barking serial killer will spend rest of his life in jail*, Barking and Dagenham Post, London, 2016, https://www.barkinganddagenhampost.co.uk/news/stephen-port-barking-serial-killer-will-spend-rest-of-his-3340208

188   *Parents of Britain's worst serial killer for a decade refuse to believe he's a killer*, ITV, London, 2016, https://www.itv.com/news/london/2016-11-25/parents-of-britains-worst-serial-killer-for-a-decade-refuse-to-believe-hes-a-killer

189   M Robinson, *'I am still shaking': Stunned parents of alleged serial killer tell of their shock as their male escort son is accused of murdering four men he met on gay websites and poisoning them with party drug GHB*, MailOnline, London, 2015, https://www.dailymail.co.uk/news/article-3278793/Man-40-appear-court-charged-murdering-four-young-men-15-months-poisoning-bodies-graveyard.html

190   M Robinson, *'I hope you die a long, slow death': Victims' relatives hurl abuse at 'monstrous' Grindr serial killer Stephen Port as he is told he will die behind bars for murdering four men*, MailOnline, London, 2016, https://www.dailymail.co.uk/news/article-3970924/Grindr-serial-killer-Stephen-Port-die-bars-drugged-raped-murdered-four-gay-men-dumping-bodies-street.html

191   *Serial killer Stephen Port lodges appeal against convictions*, BBC, London, 2018, https://www.bbc.co.uk/news/uk-england-london-45362553

192   Ibid

193   D De Simone, *Serial killer Stephen Port's murder appeal fails*, BBC, London, 2018,

ENDNOTES

https://www.bbc.co.uk/news/uk-england-london-46221475?SThisFB&fbclid=IwAR1KKLL2t3-gredy2WGNmIGmqZhOKGX_PMh4ybv4SWglUJ3yjHelNAhTT_M

194   G Burchill, *UK'S GUANTANAMO New 'jihadi jail' for Britain's most dangerous terror lags is set to open – but will include TVs, soft beds and computers*, The Sun, London, 2017, https://www.thesun.co.uk/news/3501310/new-jihadi-jail-for-britains-most-dangerous-terror-lags-is-set-to-open-but-will-include-tvs-soft-beds-and-computers/

195   T Davidson, *Grindr killer Stephen Port 'had sex with Britain's worst paedophile' in jail*, Mirror, London, 2019, https://www.mirror.co.uk/news/uk-news/grindr-killer-stephen-port-had-14323579

196   T Davidson, *Grindr killer Stephen Port 'had sex with Britain's worst paedophile' in jail*, Mirror, London, 2019, https://www.mirror.co.uk/news/uk-news/grindr-killer-stephen-port-had-14323579

197   M Robinson, *Grindr serial killer Stephen Port's drug dealer is found guilty of murdering James Bond extra with a fatal dose of chemsex drug - as victim's teenage son slams him for GRINNING at family in court*, MailOnline, London, 2019, https://www.dailymail.co.uk/news/article-7053565/Gay-drug-dealer-killed-James-Bond-actor-massive-overdose-GHB.html

198   Ibid

199   Ibid

200   S Murphy-Bates & M Robinson, *Grindr serial killer Stephen Port's drug dealer jailed for chemsex drug murder of James Bond extra tells court they are living as a woman but prison service refuses to say if the 'hustler' will serve life term in women's jail*, MailOnline, London, 2019, https://www.dailymail.co.uk/news/article-7451195/Grindr-serial-killer-Stephen-Ports-drug-dealer-jailed-31-years.html

201   R Spillett, *James Bond actor's daughter, 14, 'spoke to her father's killer when he impersonated him on the phone after giving him fatal overdose of date rape drug and stealing his bank card'*, MailOnline, London, 2019, https://www.dailymail.co.uk/news/article-7053565/Gay-drug-dealer-killed-James-Bond-actor-massive-overdose-GHB.html

202   D De Simone, *The link between a Grindr murderer and a serial killer*, BBC, London, 2019, https://www.bbc.co.uk/news/uk-england-london-48928442

203   E Pinnink & R Duggan, *The chilling link between chemsex murderer Gerald Matovu and Grindr killer Stephen Port*, MyLondon, London, 2019, https://www.mylondon.news/news/south-london-news/chilling-link-between-chemsex-murderer-16587554

204   S Murphy-Bates and M Robinson, *Grindr serial killer Stephen Port's drug dealer jailed for chemsex drug murder of James Bond extra tells court they are living as a woman but prison service refuses to say if the 'hustler' will serve life term in women's jail*, MailOnline, London, 2019, https://www.dailymail.co.uk/news/article-7451195/Grindr-serial-killer-Stephen-Ports-drug-dealer-jailed-31-years.html

205   A Walker, *Stephen Port's drug dealer found guilty of murdering actor*, Guardian, London, 2019, https://www.theguardian.com/uk-news/2019/jul/15/gerald-matovu-found-guilty-murder-actor-chemsex-drug-ghb-stephen-port

206   S Murphy-Bates, *Stephen Port's drug dealer admits supplying Barking poison killer with GHB*, Barking and Dagenham Post, London, 2019, https://www.barkinganddagenhampost.co.uk/news/stephen-port-s-drug-dealer-admits-supplying-barking-poison-killer-3347232

207   S Murphy-Bates, *Stephen Port: Jurors shown pictures of alleged serial killer's Barking flat*, Barking and Dagenham Post, London, 2016, https://www.barkinganddagenhampost.co.uk/news/crime/http-www-barkinganddagenhampost-co-uk-news-crime-court-stephen-port-3338864

208   I Cobain & M Taylor, *Far-right terrorist Thomas Mair jailed for life for Jo Cox murder*, Guardian, London, 2016, https://www.theguardian.com/uk-news/2016/nov/23/thomas-mair-found-guilty-of-jo-cox-murder

209   A Topping, *Sian Blake murder: Arthur Simpson-Kent gets whole-life sentence*, Guardian, London, 2016, https://www.theguardian.com/uk-news/2016/oct/05/sian-blake-arthur-simpson-kent-gets-full-life-sentence

210   M Robinson, *'I hope you die a long, slow death': Victims' relatives hurl abuse at 'monstrous' Grindr serial killer Stephen Port as he is told he will die behind bars for murdering four men*, MailOnline, London, 2016, https://www.dailymail.co.uk/news/article-3970924/Grindr-serial-killer-Stephen-Port-die-bars-drugged-raped-murdered-four-gay-men-dumping-bodies-street.html

211   World Prison Brief Data, https://www.prisonstudies.org/country/united-kingdom-england-wales

212   M Shales, *Barking and Dagenham police borough commander retires*, Barking and Dagenham Post, London, 2016, https://www.barkinganddagenhampost.co.uk/news/crime/barking-and-dagenham-police-borough-commander-retires-3331600

213   Office for National Statistics, *Subnational sexual identity estimates, UK: 2013 to 2015*, Section 6, fig 9, London, 2017, https://www.ons.gov.uk/peoplepopulationandcommunity/culturalidentity/sexuality/articles/subnationalsexualidentityestimates/uk2013to2015#sexual-identity-by-age-uk-countries-and-english-regions

214   R Charman, *Labour councillor, Liam Smith, claims he is victim of "dyke" smear campaign*, Pink News, London, 2008, https://www.pinknews.co.uk/2008/08/22/liam-smith-claims-he-is-victim-of-smear-campaign/

215   Ibid

216   Ibid

217   Ibid

218   J Lefley, *Labour councillor cautioned for gay insult at election*, Evening Standard, London, 2008, https://www.standard.co.uk/hp/front/labour-councillor-cautioned-for-gay-insult-at-election-6924565.html

219   C Hitchens, *Why Women Aren't Funny*, Vanity Fair, New York, 2007, https://www.vanityfair.com/culture/2007/01/hitchens200701

220   *BNP councillor defends 'erotic' film*, politics.co.uk, London, 2006, https://www.

politics.co.uk/news/2006/05/10/bnp-councillor-defends-erotic-film/

221   M Shales, *Man dies in 'unexplained' circumstances in Barking*, Barking and Dagenham Post, London, 2014, https://www.barkinganddagenhampost.co.uk/news/man-dies-in-unexplained-circumstances-in-barking-3305950 and M Shales, 21-year-old man found dead at St Margaret's Church, Barking, Barking and Dagenham Post, London, 2014

222   *Report of the Safer and Stronger Community Select Committee: Confidence in and Engagement with the Police 2014/15*, Barking and Dagenham Council, London, 2016, p35

223   E Day, *Getting away with murder? The death of Martine Vik Magnussen*, Guardian, London, 2010, https://www.theguardian.com/uk/2010/feb/22/the-murder-of-martine-vik-magnussen

224   Ibid

225   P Sawer, *Queen's sorrow over unsolved Martine Magnussen murder*, Telegraph, London, 2010, https://www.telegraph.co.uk/news/uknews/crime/7696666/Queens-sorrow-over-unsolved-Martine-Magnussen-murder.html

226   Ibid

227   A Makoni, *'Come to UK to face justice over Norwegian student's murder,' police urge suspect*, Evening Standard, London, 2021, https://www.standard.co.uk/news/uk/martine-vik-magnussen-appeal-suspect-murder-uk-b923715.html

228   E Day, *Getting away with murder? The death of Martine Vik Magnussen*, Guardian, London, 2010, https://www.theguardian.com/uk/2010/feb/22/the-murder-of-martine-vik-magnussen

229   B Masters, *Killing for company, the case of Dennis Nilsen*, Arrow, London, 2020, pp6-13

230   Ibid p14

231   Ibid p17

232   C Giordano, *Dennis Nilsen: Serial killer 'lay dying in his own filth' in prison cell*, inquest hears, Independent, London, 2019, https://www.independent.co.uk/news/uk/home-news/dennis-nilsen-death-inquest-serial-killer-prison-muswell-hill-murderer-a9168721.html

233   B Masters, *Killing for company, the case of Dennis Nilsen*, Arrow, London, 2020, p58-64

234   Ibid p66-72

235   Ibid p113

236   E Morrice, *North-east serial killer featured on international true crime podcast*, Evening Express, Aberdeen, 2020, https://www.eveningexpress.co.uk/fp/news/local/north-east-serial-killer-featured-international-true-crime-podcast/

237   B Masters, *Killing for company, the case of Dennis Nilsen*, Arrow, London, 2020, pp 115-121

238   Ibid p127

239   Ibid pp121-123

240   Ibid pp126-129

241   Ibid p326

242   Ibid pp327-328

243   *National LGBT Survey*, Government Equalities Office, London, 2018, p10, https://assets.publishing.service.gov.uk/government/uploads/system/uploads/attachment_data/file/722314/GEO-LGBT-Survey-Report.pdf

244   Local Government Act 1988, London, chapter 9, https://www.legislation.gov.uk/ukpga/1988/9/introduction

245   C Amos, *Hating Peter Tatchell*, Netflix, Los Gatos, California, 2021

246   M Thatcher, *Speech to Conservative Party Conference*, Blackpool, 1987, https://www.margaretthatcher.org/document/106941

247   C Amos, *Hating Peter Tatchell*, Netflix, Los Gatos, California, 2021

248   Z Coleman, *Peter Tatchell: "I was violently assaulted almost every week"*, Varsity, Cambridge, 2020, https://www.varsity.co.uk/interviews/19260

249   C Richardson, *The worst of times*, Guardian, London, 2002, https://www.theguardian.com/world/2002/aug/14/gayrights.comment

250   Ibid

251   Ibid

252   Ibid

253   S Daisley, *How to get away with murder*, The Spectator, London, 2017, https://www.spectator.co.uk/article/how-to-get-away-with-murder

254   H Muir, *Officers' homophobia hampered murder investigations, says review*, Guardian, London, 2007, https://www.theguardian.com/uk/2007/may/15/gayrights.ukcrime

255   Ibid

256   Ibid

257   Ibid

258   Ibid

259   Ibid

260   *Stephen Port, Crimes that shook Britain*, Sky, Title Role Productions, Manchester, 2017

261   A Topping, *How the establishment failed victims of 'black-cab rapist' John Worboys*, Guardian, London, 2018, https://www.theguardian.com/uk-news/2018/jan/05/how-the-establishment-failed-victims-of-black-cab-rapist-john-worboys

262   S Laville & V Dodd, *Police errors left rapist John Worboys free to strike - but no officers face sack*, Guardian, London, 2010, https://www.theguardian.com/uk/2010/jan/20/police-ipcc-john-worboys-errors

263   A Topping, *How the establishment failed victims of 'black-cab rapist' John Worboys*, Guardian, London, 2018, https://www.theguardian.com/uk-news/2018/jan/05/how-the-establishment-failed-victims-of-black-cab-rapist-john-worboys

264   Ibid

265   Ibid

266   Ibid

267   Ibid

268   S Laville & V Dodd, *Police errors left rapist John Worboys free to strike - but no officers face sack*, Guardian, London, 2010, https://www.theguardian.com/uk/2010/jan/20/police-ipcc-john-worboys-errors

269   A Topping, *How the establishment failed victims of 'black-cab rapist' John Worboys*, Guardian, London, 2018, https://www.theguardian.com/uk-news/2018/jan/05/how-the-establishment-failed-victims-of-black-cab-rapist-john-worboys

270   S Laville & V Dodd, *Police errors left rapist John Worboys free to strike - but no officers face sack*, Guardian, London, 2010, https://www.theguardian.com/uk/2010/jan/20/police-ipcc-john-worboys-errors

271   *Sex attacker Kirk Reid's criminal history*, BBC, London, 2010, https://www.bbc.co.uk/news/10438989

272   Ibid

273   J Fielding, *Serial sex attacker dubbed the 'Night Bus Beast' who may have preyed on 100 women is set to be free from jail in months - despite serving just nine years of his life term*, MailOnline, London, 2018, https://www.dailymail.co.uk/news/article-5756609/Serial-sex-attacker-preyed-100-women-set-free-jail-months.html

274   J King, *Officers will not be disciplined over investigation into Barking serial killer Stephen Port*, Barking and Dagenham Post, London, 2019, https://www.barkinganddagenhampost.co.uk/news/stephen-port-detectives-not-to-be-disciplined-iopc-says-3374860

275   D Campbell & R Evans, *Files shed light on alleged efforts to hide 1970s police corruption*, Guardian, London, 2018, https://www.theguardian.com/uk-news/2018/aug/19/files-shed-light-on-alleged-efforts-to-hide-1970s-police-corruption

276   S Box, Power, *Crime and Mystification*, Routledge, London, 1983, pp106-107

277   M Lockwood, *Why Stephen Lawrence is part of our organisational DNA*, IOPC, London, 2020, http://www.ipcc.gov.uk/news/our-podcasts-and-blogs/why-stephen-lawrence-part-our-organisational-dna

278   D Sillito, *Sun's Hillsborough front page 'symbol of lies and cover-up'*, BBC, London, 2016, https://www.bbc.co.uk/news/uk-36149489

279   W Worley, *Hillsborough disaster: The investigations which led to six people being charged in connection with tragedy*, Independent, London, 2017, https://www.independent.co.uk/news/uk/home-news/hillsborough-disaster-investigations-six-people-charged-ipcc-operation-resolve-david-duckenfield-a7813441.html

280   D Sales, *'The judicial system is broken': Families of Hillsborough victims slam decision to acquit two retired officers and ex solicitor accused of altering police statements in aftermath of disaster as judge rules they have no case to answer*, MailOnline, London, 2021, https://www.dailymail.co.uk/news/article-9620595/Two-police-officers-forces-lawyer-cleared-perverting-case-justice.html

281   R Spillett, *Furious Hillsborough relatives blast 'unbelievable' decision to drop charges against ex-police chief Sir Norman Bettison over 'lies' he told in aftermath of tragedy as they demand urgent review*, MailOnline, London, 2018, https://www.dailymail.co.uk/news/article-6082097/Sir-Norman-Bettison-NOT-prosecuted-misconduct-Hillsborough.html

282   R Spillett & J Middleton, *£60m, five separate jury court cases, thirty years and still NO ONE is found responsible for unlawful killing of 96 football fans at Hillsborough*, MailOnline, London, 2019, https://www.dailymail.co.uk/news/article-7735833/Hillsborough-match-commander-David-Duckenfield-CLEARED-manslaughter.html

283   D Sales, *'The judicial system is broken': Families of Hillsborough victims slam decision to acquit two retired officers and ex solicitor accused of altering police statements in aftermath of disaster as judge rules they have no case to answer*, MailOnline, London, 2021, https://www.dailymail.co.uk/news/article-9620595/Two-police-officers-forces-lawyer-cleared-perverting-case-justice.html

284   N Davies, *Crisis at police watchdog as lawyers resign*, Guardian, London, 2008, https://www.theguardian.com/politics/2008/feb/25/police.law1

285   J Crawley, *'The worst of all outcomes'*, Guardian, London, 2009, https://www.theguardian.com/society/2009/apr/08/police-complaints-commission

286   Ibid

287   S Laville & V Dodd, *Police errors left rapist John Worboys free to strike - but no officers face sack*, Guardian, London, 2010, https://www.theguardian.com/uk/2010/jan/20/police-ipcc-john-worboys-errors

288   M Hughes, *'Police could have stopped rapist,' says IPCC report*, Independent, London, 2010, https://www.independent.co.uk/news/uk/crime/police-could-have-stopped-rapist-says-ipcc-report-1873164.html

289   S Laville & V Dodd, *Police errors left rapist John Worboys free to strike - but no officers face sack*, Guardian, London, 2010, https://www.theguardian.com/uk/2010/jan/20/police-ipcc-john-worboys-errors

290   A Topping, *How the establishment failed victims of 'black-cab rapist' John Worboys*, Guardian, London, 2018, https://www.theguardian.com/uk-news/2018/jan/05/how-the-establishment-failed-victims-of-black-cab-rapist-john-worboys

291   *'Plebgate' row: Officer cleared of misconduct*, BBC, London, 2016, https://www.bbc.co.uk/news/uk-england-35481055

292   *'Plebgate' police officer guilty of misconduct*, BBC, London, 2015, https://www.bbc.co.uk/news/uk-england-35127941

293   A Mitchell, *IPCC: officers should face disciplinary hearings over Plebgate meeting*, Guardian, London, 2015, https://www.theguardian.com/politics/2015/jul/20/ipcc-

officers-should-face-disciplinary-hearings-over-plebgate-meeting

294   Ibid

295   *IPCC: Police watchdog 'woefully under-equipped'*, BBC, London, 2013, https://www.bbc.co.uk/news/uk-21277094

296   S Murphy-Bates, *Police watchdog yet to interview any officers under investigation for their handling of Barking killer Stephen Port*, Barking and Dagenham Post, London, 2017, https://www.barkinganddagenhampost.co.uk/news/stephen-port-impotent-ipcc-yet-to-interview-any-of-17-3349342

297   C Davies, *Police escape misconduct charges over case of serial killer Stephen Port*, Guardian, London, 2019, https://www.theguardian.com/uk-news/2019/jul/05/stephen-port-victim-inquests-focus-potential-police-failings

298   D De Simone, *Stephen Port: Officers refuse to answer watchdog's questions*, BBC, London, 2018, https://www.bbc.co.uk/news/uk-44970963

299   Ibid

300   Ibid

301   D De Simone, *Stephen Port: Watchdog completes serial killer Met inquiry*, BBC, London, 2018, https://www.bbc.co.uk/news/uk-england-london-45185333

302   D De Simone, *Stephen Port: 'No police penalties' in serial killer case*, BBC, London, 2019, https://www.bbc.co.uk/news/uk-48887754

303   Ibid

304   Ibid

305   *Family speaks out for justice ahead of inquest into serial killer victims*, ITV, London, 2018, https://www.itv.com/news/2018-08-12/family-speaks-out-for-justice-ahead-of-inquest-into-serial-killer-victims

306   E McConnell, *Inquest verdicts for Daniel Whitworth, of Gravesend, and Gabriel Kovrari — victims of Grindr serial killer Stephen Port — quashed*, KentOnline, London, 2017, https://www.kentonline.co.uk/gravesend/news/verdicts-into-deaths-of-serial-136050/

307   *Judge to lead Stephen Port victims' inquests*, BBC, London, 2018, https://www.bbc.co.uk/news/uk-england-london-45989879

308   *Internal police report into gay serial killer Stephen Port to be shown to families*, KentOnline, London, 2018, https://www.kentonline.co.uk/gravesend/news/families-to-see-key-report-into-gay-killings-188000/

309   C Davies, *Paramedic saw death of Stephen Port's first victim as suspicious, inquest told*, Guardian, London, 2021, https://www.theguardian.com/uk-news/2021/oct/07/paramedic-called-first-stephen-port-victim-death-suspicious-anthony-walgate

310   S Osborne, *Stephen Port: Serial killer noted as sex assault suspect on day first victim died, inquest told*, Sky, London, 2021, https://news.sky.com/story/stephen-port-serial-killer-noted-as-sex-assault-suspect-on-day-first-victim-died-inquest-told-12429423

311   M Leclere, *Grindr Killer Stephen Port's first victim's case being rejected by Met*

murder detectives was disappointing, senior officer tells inquest jury, KentOnline, London, 2021

312   C Davies, *Stephen Port laptop not inspected until he had killed three times, inquest told*, Guardian, London, 2021, https://www.theguardian.com/uk-news/2021/oct/13/stephen-port-laptop-not-inspected-until-he-had-killed-three-times-inquest-told

313   Ibid

314   L Dollimore, *Senior detective wishes he'd sent Stephen Port's laptop for analysis days after Grindr serial killer first struck and not 10 months later when he had already killed two more, inquest hears*, MailOnline, London, 2021, https://www.dailymail.co.uk/news/article-10092653/Senior-detective-wishes-hed-sent-Stephen-Ports-laptop-analysis-days-killer-struck.html

315   J Wright, Serial killer Stephen Port, 46, was 'obsessed' with watching date-rape porn and sent 'hundreds of thousands of messages about sex and drugs' to men on hook-up sites, inquest hears, MailOnline, London, 2021, https://www.dailymail.co.uk/news/article-10064565/Serial-killer-Stephen-Port-46-obsessed-watching-date-rape-porn-inquest-hears.html

316   E Tanatarova, *Parents of Grindr serial killer Stephen Port's first victim blast 'Keystone cops' for 'travesty' of an investigation when officers claimed it would be 'too expensive' to examine the murderer's laptop*, MailOnline, London, 2021, https://www.dailymail.co.uk/news/article-10120981/Parents-Grindr-serial-killer-Stephen-Ports-victim-blast-Keystone-cops.html

317   Ibid

318   Ibid

319   Ibid

320   N Enoch, *Detective in charge of investigation into murderer Stephen Port's first victim admits he made 'significant mistakes' and failed to look into Grindr killer's history, inquest hears*, MailOnline, London, 2021, https://www.dailymail.co.uk/news/article-10096979/Detective-charge-probe-Grindr-killer-Stephen-Ports-victim-mistakes.html

321   J Thorburn, *Dog walker found two victims of serial killer Stephen Port in an east London churchyard three WEEKS apart, inquest hears*, MailOnline, London, 2021, https://www.dailymail.co.uk/news/article-10136127/Stephen-Port-inquest-Dogwalker-recalls-peculiar-discovery-two-victims-serial-killer.html

322   L Dollimore, *Senior detective wishes he'd sent Stephen Port's laptop for analysis days after Grindr serial killer first struck and not 10 months later when he had already killed two more, inquest hears*, MailOnline, London, 2021, https://www.dailymail.co.uk/news/article-10092653/Senior-detective-wishes-hed-sent-Stephen-Ports-laptop-analysis-days-killer-struck.html

323   K Feehan, *Senior detective denies 'unconscious bias' in the way he investigated death of gay serial killer Stephen Port's first victim*, MailOnline, London, 2021, https://www.dailymail.co.uk/news/article-10080863/Detective-denies-unconscious-bias-investigation-killer-Stephen-Ports-victim.html

324   Ibid

325   E Tanatarova, *Parents of Grindr serial killer Stephen Port's first victim blast 'Keystone cops' for 'travesty' of an investigation when officers claimed it would be 'too expensive' to examine the murderer's laptop*, MailOnline, London, 2021, https://www.dailymail. co.uk/news/article-10120981/Parents-Grindr-serial-killer-Stephen-Ports-victim-blast-Keystone-cops.html

326   N Enoch, *Detective in charge of investigation into murderer Stephen Port's first victim admits he made 'significant mistakes' and failed to look into Grindr killer's history, inquest hears*, MailOnline, London, 2021, https://www.dailymail.co.uk/news/ article-10096979/Detective-charge-probe-Grindr-killer-Stephen-Ports-victim-mistakes. html

327   L Dollimore, *Senior detective wishes he'd sent Stephen Port's laptop for analysis days after Grindr serial killer first struck and not 10 months later when he had already killed two more, inquest hears*, MailOnline, London, 2021, https://www.dailymail.co.uk/news/ article-10092653/Senior-detective-wishes-hed-sent-Stephen-Ports-laptop-analysis-days-killer-struck.html

328   E Pennink, *Stephen Port inquests: Police chief denies 'systemic' errors*, Barking and Dagenham Post, London, 2021, https://www.barkinganddagenhampost.co.uk/news/ crime/police-chief-denies-systemic-errors-stephen-port-investigation-8439412

329   R Hooper, *'Homophobia in the Met' meant Stephen Port evidence was dismissed, inquests told*, Evening Standard, London, 2021, https://www.standard.co.uk/news/uk/ gabriel-kovari-stephen-port-daniel-whitworth-anthony-walgate-met-b964594.html

330   S Murphy-Bates, *Stephen Port: Watch Barking poison killer accuse murder victim of dealing drugs*, Barking and Dagenham Post, London, 2016, https://www. barkinganddagenhampost.co.uk/news/http-www-barkinganddagenhampost-co-uk-news-stephen-port-watch-barking-3340970

331   R Hooper, *Killer Stephen Port made up story about victim to cover up murder, inquest told*, Evening Standard, London, 2021, https://www.standard.co.uk/news/uk/ gabriel-kovari-port-metropolitan-police-daniel-whitworth-facebook-b963098.html

332   D Stuart, *Comment: Is London's gay scene self-harming through sex and drug use?*, Pink News, London, 2013, https://www.pinknews.co.uk/2013/01/22/comment-is-londons-gay-scene-self-harming-through-sex-and-drug-use/

333   P Cash, *Comment: Drug use on the gay scene needs to be acknowledged in the fight against HIV*, Pink News, London, 2013, https://www.pinknews.co.uk/2013/10/04/ comment-drug-use-on-the-gay-scene-needs-to-be-acknowledged-in-the-fight-against-hiv/

334   M Robinson, *'I am still shaking': Stunned parents of alleged serial killer tell of their shock as their male escort son is accused of murdering four men he met on gay websites and poisoning them with party drug GHB*, MailOnline, London, 2015, https://www. dailymail.co.uk/news/article-3278793/Man-40-appear-court-charged-murdering-four-young-men-15-months-poisoning-bodies-graveyard.html

335   R Spillett, *Be careful what you tweet: Number of arrests for 'offensive' social media posts soars as police target internet trolls*, MailOnline, London, 2016, https://www.

dailymail.co.uk/news/article-3624059/Arrests-offensive-social-media-posts-soar-police-target-internet-trolls.html

336   C Parker, *Police arresting nine people a day in fight against web trolls*, The Times, London, 2017, https://www.thetimes.co.uk/article/police-arresting-nine-people-a-day-in-fight-against-web-trolls-b8nkpgp2d

337   UK Government, *Communications Act 2003*, c.1, part 2, chapter 1, section 127, https://www.legislation.gov.uk/ukpga/2003/21/section/127

338   S L Gale, *Arrests for offensive Facebook and Twitter posts soar in London*, Independent, London, 2016, https://www.independent.co.uk/news/uk/arrests-offensive-facebook-and-twitter-posts-soar-london-a7064246.html

339   P Stott, *Cressida Dick has failed upwards*, Spiked Online, London, 2021, https://www.spiked-online.com/2021/07/21/cressida-dick-has-failed-upwards/

340   L Gittos, *Cressida Dick is no hero*, Spike Online, London, 2021, https://www.spiked-online.com/2017/04/24/cressida-dick-is-no-hero/

341   P Stott, *Cressida Dick has failed upwards*, Spiked Online, London, 2021, https://www.spiked-online.com/2021/07/21/cressida-dick-has-failed-upwards/

342   M Duell & J Newman, *Lawless London's murder toll soars to its highest level in a decade after 147 victims were slain on capital's streets in 2019 - with more than HALF stabbed to death in knife crime epidemic*, MailOnline, London, 2019, https://www.dailymail.co.uk/news/article-7839795/Lawless-Londons-murder-toll-soars-highest-level-decade.html

343   P Stott, *Cressida Dick has failed upwards*, Spiked Online, London, 2021, https://www.spiked-online.com/2021/07/21/cressida-dick-has-failed-upwards/

344   Ibid

345   V Dodd, *Cressida Dick to remain Met chief until 2024, ministers announce*, Guardian, London, 2021, https://www.theguardian.com/uk-news/2021/sep/10/cressida-dick-to-remain-met-chief-until-2024-ministers-announce

346   S Daisley, *How to get away with murder*, The Spectator, London, 2017, https://www.spectator.co.uk/article/how-to-get-away-with-murder